Developing Empathy

Empathy is valued across cultures, and has a profound impact on psychotherapy, our children, and our world. Why then are many human relationships *not* empathetic? This volume describes in detail the neurobiological, psychological, and social elements involved with empathy. Ideas are brought to life with case examples and reflective questions which help the reader learn ways to overcome empathetic barriers. The book shows how fear, anger, and anxiety all take away the power to feel for others, while also looking at the topic through a global lens. *Developing Empathy* is an easy-read book, backed by science, useful to the clinician, and to all readers interested in the topic.

Katharina Manassis, MD, founded and led a program in anxiety disorders at Toronto's Hospital for Sick Children. She has published over 90 papers in professional journals regarding childhood anxiety disorders and has written six related books for parents and professionals, including *Keys to Parenting Your Anxious Child* and *Case Formulation with Children and Adolescents*. She has her own private practice and is a professor emerita in the Department of Psychiatry at the University of Toronto.

Developing Empathy
A Biopsychosocial Approach to Understanding Compassion for Therapists and Parents

Katharina Manassis

NEW YORK AND LONDON

First published 2017
by Routledge
711 Third Avenue, New York, NY 10017

and by Routledge
2 Park Square, Milton Park, Abingdon, Oxon OX14 4RN

Routledge is an imprint of the Taylor & Francis Group, an informa business

© 2017 Taylor & Francis

The right of Katharina Manassis to be identified as author of this work has been asserted by her in accordance with sections 77 and 78 of the Copyright, Designs and Patents Act 1988.

All rights reserved. No part of this book may be reprinted or reproduced or utilised in any form or by any electronic, mechanical, or other means, now known or hereafter invented, including photocopying and recording, or in any information storage or retrieval system, without permission in writing from the publishers.

Trademark notice: Product or corporate names may be trademarks or registered trademarks, and are used only for identification and explanation without intent to infringe.

Library of Congress Cataloging in Publication Data
Names: Manassis, Katharina, author.
Title: Developing empathy : a biopsychosocial approach to understanding compassion for therapists and parents / by Katharina Manassis, MD, FRCPC.
Description: New York, NY : Routledge, 2017. Includes bibliographical references and index.
Identifiers: LCCN 2016046577 | ISBN 9781138693517 (hbk : alk. paper) | ISBN 9781138693531 (pbk : alk. paper) | ISBN 9781315530499 (ebk)
Subjects: LCSH: Empathy. | Compassion. | Helping behavior.
Classification: LCC BF575.E55 M355 2017 DDC 152.4/1--dc23
LC record available at https://lccn.loc.gov/2016046577

ISBN: 978-1-138-69351-7 (hbk)
ISBN: 978-1-138-69353-1 (pbk)
ISBN: 978-1-315-53049-9 (ebk)

Typeset in Sabon
by Taylor & Francis Books

To all who have taught me the meaning of empathy, sometimes without saying a word.

Contents

List of Illustrations	ix
Acknowledgments	x
About the Author	xi
Preface	xii

PART I
Understanding Empathy — 1

1 Perspectives on Empathy: Why is an Obvious Virtue so Elusive?   3

2 Nature and Nurture: The Developmental Basis of Empathy   21

3 Social Influences: Encouraging Empathy Versus Competition   38

PART II
Nurturing Empathy — 55

4 Physical Aspects: Why Empathy Requires a Healthy Body as well as a Healthy Mind   57

5 Mental Aspects: Emotional Distress and *Not* Looking Out for Number One   73

6 Taming the Fight or Flight Response   90

7 Relationships and Empathy: Treating the Other Person as a "Thou"   108

8 Beliefs and Ideals that Motivate Attention to Others' Well-Being   126

PART III
Developing Empathy: Why Bother?   143

9   Implications for Therapists   145

10   Implications for Parents   161

11   Implications for Leaders and Organizations   177

12   Implications for Everyone   193

Index   207

Illustrations

Figures

1.1	Component Processes of Empathy	11
3.1	Social Influences on Empathy over Time	39
7.1	Relationship Types by Closeness and Emotional Valence	111
11.1	Interconnection of Global Problems and Empathetic Leadership	189

Tables

2.1	Developmental Influences Toward or Away from Empathy	22
3.1	Social Influences on Empathy	53
5.1	Components of Empathy and Mental Health Conditions	76
11.1	Empathetic Communities Versus Unhealthy Organizations	190

Acknowledgments

The people who inspired the ideas in this book are too numerous to name, which makes me optimistic about the human condition despite its many problems. The members of St. Mark's United Church in Scarborough deserve a special mention though, as they welcome and include people with all sorts of off-beat ideas and quirks like me, and show them genuine empathy. Converting good ideas into a coherent, publishable work of nonfiction, however, is never easy. For all of their guidance and support in this process, a heartfelt thanks to the members of Routledge Publishing. Particular thanks to my editor, George Zimmar, whose steadfast faith in the project's many iterations allowed it to eventually reach your hands. Finally, I must thank my children for understanding, empathetically, my frequent disappearances into the basement office as I wrote this book.

About the Author

Katharina Manassis, MD, FRCPC, founded and led a program in anxiety disorders at Toronto's Hospital for Sick Children. She has published over 90 papers in professional journals in this field and has written six related books for parents and professionals, including *Keys to Parenting Your Anxious Child* and *Cognitive Behavioral Therapy with Children*. She now has her own private practice and is professor emerita in the Department of Psychiatry at the University of Toronto. She is also the mother of two young adults of whom she is very proud.

Preface

> Grant that I never seek so much…to be understood, as to understand.
>
> St. Francis of Assisi

> The forest is mankind, and the hill is the world… Trees of different names stand side by side. The trees fall and die and help the young grow. Even the crooked sticks help to build the world. And all the nations have to build that forest.
>
> Chief Walking Buffalo

The idea for this book occurred to me a few years ago as I stood impatiently in line for my morning coffee. I requested my usual type of latte, fumbled in my purse for cash, and discovered I was out of small bills. I pushed a $50 bill across the counter. "We can't accept denominations over $20", the server said. "Sorry, I don't have any small bills", I explained. "Company rules", she reiterated. "Look, I've been waiting for 20 minutes, I'm late for a meeting, and I don't have any small bills", I snapped, as the customers behind me started to stare. She thought for a moment, smiled at me sincerely, and then responded "No problem. I'll cover it today and you can pay me tomorrow… next!" Before I knew it, she was on to the customer behind me, I had my coffee, and I was on the way to my meeting. I felt relieved, but also foolish for making such a fuss at her expense. This young woman could hardly afford to pay for my over-priced latte out of her meagre wages, and yet she did so with a smile, circumventing her employer's rigid policy in order to treat me like a human being. I paid her back the next day with a generous tip, and made a point of paying for anyone in line who faced a similar predicament from that day on. I started imagining how amazing life would be if everyone behaved like this coffee server: empathetically understanding the other person's position and acting accordingly. I started wondering why it is so difficult to do so.

Seeking to understand others' perspectives, as St. Francis urges (Renoux, 2001), or "putting oneself in the other person's shoes" constitutes a simple, layman's definition of empathy. There are certainly more detailed definitions and explanations of empathy, which will be described in Part I of the book.

Importantly, as my experience illustrates, empathetic behavior can have ripple effects: experiencing empathy, we become motivated to not only repay kindness but also to "pay it forward" and behave empathetically toward others, whether they have treated us well or not. Thus, one kind act may affect multiple relationships, and sometimes even multiple generations. No wonder so many philosophers, positive psychologists, and spiritual sages have extolled the virtues of empathy!

If empathy is such a good thing, however, then why is empathetic behavior not more common? Why did the server's response surprise me? Despite recent volumes providing a sophisticated, neuroscientific understanding of empathy (see De Waal, 2009; Music, 2014), recognizing and challenging the influences that lead us *away* from empathy continues to be difficult for mental health professionals and non-experts alike. For example, as a psychiatrist, I am trained to behave empathetically with patients. Yet, I sometimes fail to do so with colleagues, family members, or other people I interact with in daily life like the coffee server. Furthermore, I know that I am not unique: many mental health professionals treat each other insensitively, even though they should know better. Many people report similar experiences in faith communities, where empathetic behavior might also be expected. Their spiritual leaders may extol the virtues of empathy, but they often provide little guidance on how to become empathetic more consistently. As I pondered these issues with a former student (now a therapist herself), she summed up the dilemma nicely: "There's no point writing about new research and new techniques if your book's not practical. Whatever the subject, you need to tell people how to apply the ideas to their lives." With respect to the quest for empathy, I hope to do just that.

This book examines empathy from a biopsychosocial perspective. That may sound like quite a mouthful, but this approach has been prevalent in thinking about a variety of medical and psychological conditions for decades (Engel, 1977). The biopsychosocial approach is useful because it acknowledges that human beings are complex, so psychological outcomes are rarely due to a single cause. More often, they are due to an interaction between the biology of the brain and social or other environmental factors. Empathy is no exception: the ability to put ourselves in another person's shoes requires certain neural substrates and life experiences conducive to empathy. The first part of the book describes how we can understand empathy in this way.

If we want to understand why empathy is sometimes absent, even though science suggests our brains are "wired" for it (see Music, 2014), we need to take a hard but practical look at ourselves and our daily lives. Therefore, Part II of the book is dedicated to the multiple potential obstacles to empathy, with chapters organized using the biopsychosocial approach. Only awareness of those obstacles will allow us to overcome them in the many relationships in which we participate. Special attention is paid to therapeutic relationships, given the pivotal role of empathy in psychotherapy and the serious consequences for clients when they feel misunderstood. Thus, the book aims to speak to both therapists and thoughtful non-fiction readers outside the mental health field. Many people, including myself, wear both of these "hats". For clarity, however, separate questions are provided at the end of each chapter for each audience, and Chapter 9 is devoted entirely to therapist implications. Separate implications are also reviewed for leaders of organizations and for parents, as these groups can profoundly influence empathetic behavior (respectively) in society and across the generations.

Here is a brief preview of what might interfere with empathy. Some authors cite the neurochemistry of high arousal: the "fight or flight" reaction that interferes with oxytocin and other "empathy chemicals" (see Music, 2014) and promotes self-absorption. Others cite desensitization to others' distress through repeated exposure to it (for example, in violent programs or video games) (see Hoffman, 2000). Still others cite genetic factors that predispose to lack of empathy or even psychopathy (Byrd and Manuck, 2014). Interestingly, individuals with these genes are typically under-aroused rather than over-aroused (Masi et al., 2014), seeming to contradict the previous hypothesis. Developmental psychologists posit that insecure attachment in childhood may interfere with the development of mental models of relationships which include empathy (see Bowlby, 1969). Moreover, these unhealthy mental models often become self-perpetuating: children who expect to be treated unkindly may show little kindness themselves, inadvertently inviting rejection and thus confirming their negative expectations. Other scholars suggest social origins for lack of empathy, particularly in societies that encourage competition and individualistic pursuit of success, where those who are vulnerable or not part of the "in group" may be marginalized or dehumanized (see Streich, 2011).

Even when these obstacles to empathy are not present, people may or may not behave empathetically. As St. Francis implies, the ability to understand others must be *sought*. Effort is needed to move from a state of pleasant co-existence with others to one where we actively seek to understand one another. What motivates that effort? Spiritual leaders have tried to provide that motivation for millennia. Most spiritual traditions have a version of the "Golden Rule" ("So whatever you wish that others would do to you, do also to them..." Matthew 7:12 English Standard Version). To urge people to follow it, they then place this rule in the context of a higher purpose for the individual and for mankind. Is it possible to find similar motivation in a modern, often secular world? Environmentalism is increasing people's awareness of the interconnection of all living beings on earth, but is that awareness sufficient to motivate empathetic behavior consistently? Perhaps, if we bear in mind the unique value of each of those beings, as the metaphor by Walking Buffalo suggests, and as many humanist philosophers have also suggested. It may take more than a philosophy to change habitual behavior though. The last section of the book explores the implications of self-focused versus empathetic behavior to illustrate why the latter is so urgently needed in relationships, including therapeutic and parent-child relationships, in organizations, and in the world.

This introductory discussion has provided more questions than answers, but that is intentional. The search for empathy cannot be concluded in a few paragraphs. I hope that these paragraphs have been intriguing enough, however, that you are interested in learning more. *Developing Empathy* is intended to be a thought-provoking book, informed by science but accessible to most readers. It does not provide a cookbook recipe for developing empathy. Like many issues involving human relationships, empathy is complex. There are no neat and simple instructions for becoming more empathetic. Instead, this book offers a guide to understanding the origins of empathy (Part I), overcoming the barriers that prevent us from behaving empathetically on a consistent basis (Part II), and the implications of empathetic behavior that may motivate us to strive for it more regularly (Part III). Important ideas in each chapter are illustrated with case vignettes. In the interest of confidentiality, these are either composites or drawn from the author's own experience. A relevant quote or two is included in each chapter as well; some are from popular culture, some I found on my travels, and some are quite ancient. Each chapter concludes with reflective questions for individuals and for therapists to allow the reader to apply key concepts to his or her own life, and act upon them if he or she chooses. Here are a few initial questions to ponder:

Reflective Questions

1 Can you recall an experience where someone treated you more kindly than you expected, as the coffee server in the example did? How did this experience affect you?
2 What are some of the stresses in your life that interfere with behaving empathetically toward others? How could you address these?
3 When thinking about your own values and ideals, what is the most compelling reason for you to seek to behave more empathetically?
4 Is there anything you want to change based on these reflections?

Questions for Therapists

1 Have you had clients who became happier as a result of psychotherapy, but did not treat others any better than before? Did you feel successful with these patients? Why or why not?
2 Which clients do you find most difficult to relate to empathetically? Why?
3 What influences outside the therapeutic hour affect your capacity for empathy?
4 Is there anything you want to change based on these reflections?

References

Bowlby, J. (1969). *Attachment. Attachment and Loss: Vol. 1. Loss*. New York: Basic Books.

Byrd, A.L. and Manuck, S.B. (2014). MAOA, child maltreatment, and antisocial behavior: meta-analysis of a gene-environment interaction. *Biological Psychiatry*, 75: 9–17.

De Waal, F. (2009). *The Age of Empathy: Nature's Lessons for a Kinder Society*. New York: Harmony Books.

Engel, G.L. (1977). The need for a new medical model: A challenge for biomedicine. *Science*, 196, 129–136.

Hoffman, M.L. (2000). *Empathy and Moral Development: Implications for Caring and Justice*. Cambridge, UK: Cambridge University Press.

Masi, G., Milone, A., Pisano, S., Lenzi, F., Muratori, Pl, Gemo, I., *et al.* (2014). Emotional reactivity in referred youth with disruptive behavior disorders: the role of the callous-unemotional traits. *Psychiatry Research*, 220: 426–432.

Matthew 7:12. *The Bible. English Standard Version*.

Music, G. (2014). *The Good Life: Wellbeing and the New Science of Altruism, Selfishness and Immorality*. New York: Routledge.

Renoux, C. (2001). *La prière pour la paix attribuée à saint François: une énigme à résoudre*. Paris: Editions Franciscaines.

Streich, G.W. (2011). *Justice beyond "Just Us": Dilemmas of Time, Place, and Difference in American Politics*. Burlington, VT: Ashgate Publishing.

Whyte Museum Blog (2011). Chief walking buffalo. http://whytemuseum.blogspot.ca/2011/05/chief-walking-buffalo.html / Retrieved August 22, 2016.

Part I
Understanding Empathy

1 Perspectives on Empathy: Why is an Obvious Virtue so Elusive?

A number of books, both for academics and more general audiences, have recently been written about empathy. As a result, it was challenging to convince my publisher that this book would be "different". Eventually I realized, however, that the biopsychosocial approach used provides an effective framework for both organizing previous ideas about empathy and addressing what is perhaps the most vexing question in this field: Why is an obvious, much-extolled virtue like empathy so difficult to practice consistently? Empathy and altruistic behavior based on empathy have been advocated by sages for millennia, yet sadly they are often elusive in modern life. Understanding the reasons for this problem and how we can work individually and collectively to address it became a central theme of this book. Part I focuses on understanding the problem, based on what is already known about empathy, Part II applies that understanding to the quest to nurture empathy in ourselves and others, and Part III explores implications for some specific audiences who may be reading this book.

Empathy: An Old Ideal Whose Time has Come Again

As a cursory look at any dating site will show, it has become commonplace to refer to oneself as a "work in progress" or to lament that one is "still on the road to finding myself". For those of us working in mental health, "lack of self-esteem" is a common presenting problem. The common thread in these examples is an emphasis on "self", and the assumption that once one is satisfied with that "self" happiness and good mental health will automatically follow.

Paradoxically, one of the best indicators of high self-esteem is a lack of preoccupation with oneself. People who like themselves don't need to worry about how they look, what impression they make, whether or not they are doing well, or how happy or unhappy they are currently. It is almost as if they have forgotten themselves, or that "self" just doesn't matter very much—instead, they are enthusiastic about life and living, they attend fully to those near them, resulting in greater empathy, and they look for ways to make the most of whatever circumstance they find themselves in. This state results in benefits for individual well-being, relationships, and communities.

If this state is so beneficial, however, then why doesn't everyone work on becoming less self-absorbed and more outwardly and relationally focused? Why do empathy and altruistic behavior often seem like the exceptions rather than the rule in our society? To find the answers to these questions, a brief historical review of ideas about collective and individual well-being is provided, before examining the nature of empathy in detail.

Collective Well-Being

Throughout evolution, human beings have banded together for mutual protection and support, as survival in a harsh environment was unlikely on one's own (see Lewis, 1992). Allegiance to one's group or tribe was an important social value, often superseding individual concerns. Those who behaved selfishly risked not only punishment but banishment from the group, often with lethal consequences. Those who developed empathy (albeit empathy limited to those within the group) generally fared better. Thus, there was a strong incentive to act in ways that benefitted others or benefitted the tribe as a whole. Conformity to the norms of the tribe sometimes resulted in cruelty, but individual selfish acts were definitely discouraged.

The invention of the printing press in the fifteenth century is often cited as the beginning of the modern age (Martin, 1995). By making the printed word accessible to large numbers of people, this invention ushered in a new era where education was no longer limited to a privileged elite, but became available to ordinary people. These people soon realized the possibility of using education to improve one's station in life. Individual achievement became a new cultural ideal, gradually replacing the old ideal of service to one's tribe or community. On the positive side, the emphasis on individual goals fostered a degree of scientific and technological discovery that had never been previously seen. It also become possible for educated people to challenge many of the old superstitions and prejudices that had been embedded in collective/tribal culture, broadening intellectual thought. Unfortunately, individualism had a dark side as well. Success and independence became regarded as virtues, resulting in arrogance among high achievers, denial of human interdependence, and disdain for the vulnerable or anyone incapable of conventional success. Obviously, these attitudes were not conducive to empathy.

To a degree, these attitudes persist today, though they are often considered politically conservative and not shared by everyone. Large organizations, for example, often have mission statements that extoll the virtues of collaboration and have staff engage in "teambuilding" exercises, but still use criteria related to individual achievement when considering employees for promotion. The poor still strive to become more affluent through individual achievement. Mass communication has resulted in another variant on this theme: emphasis on individual fame as a proxy for success. Appearances on reality television, "you-tube" videos, and pithy little "tweets" are new sources of individual acclaim.

Mass communication has had a different effect too though: increasing awareness of global issues. We are reminded daily of wars and disasters in distant parts of the world, of the striking inequities between human life in the developed and the developing world, and of the myriad ways in which we all affect and depend upon a sustainable natural environment. Though not always eliciting empathy, these reminders certainly make it harder to ignore the plight of our fellow human beings. The environmental movement has taken this awareness a step further: encouraging empathy for all creatures, and for the planet as a whole. Thus, individualism is starting to be balanced by collective thinking again. This new collective thinking is not limited to a specific tribe or group though, but rather (in Marshall McLuhan's terms) includes the "global village" (see Levinson, 1999).

Individual Well-Being

Collective/cultural ideals have affected our attitudes towards empathy, but ideas about what constitutes a good or meaningful life have as well. These ideas have also shifted over time.

As mentioned in the Preface, a version of the Golden Rule encouraging altruism exists in all major spiritual traditions. Interestingly, this has occurred despite little or no contact between some traditions, suggesting that spiritual sages independently came to the same conclusion. Perhaps this was because altruistic behavior was found to be important for social harmony. On the other hand, perhaps this related to the common observation that people easily become selfish when they feel even slightly threatened. When we feel our own or our family's survival is in jeopardy, the fight or flight reaction that results in a narrow focus on oneself is adaptive (see Music, 2014). Those who are prone to it are thus more likely to reproduce and pass along this trait. Unfortunately, even when survival is no longer threatened, the focus on oneself can persist to the detriment of one's relationships and community. People who are often anxious or have explosive outbursts of anger are particularly vulnerable to fight or flight reactions. The parts of the brain that allow us to regulate these emotions are a relatively recent evolutionary development. The admonition to treat others as one would want to be treated may therefore be an appeal to this more rational, regulatory part of the brain which would otherwise be silenced by the powerful survival-based fight or flight response. The Golden Rule encourages perspective-taking, an important component of empathy.

As scientific approaches to mental health and well-being gained prominence, spiritual ideas were put aside. Sigmund Freud was a neurologist, and started a tradition of applying the medical model to mental health issues. Distress and deviant behavior were considered signs of pathology to be identified and rooted out, much like surgically removing a tumor from the body. Psychiatry classified and re-classified mental disorders in the hope of accurately matching clusters of symptoms with effective treatments designed to eliminate them. Theoretical schools differed in their descriptions of pathology—some emphasizing internal conflict, others faulty relationship models, and still others maladaptive thoughts and behaviors—but until recently all shared a focus on improving mental health by treating pathology. Empathy only entered the picture when it was lacking: this disorder was termed "psychopathy" or "antisocial personality", and it was rarely treated successfully.

Eventually though, science led back to empathy. The discovery of mirror neurons and empathy-related hormones suggested that human beings have an innate capacity for empathy, whether or not they use it. These neural substrates of empathy are described further in the next chapter. Concurrently, psychiatrists were discovering the limitations of trying to categorize human beings according to their type of mental suffering and treating them accordingly. Many people fit more than one category (called "comorbidity") and comorbid presentations were difficult to study and treat. Moreover, even when treatment succeeded, the elimination of symptoms did not always result in a happier, more productive life. The need to build upon psychological strengths to enhance overall well-being and socially adaptive behavior was recognized. Empathy is one of those strengths. The strength-based approach is described further in the section below on positive psychology.

While mental health professionals struggled with the medical model, philosophers had been developing further ideas about empathy. The aesthetic philosopher Vischer (1873–1994) described "Einfühlung", the pleasure of contemplating a work of art to the point of projecting oneself into it. This idea of projecting oneself into something was later applied to human relationships, and elaborated by a number of twentieth century aesthetic and social philosophers. Humanist philosophers, on the other hand, did not use the word "empathy" but wrote about the centrality of inter-subjective, person to person relationships in meaningful life. Perhaps the best known of these is Martin Buber (see Buber, 1937/2004), who described a mental and spiritual connection with another person as an "I-Thou" relationship, in contrast to an "I-It" relationship where the other person is objectified. "I-Thou" implies a level of respect for and attention to the other person's experience, not unlike empathy.

Empathy in Psychiatry and Clinical Psychology

Empathy gradually gained prominence in psychiatry and clinical psychology as Rogers (1959) described it as a key therapeutic element of psychotherapy, and later Kohut (see Kohut, 1971) developed "self-psychology". Self-psychology was developed to treat personality disorders characterized by high self-absorption (mainly narcissistic personality disorders) and used empathy as its key clinical tool. Kohut found that when the self-absorbed feel understood, they become less focused on themselves and more open to different ways of relating to others. In his studies of child development, Bowlby (see Bowlby, 1969) related the development of empathy to secure parent-child attachment (see Chapter 2). His followers subsequently showed numerous benefits to such secure relationships, including decreased emotional and behavioral problems in children (reviewed in Schore, 2001).

Seligman's "positive psychology" movement, however, has represented a paradigm shift in relation to empathy (Seligman and Csikszentmihalyi, 2000). Whereas previous theorists saw empathy as a clinical tool in preventing or treating mental illness, positive psychology sees empathy as an end in itself. Positive psychology is defined as "using psychological understanding and intervention with the goal of achieving a satisfactory life rather than treating mental illness" (Compton, 2005a; Seligman and Csikszentmihalyi, 2000). The pursuit of the "satisfactory life" brought to light a number of findings related to empathy. For example, Vaillant's longitudinal study of Harvard graduates found that healthy, strong relationships were a key aspect of successful and happy living (Shenk, 2009), and empathy was an important aspect of healthy relationships. Positive psychology has also explored the benefits of spirituality. Nelson (2009) found that spirituality's association with well-being was best explained by virtues, resulting in renewed interest in virtue. Six cardinal virtues were found across cultures. One of these, "humanity", is closely linked to empathy. Humanity corresponds to behaviors that show love, kindness, and social intelligence.

Pulling together the literature on well-being (or the "satisfactory life"), Seligman eventually posited five main elements summarized by the acronym PERMA: positive emotions, engagement (in interesting activity), relationships, meaning (or sense of purpose), and accomplishments. These elements often interact. For example, the "broaden and build" theory of positive emotions (Compton, 2005b) suggests that positive emotions result in broader awareness and interest in novelty and exploration, whereas negative emotions prompt narrow, personal survival-related behaviors such as fight or flight responses. As empathy requires an outward focus, it is easier in the absence of fight or flight (i.e., when happy and relaxed) and conversely the altruistic behaviors associated with empathy often make us happy.

Haidt (2003) took the latter idea a step further in describing "virtuous cycles" based on the emotion of "elevation". Elevation is a positive emotion that occurs when people realize they have done something that benefits another person, prompting them to do more good deeds, resulting in more feelings of elevation, and so on in a positive cycle of virtue. Although empathy and altruism are distinct (see later in this chapter), it is not difficult to imagine that someone who is happy, outwardly focused, and empathetic would be more likely to engage in such a "virtuous cycle".

However, positive psychology is a broad field encompassing many aspects of personal and collective well-being in addition to empathy and altruism. The next section reviews ideas that are more specific to empathy.

Recent Ideas about Empathy

The recent literature about empathy is vast. It includes perspectives from various branches of psychology, philosophy, neuroscience, and other disciplines. Surveying this literature, however, two themes seem to emerge. First, many theories and empirical studies have sought to distinguish empathy from other constructs. Second, many theories and empirical studies have sought to parse empathy into its component processes. Both have yielded useful and often similar ideas, but the language varies by discipline. What follows is a brief summary of the two main themes this author could identify.

Empathy Versus Other Constructs

A number of authors have sought to distinguish empathy from sympathy. Sympathy is seen as a more general, "third person emotional response" (Darwall, 1998) relative to empathy. Unlike empathy, sympathy does not include any attempt to share a specific person's mental or emotional state. For instance, one can have sympathy for people caught in a flood or other natural disaster on the news, but one does not usually imagine the thoughts and feelings of a person standing in ever-deepening water at home, gasping for breath in a small air pocket below the roof, and about to drown. Few people could tolerate watching the evening news if this occurred.

A second distinction that has been discussed is the difference between empathy and self-transcendence (Cloninger, Svrakic and Przybeck, 1993). Self-transcendence is the ability to divert attention away from one's own immediate concerns to other aspects of life. It is thought to be needed in order for empathy to be possible, but it is not sufficient. When I empathize with another person, I not only transcend my own interests but also choose to focus on the well-being of the other person. I could just as easily transcend a focus on my own interests and choose to shift my focus to a starlit sky, or to a stirring symphony, or to a riveting movie. I value all of these experiences but they do not involve an effort to put myself in another person's shoes, so they do not constitute empathy.

A third distinction that has been discussed is that between empathy and compassion. Although these two terms are sometimes used as synonyms, "compassion" is more prominent in spiritual rather than psychological traditions. Karen Armstrong (2010), writing on compassion, indicates that it "calls us to always treat others as we wish to be treated ourselves". Thus, compassion focuses on a broad, behavioral principle. Empathy often results in compassionate behavior, but it emphasizes one to one relationships where people try to cognitively and emotionally relate to one another's perspective. Empathy is more intimate, more specific, and more psychologically challenging than compassion.

The distinction that has probably garnered the most attention is between empathy and altruism. Here, the difference seems to be between a state of mind (in the case of empathy) and a behavior that benefits others (in the case of altruism). Empathy has been linked to altruistic behavior, but the link is not consistent. The limitations of this link were demonstrated by Batson, as he was testing his "empathy-altruism hypothesis" (1987). Batson found that empathy generally resulted in behavior designed to benefit others (i.e., altruism) but only if the empathetic person was not overly distressed by the other person's predicament. If highly distressed, the person would act to alleviate their own distress, usually by leaving the situation, rather than being helpful to the other person (i.e. behaving altruistically). Coplan (2011) built upon these findings in her work on the importance of psychological boundaries in empathy (see below).

Component Processes of Empathy

Various biological, developmental, and social factors contributing to empathy are described further in the next two chapters. Here, we examine the psychological components of empathy that have been proposed in recent years.

Many authors have sought to distinguish the intellectual and the emotional aspects of empathy. Emotionally, one can feel distressed by others' distress or share their joy when they are happy, without necessarily attending to their perspectives on the situation. This response has been termed "affective empathy", "lower level empathy", "mirroring", or "emotional contagion". DeWaal (2009) has elaborated on this type of empathy in relation to primate evolutionary development. Primate species show empathy to varying degrees, but without the need for perspective-taking, as this aspect is most fully developed in humans.

Clinically, one often sees emotional empathy in young children or in children with limited perspective-taking ability. A poignant example I recall is of an autistic boy whose mother was crying after learning of his diagnosis. Previously, she had thought he would "catch up" on his minor developmental delays with appropriate speech therapy and occupational therapy, and eventually return to a normal course of development. With the diagnosis, however, she realized he would have a life-long developmental disability, and she started mourning the loss of the son she had always imagined he would be. The boy understood none of this, but he put his arm around her and mumbled "It's OK, Mummy." He couldn't tell me why he did this, but he obviously sensed that his mother needed comfort.

The intellectual aspect of empathy (termed "cognitive empathy", "higher level empathy", or "reconstructive empathy") requires trying to take another person's perspective on a situation. Colloquially, this is often referred to as "putting yourself in the other person's shoes". It involves different brain circuits than emotional empathy. Ideally, empathy should include both emotional and cognitive aspects, but some people seem to demonstrate the cognitive aspect without much emotional involvement. Mental health professionals, for example, sometimes become so practiced at certain empathetic responses (e.g. "That must be very difficult", "That must have made you feel so frustrated", etc.) that they recite them almost automatically without much emotion. Interestingly, this purely cognitive form of empathy is also common among con artists and other masters of deception.

A third component process of empathy has recently been suggested by Coplan (2011). She suggests that healthy psychological boundaries are needed for truly empathetic behavior. Thus, her description of empathy includes three elements: affective matching, other-oriented perspective taking, and self-other differentiation. In this model, people who have difficulty with psychological boundaries may still have some capacity for empathy, but they are prone to assuming that the other person feels as they would in a given situation. They do not take into account the other person's distinct characteristics which might result in a very different experience for that person than the one they themselves would have had.

I have occasionally experienced this difficulty when over-identifying with certain patients, as shown in the following example.

Sienna

Sienna was a junior in high school who excelled academically and was treasurer of the student council. Her parents had immigrated to Canada with high hopes for their children. Sienna's older brother was studying dentistry, and her achievements suggested Sienna could pursue a similar professional career. Despite some initial reservations (dating was not common in their culture), Sienna's parents had allowed her to go out with Jeff. Jeff was a chess player who hadn't dated much either, and his gentle humor and soft-spoken demeanor soon endeared him to the family. Over the summer, however, Sienna's family took a trip back to their homeland, and Sienna didn't see her boyfriend again until September. The first day of senior year, he sheepishly admitted that he had dated another girl in the summer, and didn't want to continue the relationship with Sienna. Sienna was devastated. She withdrew, became depressed, and her marks plummeted. At the end of first semester, she failed an examination in physics, a course needed for the university programs to which she had applied.

Sienna's family background was not unlike my own, so I identified with her plight. Given her family's expectations and the implications for her future, I assumed that the failed examination was foremost on her mind. After all, the break-up from her boyfriend was now four months in the past. Trying to be empathetic, I commented on how difficult this school failure must be, and encouraged her not to give up hope. Her response was "You're just like my parents. All you care about is my marks! Nobody cares that I've lost the love of my life!" I apologized for my mistake, and refocused the discussion on her unsuccessful attempts to get over the relationship with Jeff. In hindsight, the reason for my mistake became obvious: I had incorrectly assumed that Sienna had the same priorities that I had in adolescence. At that age, my focus was primarily on academic success rather than romantic relationships. Sienna's priorities were clearly different.

Finally, there has been some debate over whether or not empathy includes communicating one's empathetic understanding to the other person. If not, then empathy becomes a mental exercise that may make us feel more virtuous but has little impact on those around us. If yes, then that communication may or may not be helpful. Davis (1994), for example, has pointed out that empathetic communication may result in the other person feeling validated and understood, but it can also sometimes be experienced as intrusive.

As therapists, we often struggle to find the best words to convey our understanding of the client's experience, while being respectful and not saying more than the person is ready to hear. For example, when counseling a victim of child abuse the statement "you must have resented your mother for not protecting you in that situation" could result in either a feeling of validation and relief or a vehement defence of the client's mother depending upon the client's therapeutic needs. When in doubt, it is sometimes safer to make such interpretations using a general or "third person" approach such as "some people would resent their mother in that situation". The client then has the option of agreeing with "some people" or of describing why his or her situation was different.

Synthesizing these ideas, we see that empathy seems to include several component processes. These are illustrated in Figure 1.1. First, before

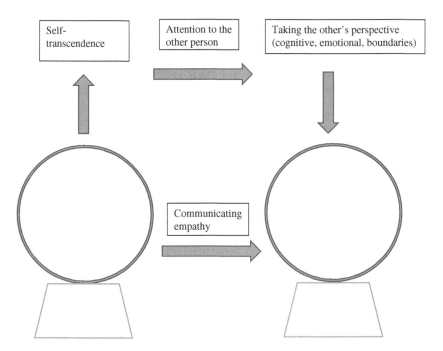

Figure 1.1 Component Processes of Empathy

becoming empathetic, we need to transcend a focus on ourselves and our own survival. Usually, this means we are not guided by fight or flight reactions, nor by preoccupation with past or future events. We are calm and alert, attending to the moment. Second, we need to direct our attention toward others. Once no longer preoccupied with our own survival, we could choose to enjoy the moment in any number of ways: appreciating a work of art or a beautiful sunset, getting caught up in the task at hand, or listening to our favorite tunes on the radio. Instead, we choose to focus on other people in an attempt to understand their thoughts and feelings. Various influences can increase or decrease the motivation to make this choice. Third, when focusing on others we attempt to cognitively take their perspective and to relate to their emotions while maintaining a clear distinction between our own feelings and theirs. Difficulty with cognitive perspective-taking, appreciation of another's emotions, or lack of psychological boundaries can all interfere with this step. Finally, we communicate our understanding of the other person's experience to them in the hope that he or she will feel understood by another human being. This communicative step depends on our ability to use language and body-language effectively, as well as on all the previous steps. It is the step most commonly taught in interviewing courses and therapy training programs. Sometimes this communication is accompanied by altruistic action towards the other person, but sometimes not.

Each of these component processes of empathy will be revisited in subsequent chapters, and related to mental health in Chapter 5. This book places somewhat more emphasis on the first two processes (transcending the focus on ourselves and directing it toward the well-being of others) than on the latter two, as the first two are more difficult to do consistently and are more readily undermined by life stress and other factors described in subsequent chapters. Perspective-taking and communication of empathy can be readily learned, for example by summarizing what you think the other person has said to you (a technique common in couples' therapy), immersion in other cultures, art forms that transport one into others' experience, exposure to others' experience (e.g., spending a day in a wheelchair to appreciate the perspective of a disabled person), repeated practice, and other methods (see McLaren, 2013). It is also important to note that communication based on empathy does not always involve a great many words. In some situations, the most empathetic response is to simply listen.

The Contrarian View

Few people would argue that empathy has a negative influence on human life. However, some have questioned Batson's premise that empathy is needed for moral or altruistic behavior. Prinz (2011) in particular has argued that empathy is *not* necessary for moral judgment or moral behavior. He points out that we can disapprove of bad behavior based on other principles (e.g., taking more than your share of a pie is wrong because it is inequitable), without necessarily having empathy for the victim. There are also some actions we consider wrong where there is no clear victim (e.g. spraying unpleasant graffiti under a bridge where few will see it). He also questions whether or not empathy is needed for moral development, as people considered morally deviant (so-called "psychopaths") often have a variety of emotional deficits besides lacking empathy. He also argues that empathy is not needed to motivate moral conduct, as emotions associated with social approval or disapproval can do the same. Finally, he points out potential pitfalls that can occur when empathy guides behavior. These include empathy promoting conformity to norms that are not necessarily moral (e.g., in collectivist societies where empathy for the group is encouraged but dissidents are punished), and empathy resulting in in-group biases (being kinder to those who are part of our group than to outsiders), proximity biases (being kinder when we can see others' suffering than when we cannot) and other forms of preferential treatment.

As a pragmatic person, I might add that empathy can sometimes result in behavior that is well-intentioned but rather useless. For example, a recent news story in our area highlighted the plight of a boy with a terminal illness whose small town rallied behind him. The boy was not expected to survive until Christmas, so the town held an early Christmas parade just for him complete with expensive reindeer floats and costumed Santa. The sight of the weak but beaming child brought tears to many eyes. I, on the other hand, thought of his rather impoverished parents, and the money they would need for his medical bills and (ultimately) his funeral. Perhaps this sounds a bit miserly, but I would have spent more money on them and less on Christmas floats.

Furthermore, empathy can sometimes make it emotionally difficult to do what is in a person's best interest. For example, as a child psychiatrist I often work with children who must face their fears despite discomfort in order to desensitize to them (called "exposure"). If I empathize with the child's distress, it becomes difficult to design and consistently encourage exposure exercises. I know, however, that these exercises represent short-term pain for long-term gain, and are necessary. I tell myself "I would want someone to give me a push so I could be more confident in the long run", but it's hard to believe when I can see that the child is clearly struggling. It can also be hard to share a difficult truth with someone if one empathizes with them. Telling someone their zipper is undone may not be too difficult, especially if one knows that this will prevent some public embarrassment, but telling someone they won't achieve their dream profession based on their level of intelligence and academic ability can be heartbreaking. One can rationalize "It's better if he/she hears it from someone who cares than someone who doesn't", but it's still not easy. Empathizing with two people who have conflicting needs can be hard too. For example, suppose a parent has one child who would benefit from a special school in a different town but another who is successful and has established friendships at the local school. Does the parent move the family? It's a tricky dilemma. In summary, empathy doesn't always make us feel good.

Finally, empathetic sentiments are sometimes used to mask self-serving goals. For example, a young newlywed might say with apparent empathy "I want to support my partner and help him/her flourish", even though a greater motivation for the marriage is to get away from an overbearing parent. Similarly, a minister might tell herself "I want to guide my parishioners in a positive spiritual direction" when her true motivation is to move up the ranks of her church. When making decisions for others we must be especially careful to distinguish empathetic from self-serving goals. For instance, "I am letting him go from a life he would not want to live" is a common justification for ending life-sustaining treatment, but it may mask the speaker's own needs (emotional, financial, or sheer exhaustion from attending to an ill relative for a long time), or even represent a projection of the speaker's wishes onto the patient.

And Yet…(Rebuttal)

One of my fondest and earliest childhood memories is of solving puzzles with my grandmother. I was six years old, and our house was full of conflict and uncertainty. It wasn't clear where the family would live, whether or not I would live with both parents, where I would go to school, and which language I would have to speak there. Moreover, the grown-ups were too busy trying to sort out these issues to pay much attention to my questions and fears. I sat in the corner miserably.

Then, my grandmother brought out a book of puzzles. She asked me to help her with them, though I realize now that she didn't really need the help of a six year old. Every time I found an answer, my grandmother smiled and I felt proud. The more answers I found, the more confident I became in my abilities, and the more fun I had. Even when I couldn't find the answer, my focus on the task in front of me seemed to block out all the other worrisome parts of my life. My grandmother eventually showed me how to do the really difficult ones, and learning this way was enjoyable too.

We didn't talk at all about feelings that day, but my grandmother somehow knew exactly what I needed. I felt understood, and she seemed to genuinely enjoy spending time with me. No reassuring word was spoken, yet I got the message that day that I was a bright, likeable girl, so wherever I ended up I would be alright. As I got older, I found in my teachers surrogate "grandmothers" who reinforced that message. I needed to learn other coping strategies too, but it was certainly a good place to start.

This example of the profound impact of empathetic moments is, to me, one of the best answers to the contrarian argument that empathy is unnecessary. Without such moments, many of us would not be the people we are today. There are other ways of learning similar life lessons, but few are as parsimonious, sometimes changing people in an instant, and few endure in memory to the same degree.

The last point raises a further question: What other virtue or ethical principle could take the place of empathy in guiding behavior? Certain codes of moral conduct might replace it, but they are usually complex and thus more difficult to apply consistently than empathy. Even the ten commandments of the Bible, a relatively simple moral code, exceeds what most people can easily remember. Short-term memory capacity is six or seven items for most of us (Miller, 1956). Moreover, using social approval or disapproval as a guide (as Prinz suggests) can have some very negative consequences. For example, in some societies committing a relatively minor offence or even belonging to a minority group can result in very harsh penalties, sometimes even the death penalty. When there is no empathy for the perpetrator or the minority group member, such irrevocable punishments are sanctioned and carried out mercilessly.

Prinz is correct that empathy is not without limitations, but that does not mean we should discard it. For example, the bias toward empathizing more with kin than with outsiders can serve as a helpful reminder: when we think of every person as someone's son or someone's daughter, our capacity for empathy increases. Try this exercise for a week and observe how your reactions to others change, particularly to those outside your immediate family.

Even apparently useless empathetic gestures, like the Christmas parade for the dying boy I mentioned, often inspire goodwill in those who observe them, resulting in indirect positive effects. For example, a parent observing the event might become kinder toward their own child; a researcher might become more determined to find a cure for the boy's disease; a person on the margins of the town might feel included by neighbors as they worked together on preparations for the parade.

Moreover, the fact that empathy can sometimes result in emotional distress should not dissuade us from practicing it. Many worthwhile endeavors are not easy. We need to be honest with ourselves though, as disentangling empathy from self-serving motives is not always easy. The reasons why these motives often compete with empathy are detailed in subsequent chapters.

Why is it Often Difficult to be Empathetic?

Much of the remainder of this book is dedicated to answering this question, as there are many influences on our behavior that cause us to veer away from empathy. These include: the many influences toward self-interest; the few influences toward aiming to understand others and step into their shoes; the influence of biases such as those mentioned in "The Contrarian View", above; the fact that emotional arousal, especially the fight or flight reaction, suppresses empathy; overexposure to horrible events, resulting in desensitization to the distress of others. Some individuals also have impairments in their capacity for empathy, which will be discussed further in Chapter 2. The next case example illustrates some of these influences away from empathy.

Marvin (Example)

It was Friday afternoon at the end of a long week. As a trainee in psychiatry, I was on call overnight at least twice a week, and I never seemed to catch up on sleep till the weekend, unless I was on call then too. This weekend, however, I had no work commitments at all. I was looking forward to an enjoyable drive through the countryside with my fiancée to view the brightly colored autumn leaves.

Most of the inpatients on the unit where I worked suffered from schizophrenia or debilitating mood disorders. Marvin, one of the patients I was assigned, had severe depression with psychotic features. Life had started deteriorating for Marvin in his last year of college. He became unable to concentrate on his work, stopped looking after himself, and withdrew from family and friends. Marvin's deterioration accelerated soon after his younger sister, to whom he had been very close, announced that she was about to marry. Marvin started hearing voices. At this point his parents, who initially thought Marvin was underachieving because he was lazy, had to admit he had psychiatric problems. Marvin was admitted to hospital, and was treated unsuccessfully with various medications for about four months. He seemed to be doing better on his most recent medication though, and there was a plan to transfer him to a hospital closer to his home in the coming days. Marvin was also eligible for a short pass outside the hospital. He said he planned to spend it with his Dad, going to a movie. I had seen Marvin earlier that day, and he seemed to be looking forward to the movie.

At around 4:30 that afternoon, Marvin's nurse approached me. She said she was worried about Marvin and wondered if it was wise to send him out on his pass. I asked what she was concerned about, "He just seems different. I feel it in my bones", was her cryptic reply. I was plowing through my last stack of paperwork before the weekend, and not in the mood for riddles. "OK. I'll take one more look at him", I curtly replied. I went to Marvin's room, ascertained that he was feeling "fine", and asked if he still planned to meet his Dad so they could walk to the movie theatre. He said he was meeting his Dad in the lobby in a few minutes. I went through my usual laundry list of questions for him: Was he hearing any voices today? Was he having any suicidal thoughts? Was he frightened or worried about anything, etc.? Marvin responded with a clear "no" to all of them. In summary, I went through the motions of clearing Marvin for his pass, and that was all I was obliged to do. Interviewing Marvin was a chore that needed to be finished in order to get on with my weekend, nothing more. Relating to Marvin empathetically, person to person, was not on my agenda that day.

Marvin left the unit a few minutes later, and I never saw him again. I was on my way out of the building when the phone rang. It was the emergency department from a nearby hospital. They had found my number on a bottle of pills that was recovered from under a bridge where Marvin had jumped. I felt sick.

The inquest into Marvin's death concluded that I had done everything that could reasonably be asked. I even got complimented on how well I had documented it. As I was a trainee, there was a recommendation that decisions involving some risk, like allowing a patient to go on a pass, should be supervised more closely in future. However, this was a general recommendation for all supervisors and trainees. I was not singled out or blamed in any way.

I never forgot Marvin though. I never again treated a patient's concerns as an obstacle to my weekend. I never again ignored the instincts of a nurse. The nurse in this example obviously had a greater capacity for empathy than I did on that day. I also learned to be extra careful when tired, sick, or otherwise not at my best. I only wish these lessons had come sooner, and not at such a terrible price.

Fortunately, not every empathetic failure has such extreme consequences. The fact that this one did is what made it so memorable. There are probably thousands of daily interactions between people that lack empathy and have little consequence…except to make the world seem a bit colder and less caring than before they happened. The traffic officer who seems to take pleasure in humiliating me for going a few miles over the speed limit, or the store clerk who sees me shivering in the rain and won't open the door because I'm two minutes early according to her watch come to mind. The outcomes in each case are the same, whether accompanied by empathy (or at least neutrality) or disdain for the other person.

Nevertheless, the extreme example of Marvin begs the question: What interfered with my capacity for empathy that day? After all, as an aspiring psychiatrist empathy was usually an integral part of my clinical work. Several factors were likely at play that day though. Fatigue or other physical discomfort can certainly impact one's capacity for empathy, as discussed further in Chapter 4. Being narrowly focused on the goal of finishing work so I could enjoy the weekend also interfered with my ability to attend to the person in front of me. This cognitive factor is described further in Chapter 5. Annoyance with the nurse's vague description of her concerns may have influenced me, as that description could not be used to justify either giving the pass or taking it away, making it rather unhelpful. Annoyance, a mild form of anger, can trigger the fight or flight reaction that competes with empathy, as described further in Chapter 6. The culture of medicine may also have played a role. In medicine, we categorize human beings according to diagnoses or clinical problems, which sometimes has a dehumanizing effect. Social and cultural factors affecting empathy are detailed in Chapter 3. Finally, feeling insecure about my trainee status may have affected my behavior. Rather than admitting doubts about the situation and asking for help, I felt a need to prove myself as someone decisive and able to take charge like a "real doctor". The roots of insecurity can stem from childhood (see Chapters 2 and 7), but social expectations and ideals (i.e., to gradually behave more like a physician and less like a trainee over the course of one's training) can contribute as well (see Chapters 3 and 8). When all of these influences combined, they created a "perfect storm" for behavior that lacked empathy. Understanding these and other influences on empathy is vital, if we are to become empathetic consistently.

What is Not Known

From the descriptions above, it is clear that a great deal of theoretical work related to empathy has been done in recent decades. Converting this theoretical understanding into practical interventions that contribute to healthier relationships and communities remains a challenge. I hope that this book begins to address that challenge. However, more research is clearly needed into the best means of strengthening the various components of empathy discussed above, addressing the limitations to empathy identified by contrarians such as Prinz, and reducing the various factors that interfere with empathy in our day to day lives.

Reflective Questions

1. Of all the aspects of empathy discussed in this chapter, which one speaks to you most? Why?
2. Do you recall situations in life where empathy was not helpful? What went wrong?
3. Do you ever recall fooling yourself into thinking you were being empathetic when you were not? What was the result?
4. What stops you from being more consistently empathetic? Is it an aspect of yourself, cultural expectations, or a bit of both?
5. Try thinking of everyone you meet this week as someone's son or someone's daughter. What do you observe?

Questions for Therapists

1. Of the component processes of empathy (cognitive, affective, psychological boundaries), which one poses the most challenges in your work with clients? How could you address these challenges?
2. Do you recall situations with clients where empathy was not helpful? What went wrong?
3. Do you ever recall fooling yourself into thinking you were being empathetic with a client when you were not? What was the result?
4. What stops you from being more consistently empathetic? Is it an aspect of yourself, professional expectations, or a bit of both?
5. Try thinking of everyone you meet this week as someone's son or someone's daughter. What do you observe?

References

Armstrong, K. (2010). *Twelve Steps to a Compassionate Life*. New York: Random House, p. 6.
Batson, C.D. (1987). Prosocial motivation: is it ever truly altruistic? In L. Berkowitz (Ed.) *Advances in Experimental Social Psychology*. New York: Academic Press, pp. 65–122.
Bowlby, J. (1969). *Attachment. Attachment and Loss: Vol. 1. Loss*. New York: Basic Books.
Buber, M. (1937). *I and Thou*. New York: Charles Scribner's Sons. Reprinted byContinuum International Publishing Group, 2004.
Cloninger, C.R., Svrakic, D.M., Przybeck, T.R. (1993). A psychobiological model of temperament and character. *Archives of General Psychiatry*, 50, 975–990.
Compton, W.C. (2005a). *An Introduction to Positive Psychology*. New York: Wadsworth Publishing, pp. 1–22.
Compton, W.C. (2005b). *An Introduction to Positive Psychology*. New York: Wadsworth Publishing, pp. 23–40.
Coplan, A. (2011). Understanding empathy: its features and effects. In Coplan, A. and Goldie, P. (Eds.) *Empathy: Philosophical and Psychological Perspectives*. New York: Oxford University Press, pp. 3–18.
Darwall, S. (1998). Empathy, sympathy, care. *Philosophical Studies*, 89, 261–282.
Davis, M.H. (1994). *Empathy: A Social Psychological Approach*. Madison, WI: Brown & Benchmark, p. 11.
DeWaal, F. (2009). *The Age of Empathy: Nature's Lessons for a Kinder Society*. New York: McLelland & Stewart, pp. 84–117.
Haidt, J. (2003). Elevation and the positive psychology of morality. In C.L.M. Keyes and J. Haidt (Eds.) *Flourishing: Positive Psychology and the Life Well-lived*. Washington, DC: American Psychological Association, pp. 275–289.
Kohut, H. (1971). *The Analysis of the Self*. New York: International Universities Press.
Levinson, P. (1999). *Digital McLuhan: A Guide to the Information Millennium*. New York: Routledge.
Lewis, D. (1992). *Millennium: Tribal Wisdom and the Modern World*. Toronto: Viking Canada.
Martin, H. (1995). *The History and Power of Writing*. Chicago: University of Chicago Press, p. 217.
McLaren, K. (2013). *The Art of Empathy*. New York: Sounds True Publishing.
Miller, G.A. (1956). The magical number seven, plus or minus two: Some limits on our capacity for processing information. *Psychological Review*, 63, 81–97.
Music, G. (2014). *The Good Life: Wellbeing and the New Science of Altruism, Selfishness and Immorality*. New York: Routledge.
Nelson, J.M. (2009). *Psychology, Religion, and Spirituality*. New York: Springer Science. p. 359.
Prinz, J.J. (2011). Is empathy necessary for morality? In: Coplan, A. and Goldie, P. (Eds.) *Empathy: Philosophical and Psychological Perspectives*. New York: Oxford University Press, pp. 211–229.
Rogers, C.R. (1959). A theory of therapy, personality, and interpersonal relationships, as developed in the client-centered framework. In Koch, S. (Ed.) *Psychology: A Study of Science, Vol. 3: Formulations of the Person and the Social Context*. New York: McGraw Hill, pp. 184–256.

Schore, A.N. (2001). Effects of a secure attachment relationship on right brain development, affect regulation, and infant mental health. *Infant Mental Health Journal*, 22, 7–66.

Seligman, M.E.P. and Csikszentmihalyi, M. (2000). Positive psychology: an introduction. *American Psychologist*, 55, 5–14.

Shenk, J. (2009). Finding happiness after Harvard. *Wilson Quarterly*, 33, 73–74.

Vischer, R. (1994[1873]). On the optical sense of form: a contribution to aesthetics. In H.F. Mallgrave (Ed.) *Empathy, Form, and Space*. Los Angeles, CA: Getty Center for the History of Art and the Humanities, pp 89–123.

2 Nature and Nurture: The Developmental Basis of Empathy

> The moment when someone can participate in another's lived story…a different kind of human contact is created.
>
> Daniel Stern (2004)

In the introduction, I pointed out an apparent contradiction between genetic and environmental ideas pertaining to empathy. One seems to suggest that those genetically predisposed to low physiological arousal are less empathetic; the other seems to suggest that high levels of arousal due to anger or anxiety (the fight or flight reaction) prevent people from behaving empathetically. The ideas in this chapter help explain this apparent discrepancy, and provide a more detailed understanding of the development of empathy generally. When seeking to become more empathetic, this understanding can prove helpful. Important findings about constitutional factors ("nature") and environmental factors ("nurture") involved in empathy are reviewed, and summarized in Table 2.1. Case examples illustrate how a child's development of empathy can go awry, and that experiences can sometimes repair the damage.

A Brain Primed for Empathy

Years ago, it was thought that empathetic behavior was largely a learned response. As neuroscientists discover more about the anatomy and chemistry of the brain, however, it is becoming increasingly clear that this organ has specific features that make us receptive to developing empathetic responses. In other words, human beings are primed for empathy.

Anatomically, the right ventromedial cortex has been found particularly important in producing empathetic responses (Shamay-Tsoory et al., 2003; Shamay-Tsoory, 2011), though with some distinct areas related to cognitive aspects of empathy and other areas related to emotional aspects. These responses are thought to occur via a system of brain cells designed to promote mimicry of others, termed "mirror neurons" (Decety and Ickes, 2011). This system transfers observational learning about others to the rest of the brain and then prompts actions, cognitions, and emotions based on that

Table 2.1 Developmental Influences Toward or Away from Empathy

Type of Influence	Impact on Empathy
Constitutional	Family history of psychopathy or autism, suggesting genetic vulnerability to lack of empathy
	Resemblance to someone your parent disliked
Early Attachment	History of trauma, loss, or mental health problems in a parent
	Memories of not feeling home was a "secure base"
	Few specific memories of childhood
	Secure relationship with a caring, non-parental adult or partner
	Participation in interpersonal or psychodynamic psychotherapy
Later Influences	Memories of authoritative parenting
	Exposure to bullying or abuse
	Highly competitive environments
	School or community environments that fostered empathy
Current Influences	Scarcity of time or money
	Physical illness
	Anxiety, depression, proneness to anger, or other mental health problems that foster a negative bias toward others
	Mindfulness or relaxation practices designed to counteract the fight or flight response

information. Mirror neurons allow us to imagine another person's experience, including his or her feelings, and respond to that person accordingly. Facial expression, posture, and cadence of speech all begin to parallel those of the other person. In this state, we no longer respond to the person with complete objectivity (i.e., as if he or she were an object in our environment) but from a position that includes an appreciation of the other person's subjective experience or, as Stern so eloquently states, we "participate in another's lived story". Termed "intersubjectivity" (Trevarthan, 1993), this state forms the basis of many close human relationships. It is made possible by the mirror neuron system.

It has been argued that mirror neurons are only one of two routes to empathy (Goldman, 1992). Mirror neuron responses are thought to be automatic neurological phenomena involving mimicry of motor actions and experiences of pain or unpleasant emotion that parallel those of another person. By contrast, shifting one's perspective to another's point of view is thought to be a less automatic, more thoughtful form of empathy. One wonders, however, if this concept is similar to the distinction between emotional empathy (i.e., responding emotionally to another's distress) and cognitive empathy (i.e., understanding a situation from another's point of view) described in Chapter 1. Alternatively, Williams (2008) has proposed in the Embodied Cognition Theory that mirror neuron coding for action provides the foundation for cognition related to others. Thus, one route to empathy (mirror neurons) may facilitate the other (cognitive perspective-taking). Recent functional imaging studies linking mirror neurons with areas of the brain dedicated to perspective taking (Schulte-Ruther et al., 2007), and the observation that practicing mimicry can improve socialization in autistic individuals (Perkins et al., 2010) seem to support this idea.

The brain chemical most consistently linked to empathy is oxytocin. Oxytocin was initially linked to the milk let-down reflex in breastfeeding (Jonas and Woodside, 2015), and for many years this was thought to be its only function. More recently, however, it has been linked to a variety of empathetic responses (see Music, 2014), and low levels of oxytocin are thought to limit empathy. Intranasal oxytocin has even been proposed as a treatment for deficits in social reciprocity found in autism (Quintana et al., 2015). Some authors have cautioned, however, that oxytocin may promote empathy only toward close kin, not acquaintances or strangers, resulting in exclusion of those outside one's immediate "tribe" (De Dreu, 2012). Other brain chemicals are likely at play in broader, more inclusive forms of empathy. A number of candidate genes for these chemicals are currently under investigation (see next section).

Constitutional Differences in Empathy

Several genetic variants have been linked to empathy or to an extreme lack of empathy termed psychopathy. Genes coding for oxytocin receptors have been most consistently linked to empathy. Recent findings suggest, however, that oxytocin genes may relate more to emotional than cognitive empathy (Usefovsky et al., 2015). Genes related to the brain chemicals vasopressin and dopamine have been associated with cognitive empathy (Ben-Israel et al., 2015; Usefovsky et al., 2015). Numerous studies have found that genes resulting in low levels of MAO-A (another brain chemical) predispose to violence and psychopathy, especially in boys (Byrd and Manuck, 2014). Genes linked to the brain chemical serotonin have been implicated in psychopathy (Sadeh et al., 2013), although serotonin also plays a role in emotion regulation (for example, regulating anxiety created by the fight or flight response) which supports the capacity for empathy. Mood and anxiety regulation has also been linked to natural opiates in the brain termed "endorphins" (Baker, 2008), so endorphin release through exercise and other activities (see Chapter 4) may support empathy as well.

Deficits in oxytocin and in mirror neuron development have been found in people on the autistic spectrum (Iacoboni & Dapretto, 2006). One of the hallmarks of autism is difficulty with taking another person's perspective, an ability needed for cognitive aspects of empathy. Despite these deficits, however, autistic individuals are not consistently violent or psychopathic, attesting to the multiple factors at play in the development of empathy.

Constitutional factors related to empathy seem to be influenced by the child's environment. For example, the MAO-A gene seems to increase the risk of psychopathy only if the affected child experiences abuse (Byrd and Manuck, 2014). Similarly, the hypothalamic-pituitary-adrenal (HPA) axis, which determines our sensitivity to fight or flight reactions and our typical stress responses, develops differently depending on whether we experience abusive or nurturing early environments (Matthews, 2002). These findings suggest that genetic factors do not destine people to lack empathy. Children who are genetically predisposed to violence or extreme lack of empathy may avoid this fate when raised in caring, supportive environments. A section below describes the nature of these supportive environments in detail.

One "constitutional" factor that is not often mentioned in the literature is the child's resemblance to a parent or someone in the parent's past. This resemblance can sometimes make it difficult for a parent to show empathy to a particular child, in turn affecting the child's development of empathy toward others. A simple example is the child who resembles a sibling to whom the parent was compared unfavorably in the past. When misbehaving, the child might be confronted with the statement "You're just like Aunt Louise!" rather than some constructive suggestion on how to change his or her behavior. This sort of parental rejection and stigmatization might make the child determined *not* to behave like Aunt Louise, but it would be unlikely to foster the development of empathy. A more subtle problem occurs when the child resembles an unwelcome part of the parent's own history, as in the following case of Danny and his father, Arjun.

Danny and Arjun

Arjun was a homicide detective in our local police force, and had moved quickly up the ranks. With any luck, he would be Chief of Police within the next few years. Much to Arjun's embarrassment, however, his son appeared to be getting into conflict with the law. Danny wasn't a malicious sort, but he associated with antisocial friends. Danny had been caught shoplifting after a friend dared him to do it, and then had been caught holding a gym bag for a friend, not realizing it contained a banned substance. When his father confronted him, Danny replied "You don't know what it's like growing up in this town. You're only interested in the next promotion!"

Arjun scolded his son severely, and grounded him for a month. He turned to me for help in understanding his boy, and "straightening him out". As I was assessing the situation, I asked him to tell me something about his own background.

Arjun reported growing up on the streets of a large city after his father died, begging and stealing food. He saw his friends taken advantage of by older men who preyed on street urchins, abusing and even crippling them so they could earn more cash from passers-by who pitied them. Arjun resolved never to be "owned" by one of these predators, and found a way to get out of his country and start a new life in North America. After completing his education, he joined the police force where he took pride in protecting the vulnerable from crime. His life of begging, stealing, and abuse seemed far behind him, and he swore never to return to it. His work and his stable family life seemed to ensure that he never would.

Now Danny was brought to his doorstep by a fellow officer, about to be arrested. Before his eyes, Arjun saw in Danny everything he had once been and subsequently tried *not* to be: a thief and a liar used by others for nefarious gain. He had fought for years to escape this fate, and now his son was playing out that fate before him. Arjun saw in his son the worst part of his own past. He could not comprehend anyone making his son's choices, and reverting to the life he had fought so hard to escape. He asked only one question: "Why?"

When I talked to Arjun's son, the answer was not difficult to find. Danny reported that his father had always spent long hours at work, and the only time he paid attention to his children was when there was a problem. Danny learned that if he failed a subject at school his Dad would come out to parent-teacher night to find out how to remedy the problem. If his sister broke curfew to stay out with her new boyfriend, his Dad would track her down. When everyone in the family was successful and well-behaved Arjun ignored them. Arjun was a problem-solver, and only engaged in relationships when his intervention was needed. Thus, rather than trying to hurt his father (as Arjun assumed), Danny misbehaved in order to relate to him.

With help Arjun was able to understand his son's perspective and recognize that Danny was not deliberately trying to upset him, and was really a caring boy who desperately wanted a relationship with his father before venturing out on his own. Empathy between father and son grew, Danny's delinquent behavior subsided, and Arjun was able to care for and guide his son in a new, healthier way. Danny eventually became a social worker, helping other youth who experienced difficulties that resembled his own.

Degrees of Empathy that May Develop

Most of us are not consistently, genuinely empathetic, nor are we the opposite. We muddle through life with some empathy, consistently toward those we see as similar to ourselves, and to a degree toward others. Although supported by limited evidence, Hoffman's theory of empathy development may be useful in understanding these "shades of grey" between self-focused interactions with others and interactions that are fully empathetic (see Hoffman, 2000). Hoffman proposes five stages of empathy development: newborn reactive cry, where the other's distress is mirrored without response; egocentric empathetic distress, where the other's distress is mirrored with efforts to reduce one's own distress; quasi-egocentric empathetic distress, where there is an attempt to help the other but from one's own point of view; veridical empathetic distress, where there are attempts to help take the other's perspective into account; and an understanding of empathy beyond the immediate situational clues (e.g., understanding the other may still be distressed even if smiling at the moment). Hoffman proposes that these stages occur in the first two years of life, and set the stage for developing a moral compass when combined with prosocial influences from the environment. Over-arousal, habituation (by which he means desensitizing to another's distress through repeated exposure to it), and the tendency to empathize more with those who are familiar and close to us than those who are unfamiliar and distant (familiarity bias and "here and now bias", see Chapter 1) are all proposed as obstacles to empathy.

As in most stage theories, however, it is not clear if the stages truly follow the timing in early development the theorist suggests, nor if everyone achieves the final stage proposed. For example, if I have a friend who becomes seriously ill but has also "pitched in" over the years when I needed help at home, my first thought upon hearing her diagnosis might be "Too bad. Now I have to find someone else to help out." My focus is on my own distress (i.e., egocentric empathetic distress), rather than hers. Alternatively, I might feel badly for her and bring her a sweet treat, not remembering she is diabetic (i.e., quasi-egocentric; helping her from my own point of view). I would hope I could move on to the latter stages, where I respond based on a deep, empathetic understanding of her experience (i.e., listening to her concerns and responding in a manner she would find truly helpful). However, I'm not sure this would always be my first reaction, and I suspect I am not alone in this regard. We now turn to early experiences that may influence the development of empathy, and help explain why fully evolved forms of empathy don't "come naturally" to many of us.

Early Environment and Empathy

As human beings, we are born into relationships. Our earliest relationships are with our parents, and experiences in those relationships continue to influence us throughout life. Trusting, caring relationships with parents make it easier to trust and care about people outside the family, paving the road toward empathy. John Bowlby studied these parent-child relationships in great detail, resulting in his Attachment Theory (see Bowlby, 1969). He defined attachment as a lasting psychological connection between human beings. Since then, a large body of research has validated many aspects of this theory, which is now used by child mental health professionals internationally.

In brief, attachment theory posits that infants develop habitual patterns of connecting with their primary caregivers when distressed or separated from them. Securely attached infants expect the caregiver to respond in consistently reassuring ways when the infant is distressed. Therefore, the infant cries vigorously when separated from the caregiver, and calms quickly when the caregiver returns. Over time, the infant learns what the caregiver does to calm distress, and becomes able to regulate distressing emotions herself. She also develops a mental model of close relationships that suggests others are caring and she (the infant) is worthy of care.

Relevant to empathy, children who feel cared for are, in turn, more likely to care for others. They are attuned to their own and others' emotions, facilitating emotional aspects of empathy. Children who feel worthy of care are also not preoccupied with bolstering their own self-worth, and so are free to look outward with curiosity toward others. Curiosity about others' mental states forms the cognitive basis of empathy. Finally, children who can regulate distressing emotions easily experience few fight or flight reactions that interfere with empathy. No wonder that multiple studies have linked secure attachment to empathetic behavior (Schore, 2001)!

Unfortunately, habitual maladaptive forms of emotion regulation often emerge in the context of insecure attachment (Zimmerman, 1999). When these persist, they intensify the focus on oneself and decrease empathy. For example, infants whose caregivers respond in consistently negative ways to their distress learn to avoid showing negative emotions (so-called "avoidant attachment"). Later in development, minimizing negative emotion tends to result in denying one's own vulnerability and need for others, and the loss of specific memories that might challenge that denial. Often, this style leads people to become arrogant, avoid intimacy, and have a limited capacity for empathy. Conversely, infants whose caregivers respond inconsistently to their distress (sometimes calming the infant, sometimes not) tend to develop "ambivalent attachment". They amplify distress signals in an attempt to get the caregiver's attention more consistently. Later in development, they may habitually dwell on negative emotion resulting in an excessive focus on past hurts and on personal vulnerability, and attempts to overcome these issues through current relationships. Within those relationships, however, the focus is on their own emotional needs rather than on empathy for their partner.

The most distorted attachment relationships occur when parents are abusive, bereaved, traumatized, or mentally ill. Termed "disorganized attachment", these relationships are very unpredictable and leave the infant without a clear strategy for regulating distressing emotions. This form of attachment has been linked to psychological problems in children most consistently, including aggression and other behaviors reflecting a lack of empathy (Schore, 2002). Sometimes, emotionally abusive parents also lack psychological boundaries, treating their children as extensions of themselves. The children, in turn, have difficulty distinguishing their own and others' feelings, a skill that is necessary for empathy.

Regardless of the specific type of insecurity, insecurely attached individuals are generally more prone to fight or flight reactions, whether they show this or not. Once these reactions occur, they attempt to regulate them in self-focused ways, limiting their ability to relate to others empathetically, especially when stressed. As they show others little empathy, these individuals may also elicit little empathy from others, confirming their negative views of relationships. Furthermore, as described in later chapters, the relationship models stemming from early attachment impact not only people's interpersonal behavior but also their physical well-being, their habitual responses to illness and to social circumstances, and even some of their beliefs.

Moreover, these suboptimal attachment patterns tend to cross generations (Raby et al., 2015). People tend to relate to their children in ways their parents related to them, even though they are often not aware of this. Of global concern, wars and international economic disparities are increasing the number of abused and traumatized children. These children's suffering will profoundly affect their own children, possibly affecting the human capacity for empathy for generations. The story of Aloofa provides an example of how, inadvertently, insecure attachment can be passed along.

Aloofa

Aloofa was raised in a war-torn country, and watched unimaginable horrors perpetrated on her family and neighbors as a teen. She helped bury many of her closest friends before fleeing to a safer land. Before the war, Aloofa's family was affluent and educated. She was trained in piano and ballet, and was an avid reader. As a refugee in her new country, Aloofa struggled to find money for food and shelter. Buying books or music was out of the question. She felt isolated, cut off from everyone she had cared about and from the culture in which she was raised. An older man who had emigrated several years earlier got her a job, and eventually married her. Unlike Aloofa, her new husband came from an impoverished background and had come to the new country voluntarily, looking for greater prosperity. Although struggling to make ends meet, he was grateful for the opportunities afforded him, and told Aloofa she should be grateful too.

Logically, Aloofa knew her husband was right. Emotionally though, she could not feel gratitude. Nightmares from her traumatic past continued to haunt her, she continued to grieve the loss of her friends and family, and it was difficult to adjust to the difference in lifestyle between that of her childhood and her new life. The difference in education level between herself and her husband also bothered her, and the couple had few common interests to talk about. She struck up a friendship with one of her co-workers though, as this woman was also well-educated but working in an entry level job due to life circumstances.

After her first child was born, Aloofa became profoundly depressed. She did not see her baby boy as a blessing; rather, she now felt alone and trapped in her apartment. As she was on maternity leave, she didn't even have the company of her co-worker any more. She tried to respond to the baby's needs, but often blamed the child for her predicament which interfered with responding empathetically. Flashbacks from her traumatic past also shifted her focus away from the baby and into her own tortured mind. Some days, she was too depressed to attend to the baby at all. Her husband eventually found a neighbor who could help while he was at work, so that the baby was not physically harmed. The attachment relationship between mother and son, however, was clearly insecure.

As the boy grew into a toddler, he seemed anxious and irritable. He was a picky eater, insisting on only a small range of foods. He slept poorly, and needed to be held by a parent in order to fall asleep. If his mother went to another room, he followed. He cried loudly if he was not included in all of her activities. At the store, he had tantrums if his mother refused to buy him candy or toys he wanted. When playing with other children, he insisted on being the boss, even if that meant pushing them around. In short, he seemed to control everything and everyone in his environment.

Behavioral problems continued as he got older. Having never experienced empathy, the boy was unable to empathize with others. He did not feel connected to his family, so sought a sense of connection in a street gang. Aloofa didn't understand why her son behaved this way and accused him of being cruel to her, "punishing me instead of being grateful for all I've done". In response to this attempt to induce guilt, he replied "You never wanted to have me. You only care about people back in the old country!" Recognizing the truth in his words, Aloofa sought counseling to deal with her troubled past. By this point, however, the chasm between mother and son was so great that even as her capacity for empathy grew, her son continued to drift away. He had become almost as cruel as the soldiers that traumatized Aloofa.

The connection between attachment and empathy doesn't always have such gloomy results though. Attachment patterns show some stability over time, but are also amenable to change. For example, insecurely attached people who experience close relationships that differ from those with parents can sometimes develop more secure attachment models, increasing their capacity for empathy (Raby et al., 2015). Psychotherapy focused on parent-child attachment can influence insecure parents to become more attuned to their infants' signals and, eventually, develop secure relationships with them (Bakermans-Kranenburg, van IJzendoorn and Juffer, 2003). Similarly, good marital relationships can buffer the effects of parental insecurity on children (Dickstein, Seifer, and Albus, 2009). Other forms of psychotherapy may help people identify maladaptive interpersonal patterns, allowing them to stop "doing what comes naturally" (i.e., automatic responses stemming from insecure attachment models) and choose to behave differently, and often more empathetically, toward others. Interpersonal therapy and psychodynamic psychotherapy are particularly attuned to these issues.

Later Environment and Empathy

Beyond attachment, other parental and non-parental influences can affect children's capacity for empathy. Effective parenting involves not only responding consistently to child distress (as described in Attachment Theory) but also setting appropriate limits, engaging in enjoyable activities together when the child is not distressed, understanding what the child needs to learn at different ages, encouraging gradual independence, and sometimes advocating for the child when he or she faces challenges outside the home. A balanced approach where the parent both cares for the child and sets reasonable expectations of behavior (so-called "Authoritative Parenting") has been linked to the development of empathy (Hastings et al., 2007).

As the child matures, influences outside the parent-child dyad become more salient. Siblings, schools, peers, and community experiences all affect our developing maps of human relationships and thus our capacity for and inclination towards empathy. Children exposed to traumatic events such as abuse or severe bullying are influenced on a physiological level as well (Matthews, 2002). Changes in the body's stress response system have been found to result from such experiences. Altered stress responses, in turn, can affect the capacity for empathy (see "Emotional states that suppress empathy" below). Highly competitive school or athletic environments can also impede the development of empathy. In these environments, adults and children learn to laud high achievers, sometimes resulting in denigrating those who are less accomplished or more vulnerable.

On the positive side, however, learning empathy still seems to be possible at school age, even in children from disadvantaged backgrounds. The Roots of Empathy program, for instance, exposes children to an infant with his or her parent on a regular basis (about every three weeks) in the classroom throughout the school year (see Gordon, 2012). Children are invited to interpret how the baby is feeling, and these efforts enhance their understanding of their own and others' feelings. This intervention, studied in several countries, has been found to reduce aggression and increase empathy among school-aged children even three years after the program ends (Santos et al., 2011).

Emotional States that Suppress Empathy

Current emotional states can "ramp up" or "ramp down" our capacity for empathy moment by moment. The fight or flight response, generated automatically by the body when we perceive threat, is thought to be the most common culprit when it comes to suppressing empathy. In this response, designed to help us cope with danger, adrenaline is released causing rapid heartbeat, rapid breathing, dilated pupils, redirection of blood flow to the large muscles, and other physiological changes. In short, the body is rapidly readied for action. The mind is affected as well. Alertness increases, mechanical reasoning ability is enhanced, and thought becomes focused and goal-oriented. As these mental abilities increase, divergent thinking decreases, thus reducing attention to the perspectives of others (Jack et al., 2013). Without attention to others' perspectives, empathy is compromised.

There are more ways of activating the fight or flight response than may be obvious at first glance. In certain psychological conditions, people are biased toward perceiving threat. Children with aggressive behavior problems, for example, perceive hostility in others more regularly than children without this condition (Dodge, 2006). On the other hand, children with anxiety disorders perceive environmental threats more readily than children without these disorders (Ouimet, Gawronski and Dozois, 2009). Both of these groups of children thus have a heightened tendency to experience fight or flight reactions (though obviously more often "fight" in the first group and "flight" in the second group). Like many developmental phenomena, these biases are thought to result from an interaction of genetic predisposition and early environment.

Physical discomfort can also be perceived as threatening, thus heightening our focus on personal well-being and decreasing our focus on others. Illness can therefore affect our capacity for empathy, which is discussed further in Chapter 4.

Behavioral economists have identified a further factor that often increases fight or flight and suppresses empathy: perceived scarcity of important resources such as food, money, or time (see Mullainathan and Shafir, 2013). When faced with such scarcity, human beings tend to become narrowly focused on the immediate need to acquire the scarce resource, losing the broader perspectives needed to plan for their own and others' well-being. Without such perspectives, behavior often becomes impulsive and lacking in empathy.

Although focusing on an immediate goal can be helpful if, for instance, meeting a deadline when time is scarce, it often results in neglect of other people's needs and concerns. For example, a working single parent may need to address her child's school difficulties, a major home repair, a stack of complicated tax forms, and an important work deadline all in the same week. As she struggles to meet the deadline and juggle the other responsibilities, she neglects her friends and snaps impulsively at her accountant. These empathetic failures seem out of character for her, but are understandable given her divided attention in the face of significant time constraints. Interestingly, this type of "tunnel vision" can also be self-defeating: in the example, the accountant who feels hurt may refuse to help with the tax forms, resulting in further problems and further time constraints.

In summary, in addition to truly dangerous situations several other factors can generate fight or flight responses, temporarily limiting our capacity for empathy. Common ones include physical illness, cognitive biases, and coping with scarce resources. Conversely, practices designed to ameliorate fight or flight reactions such as mindfulness meditation and certain relaxation practices can enhance our capacity for empathy. These will be discussed further in subsequent chapters.

Resolving the Hypo/Hyper-Arousal Paradox

With the information reviewed in this chapter so far, we can begin to reconcile the hypo/hyper-arousal paradox mentioned in the introduction. Recall that hyper-aroused emotional states generally suppress empathy via the fight or flight response. In these states, we are narrowly focused on personal needs, reducing attention to others' needs and thus reducing empathy. Chronic hypo-arousal, on the other hand, is a trait associated with callous, unemotional behavior in psychopaths (Masi et al., 2014). This trait leaves people feeling bored much of the time and craving excitement. If these people lack empathetic relationship models (for example, if they experienced abuse as children), they may seek excitement at others' expense and so behave without empathy. Thus, through different mechanisms, both hyper-aroused states and hypo-aroused/unemotional traits can limit our capacity for empathy and result in inconsiderate or uncaring behavior toward others. The mechanisms are different, but the unfortunate outcome is the same.

What is Not Known

A number of factors have been shown to influence the propensity for empathetic behavior, but it is not always clear how these factors will interact in a given individual and which one(s) will be most salient. For example, attachment has been shown to influence right brain development, including specific areas linked to empathy (Schore, 2001), but does this mean that attachment destines people to become high or low in empathy for life? Is it possible that later experiences or empathy-focused programs can eliminate empathy deficits stemming from early insecurity? Alternatively, is there a "critical period" for empathy development, after which deficits can be ameliorated but not completely eliminated?

Gene-environment interactions also merit further study. For instance, it is known that the MAO-A gene does not create a risk of psychopathy in the absence of abuse. Could something similar occur in children with a high genetic risk of hyper-aroused states (i.e., those prone to anxiety disorders) if raised in nurturing environments? The influence of social factors on empathy development requires further clarification as well, and will be discussed in the next chapter.

For now, let's examine the story of Ashley: a case vignette of someone whose view of herself and of others underwent significant change over time. As you read the story, imagine what it would be like to be Ashley. If you are a mental health professional, imagine treating her.

Ashley

Ashley was a teen from a single-parent household. She was referred to me for a diagnostic assessment after stealing a candy bar from a store. Her mother reported that she lied to her, stole food, did not apply herself at school, and associated with peers who smoked and experimented with marijuana. She believed that the root of the problem was Ashley's poor self-esteem, and requested that I "give her some self-esteem".

As I explained that self-esteem cannot be doled out like porridge, and usually requires some experiences of success and some positive relationships with others, further details came to light. Ashley's mother described how she had quit school after becoming pregnant with Ashley, hoping to marry

Ashley's father. The father had wanted nothing to do with Ashley or her mother though, and had recently been imprisoned for armed robbery. Ashley's mother reported "sacrificing everything" in order to raise her. She was proud of the fact that Ashley had a "better start in life" in that she was never physically or sexually abused, as her mother had been. She felt hurt by the fact that Ashley did not appreciate all she had done for her, and was disrespectful towards her and her new boyfriend. She also felt that Ashley was "manipulative" because she behaved well when interacting one to one with her mother, but swore, lied, and stayed out till all hours when the boyfriend was around. She felt that Ashley owed her respect and emotional support, and was being deliberately cruel when these were withheld. "Doesn't she care about what she's doing to me?" her mother asked rhetorically.

Ashley, on the other hand, described herself as her "mother's mistake". She reported that her mother's life had gone "downhill" since she was born, that her mother had never "been there" for her, and that her mother was overly focused on potential romantic partners. There had been a series of boyfriends over the years, and whenever her mother had a boyfriend she expected Ashley to behave like an obedient daughter, but as soon as the boyfriend disappeared (usually after a few months), Ashley was left to "pick up the pieces" as her mother would become depressed and abuse alcohol. She had recently decided to stop looking after her mother's emotional ups and downs, and instead focus on her peer group, who indulged in recreational drug use. She felt sorry for her mother, but explained "We're so close when she needs me for support, but then she acts like I don't exist when there's a new guy around. It hurts, and I can't get hurt again." When upset by her mother's rejection, Ashley ate sweets for comfort, resulting in the candy bar incident.

Meeting with Ashley and her mother, I agreed that there were self-esteem problems, but also commented on their relationship. I pointed out the need for Ashley to experience more consistent parenting that included both empathy for her struggles and setting firm limits with her misbehaviour. I also pointed out that the expectation that she be a confidante to her mother was not appropriate to her age. Unfortunately, her mother summarized her understanding of the discussion rather unempathetically as "I just need to be tougher with her."

I continued meeting with Ashley to provide some guidance and support regarding her relationship with her mother, and to encourage more positive ways of interacting with others at school. We eventually agreed that her mother was not "a witch" as Ashley originally stated, but rather a flawed human being who was very dependent on others to meet her emotional needs. We weighed the pros and cons of running away from home, which Ashley had considered several times, and concluded that the outcome would likely be worse than her current situation. Regarding school, we concluded that academics might not be her strong suit, but could become a stepping stone to better things ahead. She was interested in doing some form of "hands on work", and with a high school diploma she would have more options in this regard. I also encouraged looking for peers who accepted her for herself, rather than expecting her to behave a certain way to be "cool". With encouragement, Ashley eventually joined the choir at school.

Ashley's choir teacher became a role model and mentor to her for the remainder of high school. The need to attend practices consistently while maintaining her grades improved Ashley's self-discipline, traveling to music competitions was enjoyable and encouraged a healthy sense of independence, and becoming a soloist allowed her to excel. Ashley's vocal talent eventually led to a scholarship to a post-secondary music program. Most importantly, the choir teacher liked and accepted Ashley while setting firm limits on misbehaviour. By the end of high school, Ashley had become a friendly, caring, and responsible young woman. Having experienced with her teacher an empathetic relationship she had never experienced at home, she began showing empathy toward others. There was no longer any evidence of the self-esteem problems her mother had reported initially.

Several of the developmental ideas discussed earlier in this chapter can be applied to Ashley's experience. The history of incarceration for a violent crime in Ashley's father suggests she may have had a genetic predisposition to lacking empathy. However, the emotionally abusive relationship with her mother likely contributed to this problem as well. As Ashley explained, she had been badly hurt by trying to show empathy toward her mother, and so was reluctant to behave this way again in any relationship. After her unfortunate attachment experience, she probably had some bias toward perceiving others as threatening or at least uncaring. Her willingness to meet with me, however, suggested she had not given up on human relationships completely. Her fortunate experience with the music teacher then provided her with a way of relating to others with mutual respect, and a renewed opportunity to develop empathy. As she experienced success and became a role model for other choir members, her focus on her own problems and needs diminished further, allowing her to become even more empathetic. One would hope that Ashley's experience is not unique: that "course corrections" in the development of empathy can occur despite difficult beginnings.

Reflective Questions

1   Do you sometimes make assumptions beforehand about how other people will respond to you? How do these assumptions or biases affect your interactions with others? Do they nurture or hinder empathy?
2   How did your early experiences with parents and other family members shape your attitudes toward human relationships? Did they nurture or hinder your development of empathy?
3   Did you encounter people outside your family who furthered your development of empathy? How did they do this?
4   Is there anything you want to change based on these reflections?

5   Look at the summary table for this chapter (Table 2.1) and circle the influences toward or away from empathy that may have affected your own development.

Questions for Therapists

1   If you work with children, think of a specific young client you find challenging. What constitutional or environmental influences may have affected that child's capacity for empathy?
2   If you work with adults, think of a specific client you find challenging. What constitutional or environmental influences may have affected that client's development of empathy in childhood?
3   Regardless of client age, what current influences may be affecting his or her capacity for empathy?
4   Is there anything you want to change in therapy with this client based on these reflections?
5   Look at the summary table for this chapter (Table 2.1) and circle the influences toward or away from empathy that may have affected your own development. Do any of these influences still affect you when practicing psychotherapy?

References

Baker, L. (2008). Biological psychology. In: *21st Century Psychology: A Reference Handbook, Vol. 1*. Eds: Davis, S.F. and Baskist, W. London: Sage Publishing, pp. 114–124.

Bakermans-Kranenburg, M., van IJzendoorn, M. & Juffer, F. (2003). Less is more: meta-analyses of sensitivity and attachment interventions in early childhood. *Psychological Bulletin*, 129, 195–215.

Ben-Israel, S., Usefovsky, F., Ebstein, R.P., and Knafo-Noam, A. (2015). Dopamine D4 receptor polymorphism and sex interact to predict children's affective knowledge. *Frontiers of Psychology*, 6, 846.

Bowlby, J. (1969). *Attachment. Attachment and Loss: Vol. 1. Loss*. New York: Basic Books.

Byrd, A.L. and Manuck, S.B. (2014). MAOA, child maltreatment, and antisocial behavior: meta-analysis of a gene-environment interaction. *Biological Psychiatry*, 75, 9–17.

De Dreu, C.K.W. (2012). Oxytocin modulates cooperation within and competition between groups: An integrative review and research agenda. *Hormones and Behavior*, 61, 419–428.

Decety, J. and Ickes, W. (2011). *The Social Neuroscience of Empathy*. Boston, MA: MIT Press.

Dickstein, S., Seifer, R. and Albus, K.E. (2009). Maternal adult attachment representations across relationship domains and infant outcomes: the importance of family and couple functioning. *Attachment and Human Development*, 11, 5–27.

Dodge, K.A. (2006). Translational science in action: hostile attributional style and the development of aggressive behavior problems. *Development & Psychopathology*, 18, 791–814.

Goldman, A.I. (1992). Empathy, mind, and morals. *Proceedings and Addresses of the American Philosophical Association*, 66, 17–41.

Gordon, M. (2012). *Roots of Empathy: Changing the World, Child by Child*. Markham, ON: Thomas Allen Publishers.

Hastings, P.D., McShane, K.E., Parker, R. and Ladha, F. (2007). Ready to make nice: parental socialization of young sons' and daughters' prosocial behaviors with peers. *Journal of Genetics & Psychology*, 168, 177–200.

Hoffman, M.L. (2000). *Empathy and Moral Development: Implications for Caring and Justice*. Cambridge, UK: Cambridge University Press.

Iacoboni, M. and Dapretto, M. (2006). The mirror neuron system and the consequences of its dysfunction. *Nature Reviews of Neuroscience*, 7, 942–951.

Jack, A.I., Dawson, A.J., Behany, K.L., Leckie, R.L., Barry, K.P., Ciccia, A.H., et al. (2013). FMRI reveals reciprocal inhibition between social and physical cognitive domains. *Neuroimage*, 66, 385–401.

Jonas, W. and Woodside, B. (2015). Physiological mechanisms, behavioral and psychological factors influencing the transfer of milk from mothers to their young. *Hormones & Behavior*, doi: 10.1016/j.yhbeh.2015.07.018. [Epub ahead of print]

Masi, G., Milone, A., Pisano, S., Lenzi, F., Muratori, P., Gemo, I., et al. (2014). Emotional reactivity in referred youth with disruptive behavior disorders: the role of the callous-unemotional traits. *Psychiatry Research*, 220, 426–432.

Matthews, S.G. (2002). Early programming of the hypothalamo-pituitary-adrenal axis. *Trends in Endocrinological Metabolism*, 13, 373–380.

Mullainathan, S. and Shafir, E. (2013). *Scarcity: The New Science of Having Less and How It Defines Our Lives*. New York: Picador.

Music, G. (2014). *The Good Life: Wellbeing and the New Science of Altruism, Selfishness and Immorality*. New York: Routledge, pp. 105–112.

Ouimet, A.J., Gawronski, B. and Dozois, D.J. (2009). Cognitive vulnerability to anxiety: a review and an integrative model. *Clinical Psychology Review*, 29, 459–470.

Perkins, T., Stokes, M., McGillivray, J., Bittar, R. (2010). Mirror neuron dysfunction in autism spectrum disorders. *Journal of Clinical Neuroscience*, 17, 1239–1243.

Quintana, D.S., Alvares, G.A., Hickie, I.B. and Guastella, A.J. (2015). Do delivery routes of intranasally administered oxytocin account for observed effects on social cognition and behavior? A two-level model. *Neuroscience & Biobehavioral Review*, 49, 182–192.

Raby, K.L., Steele, R.D., Carlson, E.A. and Sroufe, L.A. (2015). Continuities and changes in infant attachment patterns across two generations. *Attachment & Human Development*, 17, 414–428.

Sadeh, N., Javdani, S., and Verona, E. (2013). Analysis of monoaminergic genes, childhood abuse, and dimensions of psychopathy. *Journal of Abnormal Psychology*, 122, 167–179.

Santos, R.G., Chartier, M.J., Whalen, J.C., Chateau, D. and Boyd, L. (2011). Effectiveness of school-based violence prevention for children and youth: a research report. *Healthcare Quarterly*, 2011 Apr; 14 Spec No 80–91.

Schore, A.N. (2001). Effects of a secure attachment relationship on right brain development, affect regulation, and infant mental health. *Infant Mental Health Journal*, 22, 7–66.

Schore, A.N. (2002). Dysregulation of the right brain: a fundamental mechanism of traumatic attachment and the psychopathogenesis of posttraumatic stress disorder. *Australia & New Zealand Journal of Psychiatry*, 36, 9–30.

Schulte-Ruther, M., Markowitsch, H.J., Fink, G.R., and Piefke, M. (2007). Mirror neuron and theory of mind mechanisms involved in face-to-face interactions: a functional magnetic resonance imaging approach to empathy. *Journal of Cognitive Neuroscience*, 19, 1354–1372.

Shamay-Tsoory, S.G. (2011). The neural basis of empathy. *Neuroscientist*, 17, 18–24.

Shamay-Tsoory, S.G., Tomer, R., Berger, B.D., and Aharon-Peretz, J. (2003). Characterization of empathy deficits following prefrontal brain damage: the role of the right ventromedial prefrontal cortex. *Journal of Cognitive Neuroscience*, 15, 324–337.

Stern, D.N. (2004). *The Present Moment in Psychotherapy and Everyday Life*. New York: W.W. Norton & Co., p. 58.

Trevarthan, C. (1993). The self born in intersubjectivity: the psychology of an infant communicating. In: Neisser, U., ed. *The Perceived Self: Ecological and Interpersonal Sources of Self-Knowledge*. New York: Cambridge University Press; pp. 121–173.

Usefovsky, F., Shalev, I., Israel, S., Edelman, S., Raz, Y., Mankuta, D., et al. (2014). Oxytocin receptor and vasopressin receptor 1a genes are respectively associated with emotional and cognitive empathy. Hormones & Behavior, 67, 60–65.

Williams, J.H. (2008). Self-other relations in social development and autism: multiple roles for mirror neurons and other brain bases. *Autism Research*, 1, 73–90.

Zimmerman, P. (1999). Structure and functions of internal working models of attachment and their role for emotion regulation. *Attachment & Human Development*, 1, 291–306.

3 Social Influences: Encouraging Empathy Versus Competition

> All life is sacred. All life is family.
> Anonymous quote on a stone in a cemetery near Cape Cod

When we describe empathy as the capacity to step into another's shoes, this idea highlights the dyadic nature of empathy. It implies that empathy occurs between two people, rather than three, four, or a whole group. However, much of life is not lived in dyads. In fact, it is only in early infancy that a child's world revolves around one other person: the primary caregiver. Even at this time, the caregiver's empathetic relationship with the infant is sometimes challenged by a spouse, a sibling, or another family member who also needs the caregiver's attention. As the child grows and develops, he or she participates in additional relationships outside the family. Peers, school personnel, coaches and instructors, community and congregation members, and eventually co-workers and supervisors may provide more or less empathetic experiences, and thus influence the young person's capacity for empathy. The broader influence of organizational factors in schools and companies, and national or cultural expectations becomes increasingly salient over time as well. Thus, the relatively simple exercise of learning empathy by experiencing it in relation to a steadfast, caring human being (i.e., in the context of secure attachment, as described in the last chapter) becomes complicated by increasing numbers of social and environmental factors over time. Figure 3.1 illustrates this process, with concentric circles representing the different levels of influence on empathy which affect people over time.

This chapter describes each of these levels of influence in sequence: family/small group, community/organization, and country/culture, along with evidence of their connection to the capacity for empathy. Depending on how these various groups are organized, they can either support cooperative, empathetic behavior or fuel rivalry and competition. Some groups and social environments seem to elicit caring behavior from most people, while others seem to bring out the worst in them. The table and questions at the end prompt the reader to think about these influences on empathy in relation to his or her own experiences and (for therapists) in the case of a client's

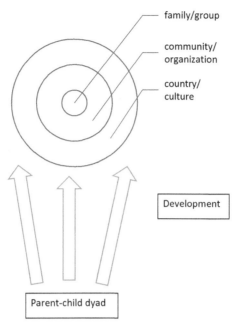

Figure 3.1 Social Influences on Empathy over Time

experiences. Let us consider how we might bring out the best, most empathetic qualities in people, until truly "all life is family".

Triads and Families

The following vignette illustrates how the addition of a third party can affect empathy in dyadic relationships using a very common example: sibling rivalry.

Jennifer and Her Boys

"Imagine how that makes your brother feel!" shouted Jennifer as she comforted her sobbing younger son whose toy Colin, the older one, had smashed just as she walked into the room.

Superficially, one might think Jennifer was helping the older boy learn about empathy. The angry tone of voice, however, was clearly undermining the empathetic message. In addition, Jennifer did not see the events leading up to this incident. Colin had been working on a science project all weekend, and finally got it to look right. He leaned it against the wall gently, waiting for the glue to dry. Then, along came his clumsy little brother and tripped over it, ruining hours of work. Colin was furious, and smashed the toy. Now, instead of getting the whole story, his mother blamed him for everything.

In Colin's mind, she wasn't saying "Imagine how that makes your brother feel", but rather "I can imagine how your brother feels, but I don't understand you at all!" He felt unfairly accused and rejected by his mother, while his sibling's destructive behavior was overlooked. Rather than feeling empathy for his brother, he now resented him more than ever.

What did Jennifer do wrong? Her reaction is certainly understandable, given the limited information she had about the situation. In most sibling conflict, however, there are two sides to the story, so it is usually unwise to assume that only one party is at fault. Besides this faulty assumption, Jennifer also encountered another common parenting problem: trying to teach children good behavior using words rather than actions. Lectures about empathy and kindness sound very hollow when children don't feel parental empathy and kindness. In this case, helping Colin fix his broken science project would have taught him much more about empathy than the admonition to imagine how his brother felt. He could still be asked to pay for the broken toy out of his allowance, as Colin must assume some responsibility for his actions and his brother shouldn't be punished for his accident by losing a toy. However, by recognizing that Colin and his brother are both hurting, Jennifer teaches them more about empathy than any verbal lesson can convey.

More generally, this example illustrates how empathy between two people can suffer (in this case, between Jennifer and Colin) as soon as a third party is involved. It is not surprising that one of the oldest stories of murder is a biblical tale of sibling rivalry: the story of Cain and Abel (Genesis 4:1–16 English Standard Version). The third person appears to threaten the relationship, competing for time, resources, and affection. Once people feel threatened, the fight or flight reaction is activated, and empathy disappears. A sibling, a spouse, or another family member can all play the role of "third party". In adulthood, co-workers, neighbors, or members of the same club or organization are added to the mix.

As the example illustrates, in each case the best solutions do not usually involve declaring one person a winner. Rather, the object of the competition (in this case, Jennifer) must find a way to address the most pressing needs of both competing parties so they are reassured enough to come out of fight or flight mode. As long as people are in this hyper-aroused state, clear thinking is not possible (as shown by Yerkes and Dodson, 1908). Once calm, people are much more likely to rationally resolve their differences and, in some cases, even develop empathy for one another. However, that cannot happen until the adrenaline rush of fight or flight subsides.

So far, we have only considered the influence of one extra person on an empathetic dyad. Many families, however, contain more than three people and at some point in life everyone must work within a small group. Families and small groups have certain similarities which can either increase or decrease a person's capacity for empathy. Rules may be spelled out more clearly in groups (family rules are often implied or "unwritten"), but interactions are often similar.

Families and small groups have both been described as systems (Skinner, Steinhauer, and Sitarenios, 2000). This means that it is usually more helpful to look at patterns of interaction within the family or group and between the family or group and outside influences, rather than blaming any one member of the family or group for problems. These interaction patterns are often circular, with one person's behavior predictably eliciting a specific behavior from another person, which in turn reinforces the behavior of the first person. For example, when a spouse repeatedly nags his or her partner to do a chore, the partner becomes irritated and less likely to do the chore, which in turn prompts more nagging. A positive example might be a parent praising a child for the specific aspects of a school assignment done well, resulting in the child regularly showing assignments to the parent, allowing for continuing feedback, praise, and well-done assignments.

Some key aspects of family systems that have been highlighted by family therapists include members' roles and responsibilities, closeness and distance in relationships, communication styles, family rules and norms, family problem-solving style, and family openness to external influences (Skinner et al., 2000). Let's examine each of these aspects in relation to the example of Jennifer's boys:

- Roles and responsibilities in families are assumed to vary with age. Thus, parents have both greater responsibility and greater authority than children. When they do not, and children are expected to assume age-inappropriate responsibility, this can be problematic. It is often seen when parents are impaired by physical or mental disability. There is also a difference in roles and responsibilities between older and younger siblings (e.g., Colin was expected to do the science project independently, which his younger brother would be unable to do), but in closely spaced siblings the difference in expectations may be small.
- Most family relationships work best when they are not overly close or overly distant. For example, if Jennifer were constantly siding with the little brother and ignoring Colin's concerns, this alliance with the brother would be considered overly close or "enmeshed", and the distance in the Jennifer-Colin relationship would be considered unhealthy. Balanced relationships where there is warmth and closeness but also clear, respectful boundaries between family members usually work best in giving people a sense of being cared for and also of being treated fairly.
- Communication in families can vary in clarity and in the nature of emotional expression. "Imagine how that makes your brother feel!" is clearly a communication tinged with negative emotion (anger) and it is indirect. That is, the statement has a different motive from what the words suggest. The motive is to make Colin feel guilty about his actions, not to stimulate his imagination or his capacity for empathy. Communication that is often indirect, that has a chronically negative tone, or that ignores emotion altogether is considered problematic.

- Some family rules and norms are obvious. The rule implied by the example, that children should not deliberately break each other's toys, is common to most families. Some rules are more subtle. For example, if Colin asked "Can I go to the movies with my friend?" and his mother responded in a critical tone "Why would you want to do that?" the implied message is that a boy of his age should not consider this activity. These implied rules often vary from one family to another, depending on parental background, parental expectations or anxiety in relation to the child, and prevailing cultural norms (see later in this chapter).
- Families solve problems in different ways, sometimes gathering input from different family members, sometimes having a parent dictate a solution, and sometimes ignoring the problem until it becomes unavoidable. The first is most likely to teach children that their opinion is valued and that they can solve problems themselves with a bit of guidance, though it does take significant time (see Manassis, 2012). It is also consistent with what has been termed "Authoritative Parenting" (Baumrind, 1967), a style considered optimal. When time is in short supply, however, most parents occasionally choose the second option: dictating a solution as Jennifer did in the example. Unfortunately, her solution was to yell at the perceived offender, which prevented further damage in the short term but resulted in heightened sibling rivalry in the long term. This lack of long-term benefit is a pitfall of many quick, parent-dictated solutions. The last option (ignoring the problem) is often seen by therapists when families only come to the office in the event of a crisis. These families disappear as soon as the crisis has passed, even though their problems have not been solved, setting the stage for the next crisis.
- The degree of family openness to external influences varies. Some families appear almost impenetrable to outside influence. This stability makes it difficult for the family to adapt to changing life stages and life circumstances. Other families show very little stability, seeming to change their norms and routines whenever there is a new cultural trend, which can be anxiety-provoking for some family members. As therapists, we often hope for families who are in the middle of this range, open to trying new behaviors that might improve family functioning but with enough stability and routines to keep regular appointments and limit members' anxiety. Without further information, it is not clear where Jennifer and her family would fall on this spectrum.

Before reading the discussion of groups that follows, reflect upon your own family or family of origin with respect to these characteristics. How does/did each of them affect your capacity for empathy? What changes in your family would allow or would have allowed you to develop empathy more readily? Is/was yours a close-knit family with highly empathetic relationships among members? Does/did this help or hinder your capacity for empathy for those outside the family? If empathy is or was lacking in your family, what other relationships have allowed you to experience it? Are there circular patterns in family relationships that interfere or interfered with your capacity for empathy?

Triangles, where empathy for one person seems to compete with empathy for another, are also not unique to family situations. Here is an example relevant to mental health practitioners:

Dorothy

Dorothy was a social worker in a suburban community. One of the most gratifying aspects of her work was doing home visits to elderly people who needed her support. However, Dorothy was also the mother of a teenage girl, Abby, who had significant mental health problems. Abby often cut herself when upset, had an on-again/off-again relationship with her therapist, and acted out at school prompting frequent calls home. Dorothy didn't blame Abby: she was born at a time in Dorothy's life when she was married to a man who threatened and abused her in front of the child. Abby still had nightmares about what she witnessed at home, and her difficulty regulating her emotions likely related to her traumatic past. Dorothy had left the relationship and was now raising Abby on her own.

One day, Dorothy arrived at the home of Iris and George, a debilitated elderly couple whom she had helped access community services so they could remain in their own home. Iris was distraught: George had been hospitalized in the city after a suffering a stroke, and the prognosis was not good. Iris was no longer able to drive, so she had no way of seeing him, and the doctors had provided little information. As Dorothy was comforting Iris and trying to communicate with the hospital, Abby called. She had cut herself while dissecting a frog in biology class, fainted, and was now panicking in the school office because the inadvertent "cutting" had reminded her of times in the past when she had deliberately cut herself in response to traumatic memories. She desperately wanted Dorothy to come to the school and take her home. What was Dorothy to do?

Dorothy seems to be faced with the challenge of prioritizing empathy for her daughter versus empathy for Iris, her elderly client. Upon reflection though, it becomes clear that she cannot neglect the needs of either person in the long run. To neglect Abby's needs would be irresponsible parenting; to neglect Iris's needs would be unprofessional. It is really a question of whose needs to attend to first, and how to show empathetic concern for each party even if she cannot help both at the same time.

In this case, she asked the school to watch Abby for a short time until she could get there, connected Iris with her husband's nurse, and agreed to come back to Iris to help clarify her husband's overall medical condition and arrange a hospital visit the next day. Then, she picked up her daughter, comforted her at home, and informed her daughter's therapist of what was happening. Most importantly, she listened carefully to both Abby and Iris, tried to contain her own anxiety about their competing needs for her attention (remembering that empathy is compromised when we become anxious about the other person—see Chapter 1), asked for their patience, and assured them both that she would do her best to address their respective problems as soon as feasible.

Small Groups

Similar to families, small groups, whether peer groups, work groups, or therapeutic groups, can also be thought of as systems, and face similar challenges. Therefore, all of the family-related issues above could also be applied to these group situations. If you are currently struggling in a group situation, reflect upon the questions regarding families one more time.

Apart from their challenges, Yalom and Leszcz (see Yalom and Leszcz, 2005) have highlighted the many potential strengths of groups, especially when conducted with therapeutic goals. Some of these strengths are quite relevant to empathy. These relevant group strengths include: a) universality—members recognize that other members share similar feelings, thoughts, and problems; b) altruism—members gain a boost to self-concept by extending help to other group members; c) instillation of hope; d) developing better ways of relating to others socially; e) cohesiveness—the feeling of trust, belonging, and togetherness with other group members; f) self-understanding (aids understanding others); and g) release of strong feelings (and strong feelings could interfere with empathy). Notably, the same strengths can be found in well-functioning families.

Where have you experienced these strengths in a well-functioning group? Even if you have never participated in a therapy group, you might recall a well-run after school activity, a team sport, an interest group (e.g., book club, gardening club, choir, band), or a small, cohesive social group that fits this description. How did these experiences contribute to your capacity for empathy? Is there a current group you belong to that could be improved to approximate this ideal?

Groups have their dark side too though. The degree of individual responsibility felt for one's actions can decrease in some groups. For example, groups of sports fans rioting after losing a match often destroy property and engage in behavior they would not condone as individuals. This "diffusion of responsibility" (Leary and Forsyth, 1987) is a common risk in group activities, and can interfere with empathy. It can be exacerbated by alcohol and other substances, and we are wise to be mindful of this risk.

Even more concerning, pressure to adhere to group norms in order to feel that one "belongs" can be abused, resulting in mistreatment of outsiders. There appears to be a biological basis for this, in that we use the same, emotional brain areas when thinking about fellow group members as when thinking about ourselves, but different, more deductive and utilitarian brain areas when thinking about outsiders (Mitchell et al., 2006). Oxytocin exacerbates this tendency, increases trust among members and also defensiveness toward outsiders (De Dreu, 2012), but endorphins, serotonin, and other brain chemicals help regulate these defensive responses that often result in exclusion (Jamner and Leigh, 1999).

In the extreme, group cohesion and suspicion of outsiders can be abused by unscrupulous leaders. Cults, gangs, extremist groups, and totalitarian regimes all insist on strict adherence to their group norms, often with severe penalties for any deviations. Some people are forced to belong to such groups (see National/cultural influences, below), but others join them by choice. The choice to relinquish one's own ethical standards in order to be accepted by a group, please a charismatic leader, or conform to an extreme ideology is a troubling one. It robs the individual of any capacity for empathy toward people who are not part of the group. Membership in extreme groups has been linked to insecurity, mental health problems, poverty, feeling marginalized from more prosocial groups or from mainstream society, and anomie (lack of a sense of life purpose) (see various authors in Piven, 2002). These and other factors are still being studied by those aiming to curb extremism.

Community/Organizational Influences

When a group expands beyond a number that can comfortably sit around a table and converse, sub-groups invariably form and a means of organizing these is needed. In many companies, these sub-groups are formed deliberately with the goal of looking at specific issues in detail (called a "task force" or "sub-committee") and then reporting back to the larger group. In other cases, group expansion and sub-grouping happens without such planning. Sub-groups often have the small-group dynamics discussed above, but additional issues relevant to empathy may arise in larger organizations.

In large organizations, people face the additional challenge of working together in efficient and effective ways without necessarily communicating directly about each decision. Rules and policies are therefore needed, and these may benefit some members of the organization more than others. If everyone has been consulted in developing the policies, people may be willing to make sacrifices for the greater good of the organization; if not, they may resent the policies. New people joining the organization certainly have not had a say regarding the policies, and may need explanations of how and why they came about. People enforcing the policies also need to be mindful of the need for "exceptions to the rule" depending on individual circumstances, as policies can sometimes result in cruelty if applied rigidly and indiscriminately. In short: rules are supposed to be made for people, not the other way around. Here is an example of a rather troubled organization.

The Unhealthy Clinic

Once there was a small group of health care providers who banded together to form a clinic. The members of the group knew each other either from medical school or from having worked together in other settings, and they respected one another's unique talents and abilities. When hiring staff, they interviewed together to make sure the prospective worker would fit well with the group. When making decisions about the clinic, they made them jointly. When collaborating on cases, they talked about the client's symptoms and characteristics in detail, and were honest about what interventions had worked or not worked. They commiserated about professional difficulties, and enjoyed sharing their successes.

As the reputation of the clinic grew, more providers joined and more staff were hired. It was no longer possible for everyone to participate in hiring and other clinic decisions, so guidelines were drawn up for these procedures, and people were informed of the results by e-mail. Some people complained about their ideas not being included, so committees were formed. Soon, people were spending several hours each week in committee meetings. Some committees were known to be more influential than others, and getting nominated for one of these was considered prestigious. Committees sometimes went beyond their assigned tasks, spending time discussing how to best promote their members' interests in the organization.

Case collaboration time was now in short supply, so communication about clients was based on diagnosis (i.e., a short-hand summary of symptoms) rather than detailed client characteristics. Funding from the government also became tied to diagnosis around this time, so clients with certain diagnostic categories were preferred, while others were considered less desirable, and still others were excluded from the clinic entirely. Soon, the small, mutually respectful group of providers focused on clients had changed into a large organization with a staff hierarchy based on committee memberships and a client hierarchy based on diagnosis.

As the clinic grew, an expert administrator was hired to ensure that the most modern and efficient procedures were followed. He quickly informed the health care providers that greater transparency and greater accountability to various stakeholders was needed. To ensure transparency, every staff member had to document their daily activities on a spreadsheet, divided into ten-minute increments. The only activity that could not be included was the significant time it took to fill out the spreadsheet every day. To improve accountability to stakeholders, some people from outside health care were added to the committees, which nobody seemed to mind initially. Whenever one of these people raised a concern, however, the administrator responded by ensuring that everyone received mandatory training in the relevant area. At first, there was annual mandatory training in first aid, which made sense in a medical clinic, and the occasional fire drill. Over time, however, other annual mandatory training sessions were added. These related to disaster preparedness, preparedness for unusual disease outbreaks, cultural sensitivity, sensitivity to the disabled, gender sensitivity, sensitivity to workplace bullying, and even training on work-appropriate footwear. Because much of the training was evaluated using online tests, the most computer-literate people usually did best on it, regardless of how well-prepared or sensitive they were.

Soon, the amount of time people spent documenting their daily activities, attending committees, and attending mandatory training sessions was so great that they were seeing very few clients and hardly ever talking to their colleagues informally. Interactions that did occur were often terse and lacking in empathy, as people were stressed by their various new job requirements.

Moreover, everyone knew that the health care providers who had started the clinic had very little power any more. In fact, one of them was fired after a dispute with the administrator about wearing sandals to work. The real power seemed to reside with the administrator. Those who wanted to be promoted spent large amounts of time ingratiating themselves with the administrator, even if this meant denigrating colleagues or reporting those colleagues who were non-compliant with certain procedures. The primary goal of many staff was no longer providing health care. Instead, it was to be promoted to an administrative position where they didn't have to see clients at all. At that point, they were sure they would be successful and happy.

What's Different in a Well-Functioning Community?

This rather facetious tale of the unhealthy clinic is a composite of organizations I have worked for over the years, but unfortunately all of the problems described really did occur. As these problems are obvious from the story, I will not review them except by contrast to a well-functioning community. Community implies not only a group of people living in the same area, but also a feeling of fellowship with other members of the group. To create that feeling of fellowship, a community must have certain attributes which will now be described.

Unlike the organization above which is driven by competition and hierarchies, a well-functioning community recognizes the interdependence of its members, and so values the unique contribution of each member and recognizes each member's unique needs. Even the most vulnerable members are valued, as they remind us of our own fragility and often elicit empathy in extraordinary ways. Vanier (see Vanier, 1998) has written of this poignantly in his descriptions of the L'Arche communities for the mentally disabled, as has Solomon (see Solomon, 2012) in his book about families raising children with differences or disabilities.

Some leadership is still needed in a community, but it is provided primarily to serve the community, rather than to elevate the status of the leader. Subgroups whose members support each other may exist, but membership in these is not rigidly defined, nor do members plot against those outside the subgroup. Similarly, the community as a whole defines itself in certain ways, but is also open to considering new members and new ideas. An apt metaphor for a well-functioning community is that of a cell: it has a membrane to protect it and define its shape, but the membrane is semi-permeable so allows exchange of molecules with its surroundings. Similar to a community leader, the nucleus coordinates the cell's activities, but it cannot effect change without organelles that each have a specialized function, nor without the plasma that holds and supports those organelles. Like community members, components of a cell are interdependent and so all components matter.

Community leaders also resist the urge to slot human beings into categories that deny individual difference. For example, mental health research increasingly recognizes the need to start from the perspective of the participants (a so-called "emic" or "qualitative" approach) to discern meaningful themes and questions to study, before testing specific hypotheses in various populations (a so-called "etic" or "quantitative" approach) (see Headland, Pike, and Harris, 1990).

Perhaps most importantly, the humane values of the community are lived out in daily, person to person interactions, rather than being usurped by inhumane procedures. Leaders do not force subordinates to engage in hours of activities they find meaningless and stressful for the sake of making the leadership look good. Thus, their empathy toward community members and those touched by community members is not limited to verbal interactions, but is reflected in thoughtful, caring actions that recognize the dignity of each person. If procedures are starting to matter more than the people they were designed for, time is taken to reflect upon and revise how things are done.

National/Cultural Influences

There are two important aspects of culture in relation to empathy: the effect of cultural difference on empathy and the effect of cultural norms on empathy. The role of cultural difference is described first. Then, cultural characteristics and norms that relate to empathy are reviewed briefly. These are described in more detail in Chapter 8.

Cultural Difference

There is some debate about whether we empathize more easily with people of the same culture as ourselves or it makes no difference, with various findings supporting both positions. Soto and Levenson (2009) seemed to resolve this. They had people rate videotaped interactions of women of four different ethnicities talking about relationships with dating partners. Some raters showed greater physiological response when the woman was of their own ethnicity, but no significant difference in empathetic accuracy emerged. In other words, people were able to identify what the woman was feeling and rate the intensity of her feelings regardless of their own ethnicity or the ethnicity of the woman. These findings suggest that at the least the cognitive aspects of empathy seem to apply regardless of ethnic difference, but empathy may not "come naturally" toward people of other ethnicities as emotional responses are stronger toward one's own ethnic group.

Like all research findings, however, we need to treat these results with a healthy skepticism. An experimental challenge may or may not be reflected in real-life behavior. In other words, just because the research subjects were able to empathize with someone of a different ethnicity when asked to do so in the laboratory doesn't necessarily mean they would do this consistently in real life. Also, the emotional responses to a troubled romantic relationship represent a fairly universal human experience, so are readily understood across cultures. The experience of being treated differently because of one's race or ethnicity, on the other hand, is not universal and may be harder for someone of a different race or ethnicity to grasp.

For example, as a middle-aged white woman wearing slacks and a turtleneck, I am rarely stopped at the airport for extra screening before a flight. If I were a person of color or I wore a hijab my experience would likely be different. I experience empathy for those who are stopped more frequently at the airport, but do I fully understand their perspective? I have to consciously remind myself that they are not just inconvenienced at the airport, but often singled out preferentially by police and sometimes regarded with suspicion by their neighbors simply because of their appearance.

Potential difficulty empathizing with those of different cultural backgrounds from our own has been a particular concern in the helping professions. Therefore, Wang and colleagues (2003) have developed a measure of ethnocultural empathy, the ability to empathize across cultures. This instrument, The Scale of Ethnocultural Empathy, has cognitive, emotional, and communicative components reflecting the different aspects of empathy that may be challenged by ethnocultural difference. In a pilot study, Fleming and colleagues (2015) showed that dental and nursing students' ethnocultural empathy on this measure could be improved through a brief workshop intervention, with gains maintained at one month post-workshop.

Moreover, differences other than ethnicity may affect our ability to empathize with others. Age, gender, socioeconomic level, educational level, disability, or sexual orientation may all make it easier or more difficult to empathize with another person. Here are some brief examples of each:

- Age: It is not always comfortable entering a room full of people from a different generation and trying to join the conversation. For instance, as a middle-aged adult, I may not be aware of the current trends in social media discussed by a room full of teens; I may not share the memories of World War II or the post-war years discussed in a room full of older adults.
- Gender: The book *Men are from Mars; Women are from Venus* (see Gray, 1993) was a bestseller for good reason: the genders often communicate differently, sometimes making empathy for someone from the opposite gender challenging. When it comes to expressions of romantic interest, this can become even more delicate as what one gender considers a harmless flirtation may be perceived as harassing or even threatening by someone of the opposite gender.

- Socioeconomic level: As a psychiatrist from a rather impoverished background, I sometimes find it difficult to empathize with families from a wealthy background. For example, a wealthy parent may express concern that their child is too anxious to go to overnight summer camp, even though the child is otherwise functioning at a high level. In my family, we couldn't afford to go to such a camp, and there were many more pressing concerns. I have to remind myself that for the parent in front of me, it is considered socially deviant to not cope with camp.
- Educational level: Some of the least happy couples I have seen in my practice were those where there was a substantial difference in educational level. For instance, one partner may have no post-secondary education and be content to work in a factory and watch the ballgame on television while the other, more educated partner may want to attend lectures, discuss current events, and go to the symphony. Empathy for one another's position can be difficult to develop in these cases.
- Disability: When people who are not disabled spend a day in a wheelchair or blindfolded, their empathy for people with disabilities invariably increases. A business owner who previously grumbled about the high cost of creating an accessible environment, for example, may recognize the necessity of doing so. Disfigurement creates a further empathetic challenge. In this case, we need to overcome our own fearful or even disgusted reactions to someone's appearance in order to relate to that person as a human being.
- Sexual orientation: Exclusion and disadvantage related to this factor continues in society. The right to marry, to adopt children, and to have access to pension benefits when a partner dies are just some of the issues that are still contentious. Moreover, even heterosexuals who consider themselves progressive sometimes make remarks that are insensitive from the perspective of someone who is not.

What all of these differences share is the importance of not making assumptions about the other person's feelings. When in doubt, an attitude of respectful curiosity is usually best. "What is it like for you when this happens?" is often a good question, or "It seems to bother you when I do that. Can you tell me why?" If the interaction still seems tense or awkward, it may help to acknowledge the difference in background openly, for example "I know I'm talking from the perspective of a white, female physician. Tell me how that's different from your perspective."

Cultural Characteristics and Norms

Several cultural characteristics and norms have been linked to empathy or lack of empathy. The most consistent finding relates to the financial gap between the wealthiest members of a society and the poorest members of a society. Epidemiologists have linked a large gap to low levels of empathy. In addition, societies with a large gap tend to show higher crime rates, lower average physical and mental health, and more negative attitudes toward their most vulnerable members relative to societies with a small gap (see Wilkinson and Pickett, 2009). Competition among individuals and groups is emphasized, and there is limited support for those who are not seen as potential "winners". In such competitive societies support for parents raising young children also tends to be limited, impacting parent-child relationships and thus affecting empathy in the next generation (see Hrdy, 2009).

Cultural norms emphasizing materialism and acquisition of goods have also been linked to low empathy (Music, 2014). In such cultures, the less affluent are perceived as outsiders as they cannot participate in consumer culture to the same extent as their neighbors, often resulting in unfair stereotyping of the poor and financial policies that reduce their chances of escaping poverty. Immigrants, who are often poor when arriving in a new country, may be particularly targeted, contributing to racism and ethnic conflict.

Authoritarian cultural norms often have an adverse effect on empathy in a society. Even a passing glance at recent history reveals that many of the most egregious abuses of human rights have occurred when leaders expect and enforce obedience without question. One might think that people who deliberately harm others when told to do so are the exception rather than the rule. Unfortunately, the psychologist Stanley Milgram (1963) demonstrated that this is not true. Most people in his experiments were willing to administer increasingly severe, even lethal electric shocks to another person when told to do so. The shocks were not real and the experiments would be considered unethical by today's research standards, but the conclusion was inescapable: in an authoritarian environment, human beings usually prioritize obedience over empathy.

Conversely, cultural norms that include empathy have been related to a number of social benefits. For example, empathy is a good predictor of forgiveness (Fincham, 2010), which can aid reconciliation after systemic injustice has occurred in a society. Several countries have recently undertaken truth and reconciliation commissions after recognizing the harm done by such injustice. South Africa's commission in relation to Apartheid (forced racial segregation) is perhaps the most famous. Canada has recently conducted such a commission in relation to the mistreatment of First Nations youth in residential schools.

Cultures that recognize the interdependence of their members, an attitude closely linked to empathy, also foster a sense of community (see Geertz, 2000). Community involvement in the form of volunteering and random acts of kindness has been linked to increased happiness (Meier and Stutzer, 2008; Lyubomirsky et al., 2005). As people become more contented, they also become more prosocial, outward looking, and generous (Konow and Earley, 2008), often resulting in "virtuous cycles" of life satisfaction and altruistic behavior. Furthermore, contact with community members that are different from oneself results in relating to those community members in humane, empathetic ways, reducing stereotyping and healing community divisions.

Finally, cultural norms that include empathy can reduce negative attitudes toward outsiders. Highly empathetic people eventually regard all others as members of the same group: the human family. They see past differences in wealth, status, educational level, ability, race, gender, age, ethnicity, sexual orientation, immigration status, and all other divisions. They approach the ideal of compassion: broadening group membership to include everyone. The urgent need to foster this ideal in order to address global problems has been identified by many, and articulated eloquently in the Charter for Compassion developed by Armstrong (see Armstrong, 2010) and other spiritual leaders (see www.charterforcompassion.org).

What is Not Known

The effect of each type of social influence on empathy could be studied further, and we could all benefit from greater awareness of these influences. For example, as a mental health professional I am often sadly surprised by how willing my colleagues are to blame one person in their family for an empathetic failure without considering the influence of the overall family system. I'm sure I have done the same from time to time. As professionals in this field we should know better, but somehow it's different when it comes to our own families.

Fostering empathy within groups without denigrating outsiders continues to be a challenge. Oxytocin seems to be working against us in this regard (De Dreu, 2012), so more needs to be learned about the neurochemistry of inclusiveness as well as the psychological factors that promote it.

At the organizational level, an intriguing question is: can a very large organization function like a healthy community or not? Naomi Klein (see Klein, 1999) suggests that in large corporations this may not be possible. However, some Scandinavian countries are quite large and still seem to promote community-focused values (see Wilkinson and Pickett, 2009). We need a better understanding of how to create humane organizations where empathy can flourish.

Finally, given the myriad of differences that seem to divide us, we need to know more about how to recognize our human commonalities both cognitively and emotionally. Learning about the experience of those unlike ourselves is a good place to start, but it may not overcome long-held prejudices or strong emotional reactions to certain differences. In other words, we still have a long way to go before reaching the ideal of compassion for all.

Reflective Questions

1 Think about the social influences on your own capacity for empathy, and fill these in on Table 3.1.
2 Do you want to address any of these influences? How?

Table 3.1 Social Influences on Empathy

Level of Interaction	Influence
Family/Small Group	
Community/Organization	
Country/Culture	

Questions for Therapists

1 Think about a client who seems to show little capacity for empathy. Consider the possible social influences on your client's capacity for empathy, and fill these in on Table 3.1.
2 Do you want to address any of these influences with the client? How?
3 If you see families, think about a family characterized by competition rather than empathy or mutual support. Based on the ideas in this chapter, how could you help this family?

References

Armstrong, K. (2010) *Twelve Steps to a Compassionate Life*. New York: Random House, Inc.
Baumrind, D. (1967). Child care practices anteceding three patterns of preschool behavior. *Genetic Psychology Monographs*, 75, 43–88.
De Dreu, C.K.W. (2012). Oxytocin modulates cooperation within and competition between groups: An integrative review and research agenda. *Hormones and Behavior*, 61, 419–428.
Fincham, F.D. (2010). Forgiveness: integral to a science of close relationships? In M. Milulincer and P. R. Shaver (Eds.) *Prosocial Motives, Emotions, and Behavior: The Better Angels of Our Nature*. Washington, DC: American Psychological Association, pp. 347–365.
Fleming, B.D., Thomas, S.E., Burnham, W.S., Charles, L.T., Shaw, D. (2015). Improving ethnocultural empathy in healthcare students through a targeted intervention. *Journal of Cultural Diversity*, 22, 59–63.
Geertz, C. (2000). *The Interpretation of Cultures*. New York: Basic Books.
Genesis 4: 1–16. *The Bible. English Standard Version*.
Gray, J. (1993). *Men Are from Mars, Women Are from Venus*. New York: HarperCollins.
Headland, T.N., Pike, K.L., and Harris, M. (Eds.) (1990). *Emics and Etics: The Insider/Outsider Debate*. Newbury Park, CA: Sage Publications.
Hrdy, S. (2009). *Mothers and Others: The Evolutionary Origins of Mutual Understanding*. Cambridge, MA: Belknap Press.
Jamner, L.D. and Leigh, H. (1999). Repressive/defensive coping, endogenous opioids and health: how a life so perfect can make you sick. *Psychiatry Research*, 85, 17–31.
Klein, N. (1999). *No Logo: Taking Aim at the Brand Bullies*. Toronto: Knopf Canada.

Konow, J. and Earley, J. (2008). The hedonistic paradox: Is homo economicus happier? *Journal of Public Economics*, 92, 1–33.

Leary, M.R. and Forsyth, D.R. (1987). Attributions of responsibility for collective endeavors. *Review of Personality and Social Psychology*, 8, 167–188.

Lyubomyrsky, S., Sheldon, K.M., and Schkade, D. (2005). Pursuing happiness: the architecture of sustainable change. *Review of General Psychology*, 9, 111–131.

Manassis, K. (2012). *Problem Solving in Child and Adolescent Psychotherapy*. New York: Guilford.

Meier, S. and Stutzer, A. (2008). Is volunteering rewarding in itself? *Economica*, 75, 39–59.

Milgram, S. (1963). Behavioral study of obedience. *Journal of Abnormal and Social Psychology*, 67, 371–378.

Mitchell, J.P., Macrae, C.N., and Banaji, M.R. (2006). Dissociable medial prefrontal contributions to judgments of similar and dissimilar others. *Neuron*, 50, 655–663.

Music, G. (2014). *The Good Life: Wellbeing and the New Science of Altruism, Selfishness, and Immorality*. New York: Routledge, pp. 169–177.

Piven, J.S. (2002). *Jihad and Sacred Vengeance: Psychological Undercurrents of History Volume III*. New York: Writers Club Press.

Skinner, H., Steinhauer, P., and Sitarenios, G. (2000). Family Assessment Measure (FAM) and process model of family functioning. *Journal of Family Therapy*, 22, 190–210.

Solomon, A. (2012). *Far from the Tree: Parents, Children, and the Search for Identity*. New York: Scribner.

Soto, J.A. and Levenson, R.W. (2009). Emotion recognition across cultures: the influence of ethnicity on empathic accuracy and physiological linkage. *Emotion*, 9, 874–884.

Vanier, J. (1998). *Becoming Human*. Toronto: Anansi Press Ltd.

Wang, Y.W., Davidson, M.M., Yakushko, O.F., Savoy, H.B., Tan, J.A., and Bleier, J.K. (2003). The Scale of Ethnocultural Empathy: development, validation, and reliability. *Journal of Consulting Psychology*, 50, 221–234.

Wilkinson, R. and Pickett, K. (2009). *The Spirit Level: Why Greater Equality Makes Societies Stronger*. London: Bloomsbury Press.

Yalom, I. and Leszcz, M. (2005). *The Theory and Practice of Group Psychotherapy*, 5th Edition. New York: Basic Books.

Yerkes, R.M. and Dodson, J.D. (1908). The relation of strength of stimulus to rapidity of habit-formation. *Journal of Comparative Neurology and Psychology*, 18, 459–482.

Part II
Nurturing Empathy

4 Physical Aspects: Why Empathy Requires a Healthy Body as well as a Healthy Mind

> If compassion does not include yourself, it is incomplete.
>
> Jack Kornfield

In Part II of this book, I shift from describing what is known about factors that influence our capacity for empathy to examining each of those factors in detail using the biopsychosocial framework mentioned in the introduction (Engel, 1977). Influences nudging us toward and away from empathy are discussed in each area, with the goal of finding specific strategies for strengthening our own and our clients' capacity for empathy. This first chapter of Part II is dedicated to biological factors related to empathy and, more specifically, influences related to brain chemistry, bodily comfort, and bodily discomfort. It reviews how healthy or unhealthy physical states can influence the capacity for empathy. Chapters 5 to 7 look at psychological factors related to empathy, starting with the most obvious (psychiatric symptoms, discussed in Chapter 5), then moving to habitual coping strategies for dealing with intense emotion that we may or may not be aware of (Chapter 6), and finally the relationship patterns associated with early attachment that we are often unaware of (Chapter 7). In Chapter 8, I shift to the social sphere, as norms and ideals related to empathy are examined in detail. To begin, we look at the importance of a compassionate attitude toward oneself, especially when it comes to bodily health, as the lack of this attitude is such a common impediment to empathy.

Self-Compassion and the Body

The Golden Rule of treating others as we would like to be treated ourselves includes an important assumption: it assumes we treat ourselves well. In truth, we don't always treat ourselves well, particularly when it comes to physical well-being. The mistreatment of the body is most obvious in those with eating disorders, who become overly focused on perfecting unrealistic physical ideals. In order to achieve these ideals they starve, purge, or undertake extreme exercise regimens that harm rather than enhance physical health. When the brain is deprived of calories, thinking becomes more narrowly goal-focused (Samelson, 2009), reducing empathy and keeping people stuck in their unhealthy eating patterns. Excessive preoccupation with one's own imperfections also interferes with the ability to transcend the focus on "self" in order to engage with others (Nobel and Manassis, 2012), thus further impairing empathy. Methods for helping these clients are described in detail in volumes specific to these conditions (e.g., see Fairburn and Brownell, 2002), and the issue of overcoming unhealthy self-preoccupation is revisited in Chapter 6.

As the quote implies, however, neglecting ourselves, particularly neglecting our physical selves, may be even more common than mistreating ourselves. In Western societies, neglect of the body is often seen as an acceptable compromise in striving for success or in avoiding emotional pain. We see our good health as a means to an end, a way of competing with others or experiencing pleasure, rather than a gift to be cherished in its own right. We rarely think about how neglecting our health might affect those around us. To experience pleasure, we engage in cycles of intoxication and withdrawal from alcohol and other substances, destabilizing our emotions and thus weakening our capacity for empathy. To save time, we neglect dental hygiene and other basic self-care, not thinking about the cost to our families of treating cavities, infections, and other complications months later. We allow ourselves to spend much of the day in fight or flight mode as we strive for success, without stopping to reflect on the impact upon others. We maintain poor eating, sleeping, and exercise habits, eventually developing chronic illnesses stemming from these unhealthy habits (hypertension, Type II diabetes, and cardiovascular disease among others). In some cases, this can tragically result in what is perhaps the ultimate empathetic failure: leaving those we love by early death due to neglected health.

The so-called "helping professions" may be particularly vulnerable to these self-abusive behaviors. As physicians or therapists we often fool ourselves into thinking that long-term altruistic goals justify short-term neglect of health. For example, while writing this book (which I saw as at least somewhat altruistic in nature) I had to make a conscious effort to include some healthy exercise in my day, even if that meant living with some anxiety about meeting my publisher's deadline. Below is an example from my practice of a client who faced a similar dilemma.

Tammy's Struggles

Tammy came from a very deprived background. She never knew her mother, and was frequently humiliated by her stepmother and told she was "trash". When she was 13, her stepmother died suddenly of a heart attack. Tammy found her and tried to revive her, but failed. In response to the emotional abuse, Tammy had sometimes silently wished her stepmother would "drop dead". Now that it had actually happened, she felt guilty and responsible for her death. Emotions were not readily expressed in Tammy's family though, so she kept her feelings to herself.

I met Tammy in her last year of high school because she was experiencing anxiety. She was a straight "A" student and hoped to get into medical school. I wondered if her career goal related, at least in part, to the guilt-ridden memory of losing her stepmother, but did not confront her with my suspicions right away. My bigger concern was how, in the pursuit of her goal, Tammy was neglecting her health. She studied until all hours of the night, and was often sleep-deprived and grumpy. She knew that extra-curricular activities would look good on her medical school application, so she signed up for five of them. She was constantly driving to various volunteer activities. She struggled with her weight because she felt she only had time to consume fast food.

One day, she planned to drop off her dog at the vet on the way to one of her activities. Unfortunately, she was so preoccupied with the upcoming activity that she left the dog in the car on a hot day. It was rescued by a passer-by just in time, but Tammy felt horribly guilty. After that, she became even more determined to work hard and get into medical school "to make a positive contribution". It took some time for her to realize that she would contribute to the well-being of others far more effectively if she took care of herself than if she did not.

Although not everyone is driven by intense guilt, many people follow Tammy's pattern of neglecting their health for the sake of an altruistic future goal. The problem with this approach is that like Tammy they often become grumpy and forgetful as a result of this neglect, compromising their capacity for empathy. Often, this results in inadvertent empathetic failures: road rage, careless emails that upset the recipient, losing items that are important to others, or frank neglect of others as Tammy neglected her dog. In summary, inattention to the moment for the sake of a saintly future often backfires.

By contrast, attending to bodily needs helps center people in the moment, and often makes them grateful for their health and strength. In this attentive, present-focused frame of mind, empathetic responses to others one encounters become possible. Termed "mindfulness", this frame of mind is one that can be cultivated with practice as described by Kabat-Zinn (see Kabat-Zinn, 1994). Not surprisingly, mindfulness programs often start with a very simple, but very physical exercise: consciously eating a raisin. By focusing on every subtle sensation one encounters in consuming this tiny morsel of food, eating becomes an appreciated, conscious, moment-by-moment experience. The tendency to mindlessly overeat is also reduced. The ability to experience mindfulness throughout the day is challenging, but the associated physical and mental health benefits suggest it is well worth the effort of practicing this approach.

Encouraging Self-Compassion

The previous discussion seems to suggest that mindfulness meditation is necessary to encourage the moment-by-moment, self-compassionate attitude that facilitates empathy. However, meditation is not for everyone, as the following example shows, so alternatives should be considered when working with certain clients.

Jack

Jack was an older teen I had been treating for an episode of depression. Usually, I saw him alone but on this day his mother insisted on attending. She ordered him to roll up his sleeves and he sheepishly agreed, showing numerous superficial horizontal cuts that had prompted an emergency room visit the previous night. When asked what caused him to do this to himself, he replied "I had so much work due, and then I thought about exams next week, and then my girlfriend was on my case about how I need to spend more time with her…and I just freaked out." He denied any desire to end his life, but had clearly been feeling overwhelmed and inflicted the cuts "to take out all the stress".

I was reluctant to change Jack's medication, as his mood was well-regulated "29 days out of 30", but once a month or so he became distressed enough to engage in self-injury. To address this pattern, I suggested looking at alternative ways of coping with stress. I pointed out that there is good evidence for mindfulness meditation as a means of both coping with stress and preventing relapse of depression (see Williams, Teasdale, Segal, and Kabat-Zinn, 2007).

Jack's response was, "I don't do meditation." He was not the first adolescent boy I had treated who displayed this attitude. I tried exploring the reasons for his reluctance, examined the pros and cons of trying this practice, referred him to some teen-friendly information on the subject, and eventually urged him to think about it, but to no avail. Jack considered meditation "hokey" and would have no part of it.

Looking at a variety of other "stressbusters", we eventually found one he was willing to pursue: exercise. He found that "running it off" was a great way of relieving stress and produced similar calm feelings to those he experienced after cutting himself (i.e., the calmness experienced after endorphin release, which both activities trigger). The only issue to address was how to get a work-out if he was distressed at night, when he couldn't safely go out and run in his neighborhood. Jack felt an exercise bike and a punching bag would help, and his mother agreed to help pay for these. The strategy worked. Jack eventually exercised for fun, not just to relieve distress, and his mood remained good.

As this example shows, attending moment by moment can be enhanced by demanding physical activities that require some concentration. These activities also release endorphins, brain chemicals that reduce pain and help regulate mood and anxiety symptoms (Baker, 2008). When these symptoms are kept in check, self-preoccupation is reduced, further increasing our capacity for empathy. People who are contented with themselves and their bodies are also more inclined to attend to the needs of others, often becoming more generous and altruistic (Music, 2014).

Prayer is another alternative to mindfulness practices that many people find helpful in centering themselves in the moment and developing a less self-absorbed, more empathetic frame of mind. Silent prayer that encourages "listening to God" rather than pleas for divine intervention (see Barnes, 2005) resembles meditation, and may thus be particularly helpful.

Almost any activity that focuses the participant on the "here and now" can serve this function. I often find figuring out the "puzzle" of children and youth I assess in my practice very centering. As I am trying to sensitively elicit information in order to understand the various factors contributing to their problems, I am fully engaged in the process and my own worries or ambitions fade into the background. The same experience has been described to me by expert tradesmen. For example, "When I am doing carpentry (or cooking, or plumbing, or another skilled trade), I am focused on doing the best job possible, nothing else" is a common description by someone who is dedicated to their craft.

In addition to practicing centering ourselves in the moment, maintaining certain attitudes can support self-compassion. These can include setting reasonable expectations for ourselves. For example, I had some pretty lofty goals when writing this book, but had to remind myself that a lifetime's worth of knowledge and experience could not be condensed into one volume. Avoiding comparisons between ourselves and others is also important. There will always be people who are smarter, more competent at certain tasks, and better looking, but they are not you. You are unique, and therefore able to contribute something unique to those around you and to the world, whatever it may be. Remembering how far we have come since experiencing the vulnerability and mistakes of youth is important too, as it remind us of our strengths. Focusing on what we have not done, by contrast, results in preoccupation with our own shortcomings, often impeding empathy for ourselves. Finally, self-compassion implies self-respect. Prioritizing being on time for the next meeting over basic self-care, for instance, is unkind and disrespectful to yourself. There is always time to brush teeth, comb hair, and make oneself look presentable. If you don't respect yourself enough to like what you see in the mirror, how can you expect respect from others? Respectful relationships are central to empathy, and that includes self-respect.

In summary, self-compassionate attitudes toward ourselves that include some means of centering ourselves in the moment are often conducive to empathy. These attitudes include attending to bodily health without becoming overly preoccupied with it, recognizing that this is sometimes a fine balance. To avoid either over-doing health-focused activities or neglecting the body, one must usually develop daily or weekly habits that strike this balance. Change is difficult though, so don't expect the new habits to take hold immediately. Most people must persevere at least 66 days with a new habit before it becomes an enduring lifestyle change (Lally, van Jaarsveld, Potts, and Wardle, 2010). For most of us, it also requires the occasional reminder that when we are busy we need to look after ourselves most of all, and (for mindfulness) the old aphorism that "Life happens while you're making other plans."

Strengthening the Biological Substrates of Empathy

I am a very tense traveler, and not always empathetic toward those I meet along the way. The airport security screening frightens me, as I once forgot to take my shampoo out of the carry-on luggage and got selected for extra scrutiny, almost missing my flight. The memory still haunts me, and generates a fight or flight reaction every time I fly. I get even more anxious if I have to make a connecting flight. I don't mind jogging through the airport to get to the gate on time, but getting stuck in multiple line-ups along the way raises my blood pressure. Once I arrive at my destination I should relax and get some rest, but changes in time zone and environment prevent that. Even though I take melatonin (an over-the-counter remedy for jetlag), I never sleep quite as well in a hotel bed as I do at home. When it comes to food, I enjoy a variety. However, I am by nature a "grazer" who eats small quantities frequently during the day. When I eat abroad, I am invariably presented with super-sized restaurant meals which leave me feeling uncomfortably full and sluggish. I also miss my favorite music, my spacious bathtub, the water splashing down a small stone fountain in my meditation corner, the favorite paintings that draw me in, and hugging my now grown-up children. None of these experiences exist when I travel. If it wasn't for the in-room coffee at the hotel triggering regular bowel movements, I don't think I could cope. In short: my physical state when traveling often makes me unusually grumpy and unkind.

As my experience illustrates, a degree of physical comfort is needed for most of us to behave empathetically. Sleep deprivation, upset stomach, and lack of familiar sensory experiences can all focus our attention on ourselves as we struggle to return to our usual state of comfort. While engaged in this struggle, we do not always attend to the feelings and needs of those around us. Unpredictable circumstances often bring on a fight or flight reaction which can further increase our discomfort and decrease our capacity for empathy (Music, 2014). Returning to at least some of our usual health routines is important in restoring an empathetic frame of mind.

Even when basic comforts are provided, people vary in their capacity for empathy. As discussed in Chapter 2, some biological substrates of empathy are "hard-wired" genetically, and thus cannot readily change. However, others are amenable to environmental influence. For example, when raised in nurturing environments with one or more consistent, caring parents children develop a physiological stress response system that reacts flexibly to circumstances, rather than being "stuck" in either a heightened or dampened state (Matthews, 2002). They do not develop fight or flight reactions at the drop of a hat, nor do they remain callously unemotional in the face of truly horrible events. Thus, they can respond to others in ways that are consistent with the situation, and thus often consistent with the other person's empathetic needs. Good care for our children will thus strengthen the biological substrates of empathy for generations to come.

Practices that dampen the sympathetic nervous system associated with fight or flight and strengthen its opposite, called the parasympathetic nervous system, support an empathetic frame of mind. The centering practices described in the previous section certainly fit this category, but other forms of physical relaxation also facilitate this calming part of ourselves. Simply breathing slowly and deeply enough to stretch the diaphragm (a muscle at the base of the lungs), for example, can reliably trigger the parasympathetic nervous system. We breathe this way automatically as infants, but shift to shallow, rapid breathing later. Therefore, most people need to practice breathing from the diaphragm daily for a few weeks in order to re-learn this natural calming technique.

Enjoyment of physical pleasures can contribute to empathy as well. The opportunity to engage with others while sharing a communal meal, for example, often draws people together and helps them understand each other better. Similar experiences can occur when people hike together, bike together, or attend the same gym. Anything that releases endorphins will reduce discomfort and thus enhance the capacity for empathy, which can include certain foods (e.g., dark chocolate, spicy foods), scents (e.g., vanilla or lavender), meditation, laughter, aerobic exercise, and sexual activity (Goldstein, 1980). Sexual activity can further contribute to empathy when practised in the context of loving relationships, where partners attend to one another's pleasure rather than focusing exclusively on their own.

Enjoyable activities that release oxytocin also nurture our capacity for empathy. Hugging, singing, dancing, praying, watching an emotional movie, exercising with a friend, or just being kind to someone else all contribute to oxytocin release (see Zak, 2012).

Thus, from turning on the parasympathetic system through relaxation and healthy routines to stimulating endorphins or oxytocin, there are a host of activities that can strengthen the biochemistry of empathy. Unfortunately, we often consider ourselves too busy with matters we consider more important to engage in these activities. This dilemma reminds me of a bit of folk wisdom attributed to the Cherokee (see Unknown Author). In the story, a grandfather describes to his grandson two wolves battling inside him: one characterized by (among other qualities) anger, arrogance, and ego and the other characterized by (among other qualities) humility, kindness, and empathy. The grandson asks which wolf wins the battle. The grandfather replies "The one you feed." May we all take the time to feed the biological substrates that support empathy.

Reactions to Illness and Empathy

Illness usually intensifies the focus on ourselves. This makes sense, as illness represents a threat to well-being and ultimately to life itself. Therefore, to ensure survival, illness elicits stress responses similar to those we experience when we fight or flee in response to danger. These survival-focused responses readily override the neural circuits related to empathy. Certain illnesses and certain medications can have further adverse effects on these circuits.

People surrounding the ill person may not be treated as well as usual, but they typically understand that the person is behaving "out of character" due to illness. Moreover, they may feel a duty to aid in the person's recovery, so they ignore the individual's unpleasantness and do their best to help restore the person to health. If the ill person is persevering in very difficult circumstances, the courage displayed by doing so may even be inspiring to his or her caregivers.

Beyond the neurobiological effects of illness, people may also struggle with the effect of illness on their autonomy and typical interpersonal style. Sick people are expected to do what the doctors and nurses tell them to do. Some people are very resistant to doing as they are told. Others hope the medical professionals will "fix them", and therefore take a very passive approach to their own recovery.

On the positive side, sometimes the vulnerability of being ill or incapacitated may help us recognize that we need others. This recognition of our own interdependence with others may increase our capacity for empathy. For example, when ill we may have to ask others to help mind the children or cover certain duties at work. Sometimes we expect negative responses to such requests and are pleasantly surprised by others' willingness to help. These experiences create a more positive view of the helpers, and often of other human beings generally, increasing our capacity for empathy.

There are also differences among cultures in how patients are expected to behave (Manassis, 1986). For instance, in some cultures, doctors are seen as authority figures that patients are expected to obey and not question; in others the patient is seen as a consumer of medical services and encouraged to take a more skeptical attitude toward medical advice. All of these factors can affect empathetic behavior in the patient and the medical staff.

The following examples show two contrasting responses to illness, which are discussed further in the next section.

Hank and Lois

As I walked into the hospital room, I hardly recognized Hank. My eccentric but loveable uncle with his dry wit and easy charm was gone. Instead, he weakly mumbled "Look what they expect me to eat. I asked for toast and they brought these stale rolls!" When I tried to be encouraging, he launched into a critique of the nursing staff. When I tried to empathize, he continued "You don't know the half of it! The interns are clueless, and the real doctors never show up till it's an emergency. Maybe I need to lower the bedrail and take a fall to get their attention!" Trying to distract him with some news of his favorite sports team didn't work either. Every topic of conversation was shut down in favor of ongoing, hospital-related complaints. The listener's only option was to nod with concern. Trying to alleviate his distress by fluffing the pillow or providing a treat elicited thanks followed by an immediate sigh of "It's nice you're trying, but..." followed by a description of the symptoms that had not been alleviated. When I left I was sad, but also frustrated by being made to feel so useless.

Visiting my old colleague Lois in the hospital was a different experience. Lois was a doctor, and doctors have a reputation for being bad patients. Lois lived up to that reputation. She ordered the nurses around as though she were in charge of the floor. She was constantly trying to look at her chart so she could tell the medical team how to better manage her case. When I tried to empathize about how difficult it must be to have so little say in her care, she replied "I can handle it...but somebody has to keep the house staff on their toes!" Lois had her friends bring in food that was not part of her hospital diet. Smoking was strictly forbidden, yet somehow Lois bartered with another patient for cigarettes and got an orderly to wheel her to the smoking area. Lois fell and hit her head after getting up to go to the bathroom when told to stay in bed. When I wondered aloud if this was wise, she replied indignantly, "I'm not going to beg some young thing for a bedpan so I can go to the loo!" I wasn't surprised by her remark: Lois never asked for help, even when she clearly needed it. Moreover, she thought her extreme self-sufficiency was a positive trait, and had little idea how it affected those around her. As I left, I couldn't help but worry about her recovery.

Understanding "Bad Patients"

Hank and Lois can be forgiven for their exasperating responses to illness. Nobody is at their best when physically unwell, which is why most people try to show empathy toward those who are ill rather than expecting it from them.

However, responses to illness may also reflect long-standing attitudes toward others rooted in early attachment experiences (see Chapter 2). When our health is challenged to the point where daily activities are affected, we invariably rely on others' support. The experience reminds us that we are not truly independent of our fellow human beings, but rather interdependent: sometimes we need others' help, and sometimes they need ours. This recognition of interdependence brought on by health challenges is embraced by some and considered threatening by others.

Those whose early attachment experiences were secure have the least difficulty moving flexibly along the spectrum from needing help to being relatively autonomous to helping others. Those whose early attachment experiences involved minimizing feelings of vulnerability (the "avoidant" or "dismissive" style) are likely to behave like Lois: rejecting help and insisting on making their own decisions, often to the detriment of their recovery. Those whose early attachment experiences involved exaggerating distress in order to get attention (the "ambivalent/resistant" or "preoccupied" style) are more likely to behave like Hank: whining and complaining about every minor discomfort with little effort to help themselves. They seem to take advantage of their role as a patient, making everyone else do more care than is reasonable. Those with traumatic or "disorganized" attachment experiences respond unpredictably to illness, as they do to any stress, often impeding recovery. Awareness of these different coping styles can be helpful to mental health professionals consulting to hospital services or, more generally, working with those who are physically ill.

A Mental Health Professional's Perspective

Fortunately, I have been spared serious illness, but when recalling the physical vulnerability imposed by pregnancy, I quickly realized I am more of a "Lois" than a "Hank". Some women describe pregnancy as a joyous experience, reminding them of the miraculous little being growing within, and of the opportunity to nurture new life. They talk to their baby-to-be, laugh when it kicks, pick out favorite decorations for the nursery, and even play soothing music near their bellies for the little one. By contrast, I loved my children dearly once they were born, but was miserable while carrying them. Rather than focusing on the miracle of new life, I worried about how I was going to keep up with my responsibilities with my body in this altered state. I fretted about being late for work, as I had to pull over and vomit at the side of the road in the mornings. The need for frequent obstetric appointments meant that I had to ask others to cover my duties, and I hated owing people favors. Hormonal changes made it difficult to maintain an even mood and a professional demeanor. In the latter stages of pregnancy, sleep became unpredictable as well, so I was often tired and frustrated by my slower pace and reduced efficiency. The only bright spot was occasionally being offered a seat on the train. Otherwise, I was much happier after the baby's birth when I was able to regain some sense of autonomy and control over my life.

Like many with this coping style, I eventually realized that my sense of autonomy and control was exaggerated, but not until I was much older. At the time of my pregnancies, it seemed normal to me. As a result, my capacity to empathize with those with different coping styles was limited early in my career. My clinical skills with "whiny" patients like Hank were quite poor, until I realized that we all need help sometimes, and complaining may be the only way to get it in certain situations. As I started to advocate for the needs of my children in the education system, for instance, I quickly learned that indeed "the squeaky wheel gets the grease". Those who cannot stop "squeaking" when ill, however, need our support in developing effective ways of participating in their own recovery. Conversely, those who insist on controlling their own medical decisions need our support in learning how to allow others to help.

One further type of patient or client that challenges our capacity for empathy is the patient who seems to be "faking" physical symptoms. The child who complains of tummy aches before school but is fine once brought there, the man with "whiplash" after a minor car accident who wants to be declared disabled to avoid work, and the woman who arrives in the emergency department with numbness that does not follow the anatomical distribution of any particular nerve are all examples of this dilemma.

It is important to remember that the causes of these ailments may or may not relate to conscious deception (see American Psychiatric Association, 2013). For example, anxiety can cause blood to flow to large muscles and away from internal organs, causing cramping and stomach pain. Most children are not aware of this process, so they genuinely believe they are ill when experiencing tummy aches. The man with whiplash may have some pain but become overly focused on it, intensifying the experience, perhaps due to fears of not being able to manage his usual duties at work; perhaps due to other issues. The woman with unusual numbness may be experiencing a "conversion reaction" where a past, often traumatic event results in apparent disability.

These patients challenge us to understand the interplay of mind and body in the experience of distress. Most of the time, they are not deliberately trying to manipulate their caregivers or therapists, but rather expressing emotional hurt in somatic ways. Helping them express that hurt in words, drawings, or (in children) play is often more helpful than showing them laboratory results that prove the illness is "all in the mind".

Witnessing Illness and Disability

Those with chronic illness or disability stretch our capacity for empathetic relationships, yet at the same time show us how meaningful life can be even in the absence of success as conventionally defined. Jean Vanier has described this experience eloquently with respect to the mentally disabled and the L'Arche communities he has established for and with them (see Vanier, 1998). In my own experience of raising an autistic child, I sometimes struggle to be empathetic when he experiences apparently minor changes as catastrophic. Yet, I am also surprised at how attuned he can be to my emotional states, considering the disorder has been linked to impairments in "theory of mind", a capacity needed for the cognitive aspects of empathy. Overall, I have to admire his courage for persevering with (for the most part) an optimistic attitude, despite a number of physical as well as mental challenges. Solomon (see Solomon, 2012) describes similar family experiences in relation to a number of other differences and disabilities in children.

Those encountering disability later in life may struggle even more emotionally than disabled children do. It is extremely difficult for someone in their forties or fifties to adapt to the "new normal" of being suddenly impaired when he or she has been highly autonomous and accomplished previously. Sometimes, the person becomes depressed. Sometimes, he or she may even question the value of continuing life in this newly debilitated state. Imagine, for example, an apparently healthy, vigorous executive who has a serious stroke that leaves him conscious but unable to move or speak. *The Diving Bell and the Butterfly* is a recent book and film about a man in such a state, and his battle to return to a meaningful life (see Bauby, 1997).

For those around the person there are different challenges. For example, how does one show empathy when there is no means of communicating and ascertaining what the other person is thinking? Except for the most intuitively gifted, most people have to rely on their knowledge of the person's character based on past experience, and make an educated guess regarding the person's experience based on this knowledge. Sometimes, disfigurement poses an additional challenge. In this case, the other person may have to overcome their own revulsion or disgust before being able to show empathy. Consistent with Batson's (1987) findings (see Chapter 1), becoming distressed in response to the ill person's distress can also interfere with empathy. For those previously in a close relationship with the newly disabled person, adapting to changes in the role of each partner and in the relationship as a whole may be difficult. The experience of sudden, devastating illness can also be emotionally traumatic for both patient and loved one. When faced with emotional trauma, people feel overwhelmed and disorganized. In this state, they may try to regain a sense of control by seeking a simple, organized explanation for events, even if that explanation involves blaming themselves or others, compromising empathy.

Finally, witnessing the ravages of disease and disability in others can heighten our own appreciation of health and wellness, an "attitude of gratitude" that connects us to the moment by moment frame of mind needed for empathy. People in hospital are restricted in their movements, live in artificial light that obscures the difference between day and night, and are generally deprived of many familiar sensory experiences which they would have at home. Driving away after a hospital visit, I often find I have a heightened awareness of sensory experience: I notice the sun beating down on my left forearm through the car window, the sensations in my muscles as I hoist snow out of the driveway, and (in summer) the plants brushing against my skin as I weed the garden. Perhaps because these are all things my friend in the hospital cannot experience, I experience them more deeply. It reminds me that the original description of empathy was Einfühlung, a German word referring to one's ability to emotionally enter into the essence of a painting (Vischer, 1994).

Social Determinants of Health and of Empathy

The link between physical well-being and empathy has implications that go beyond our individual relationships (discussed further in Part III of this book). The reason for this is that in many parts of the world physical health is chronically compromised. For example, when people are starving, it is natural for them to become preoccupied with obtaining food for themselves and their families, even if this requires a lack of empathy toward those outside their immediate circle (Samelson, 2009). When children are born to malnourished mothers, there may be effects on neural development which further compromise their capacity for empathy. Expecting people who live in these circumstances to work towards peace and engage in practices that protect the natural environment is simply not realistic. Their own and their children's survival will always be their first priority.

Even in North America, the urban poor often live in so-called "food deserts" (Cummins and Macintyre, 1999) where store shelves are stocked with unhealthy snacks and access to fresh fruits and vegetables is difficult or impossible. These circumstances result in high rates of obesity, cardiovascular disease, and other chronic health conditions that require attention, making it difficult to focus on others' well-being.

In recent years, medical practitioners have come to realize that treating diseases is only a small part of improving population health. Addressing poverty, discrimination, and other social factors affecting health will help more people become healthy more of the time than any "miracle cure" (Marmot, 2005). It is also necessary in order to build the foundation for a more empathetic society.

Summary

There are a number of possible biological impediments to empathy as listed below. These can include being unkind to ourselves through:

- Intoxication and withdrawal cycles from substance abuse
- Neglect of health habits: lack of attention to sleep, eating, dental hygiene, exercise
- Excessive focus on one's body in a starved state (as in eating disorders or extreme poverty)
- Ignoring self-care for the sake of an altruistic future goal (common in health professionals)
- Lack of self-compassionate attitudes

Further impediments to empathetic behavior can include:

- Change in usual health routines
- Biological differences in the neurochemistry needed for empathy (see Chapter 2)
- Biological effects of illness or its treatment on our state of mind
- Reactions to being sick based in early attachment experiences
- Lack of understanding for somatic symptoms that usually result from the interplay of biology and psychology
- Difficulty adapting to chronic illness or disability
- Fearful, traumatic, or disgusted reactions to another person's illness

On the other hand, some biological considerations important in enhancing our capacity for empathy include:

- Good health habits (i.e., attention to sleep, eating, dental hygiene, exercise)
- Mindfulness, whether through meditation, prayer, exercise, or attention to the task at hand
- Cultivating self-compassionate attitudes
- Addressing physical discomfort so we can focus less on ourselves and more on others
- Diaphragmatic breathing and other relaxation practices which support the parasympathetic nervous system
- Activities that enhance endorphin release (tastes, smells, laughter, exercise, sex, meditation) or oxytocin release (hugging, singing, dancing, praying, watching an emotional movie, exercising with a friend, or being altruistic)
- Communal meals and shared physical activities
- Ensuring nurturing environments for our children, so they can develop a flexible stress response system conducive to empathy
- Illness sometimes helps us recognize our own interdependence with others, increasing empathy
- Learning to empathize with those who are physically vulnerable or not conventionally successful
- Admiring the perseverance and courage of the seriously ill or disabled
- An "attitude of gratitude" in relation to our own health and wellness
- Working towards addressing the social determinants of health

Most of us can improve in at least one of these areas. Use the reflective or therapist questions on the next page to identify your goals for enhancing the biology of empathy in your own life.

Reflective Questions

1. What aspect(s) of your own health could benefit from a self-compassionate attitude?
2. Who would be affected if your health suddenly deteriorated?
3. What health practices might strengthen your capacity for empathy?
4. Are you more like Lois or Hank when coping with illness? For which of these characters do you feel greater empathy? Why?
5. How have people with disabilities or serious illnesses affected your capacity for empathy?

Questions for Therapists

1. Which of your clients could benefit from a more self-compassionate attitude? In what way?

2 How could you foster a more self-compassionate attitude in each of these clients?
3 What health practices related to the capacity for empathy do you often recommend? Do you plan to recommend any others?
4 How do clients with physical illnesses challenge your capacity for empathy? Do you work better with those more like Lois or those more like Hank?
5 Do you have an approach to working with clients whose medical symptoms are not entirely explained? What seems to be helpful for them?

References

American Psychiatric Association (2013). *Diagnostic and Statistical Manual of Mental Disorders, (DSM 5)* 5th Edition. Washington, DC: American Psychiatric Association.
Baker, L. (2008). Biological psychology. In: *21st Century Psychology: A Reference Handbook, Vol. 1.* Eds: Davis, S.F. and Baskist, W. London: Sage Publishing, pp. 114–124.
Barnes, S. (2005). *The Art of Listening Prayer.* Gainesville, GA: Ashland Press.
Batson, C.D. (1987). Prosocial motivation: is it ever truly altruistic? In L. Berkowitz (Ed.) *Advances in Experimental Social Psychology.* New York: Academic Press, pp. 65–122.
Bauby, J.D. (1997). *The Diving Bell and the Butterfly: A Memoir of Life in Death.* New York: Vintage Books.
Cummins, S. and Macintyre, S. (1999). The location of food stores in urban areas: a case study in Glasgow. *British Food Journal*, 101, 545–553.
Engel, G.L. (1977). The need for a new medical model: A challenge for biomedicine. *Science*, 196, 129–136.
Fairburn, C.G. and Brownell, K.D. (Eds.)(2002). *Eating Disorders and Obesity, Second Edition: A Comprehensive Handbook.* New York: Guilford Press.
Goldstein, A. (1980). Thrills in response to music and other stimuli. *Physiological Psychology*, 8, 126–129.
Kabat-Zinn, J. (1994) *Wherever You Go, There You Are: Mindfulness Meditation in Everyday Life.* New York: Hyperion Books.
Kornfield, J. (1993). *A Path with Heart.* New York: Bantam Books.
Lally, P., van Jaarsveld, C.H.M., Potts, H.W.W., and Wardle, J. (2010). How are habits formed: Modelling habit formation in the real world. *European Journal of Social Psychology*, 40, 998–1009.
Manassis, K. (1986). The effects of cultural differences on the physician-patient relationship. *Canadian Family Physician*, 32, 383–389.
Marmot, M. (2005). Social determinants of health inequalities. *The Lancet*, 365, 1099–1104.
Matthews, S.G. (2002). Early programming of the hypothalamo-pituitary-adrenal axis. *Trends in Endocrinological Metabolism*, 13, 373–380.
Music, G. (2014). *The Good Life.* New York: Routledge. pp. 29–36.
Nobel, R. and Manassis, K. (2012). Perfectionism in relation to outcome of school-based CBT for children. *Journal of Rational Emotive & Cognitive Behavioral Therapy*, 30, 77–90.

Samelson, D.A. (2009). *Feeding the Starving Mind*. Oakland, CA: New Harbinger. pp. 65–67.

Solomon, A. (2012). *Far from the Tree: Parents, Children, and the Search for Identity*. New York: Scribner.

Unknown Author (traditional Native American). *The Cherokee Tale of Two Wolves*.

Vanier, J. (1998). *Becoming Human*. Toronto: Anansi Press Ltd.

Vischer, R. (1994) (reprint and translation from the original German). On the optical sense of form: A contribution to aesthetics. In *Empathy, Form, and Space: Problems in German Aesthetics, 1873–1893* (Texts and Documents Series). Santa Monica, CA: Getty Center for the History of Art, pp. 89–123.

Williams, M., Teasdale, J., Segal, Z., and Kabat-Zinn, J. (2007). *The Mindful Way Through Depression: Freeing Yourself from Chronic Unhappiness*. New York: Guilford Press.

Zak, P.J. (2012). *The Moral Molecule: The Source of Love and Prosperity*. New York: Dutton Press.

5 Mental Aspects: Emotional Distress and *Not* Looking Out for Number One

> We must learn to regard people less in the light of what they do or omit to do, and more in the light of what they suffer.
>
> Dietrich Bonhoeffer (1997)

Whereas the last chapter focused on physical factors related to empathy (the "biology" in the biopsychosocial model), this chapter and the next two are dedicated to psychological factors that can affect empathy. Although some aspects of these chapters may be of greater interest to therapists than parents or leaders, the examples are based on struggles common to many people. Chapters 5 to 7 can be thought of, metaphorically, as different layers of an onion. Chapter 5 focuses on fairly obvious mental health symptoms, which can be thought of as the outer layer of the onion. Their main influence on empathy is to increase self-preoccupation, and even though not all of us suffer from serious mental illnesses, we all experience emotional distress to a degree. In these distressed states, it is more difficult to *not* look out for number one (i.e., focus on self-interest) than otherwise. Chapter 6 explores habitual coping styles (or defenses, depending on one's perspective—see Vaillant, 1993) which we use to manage intense emotions, whether or not we are aware of them. Some of these result in greater empathy and selfless behavior than others. Chapter 7 delves into expectations we have of ourselves and others in relationships that are often not entirely conscious (i.e., the inner layers of the onion). To begin this chapter, ideas about mental health and mental illness are placed in a historical context.

Mental Health and Mental Illness: A Historical Perspective

In pre-industrial societies, mental health and mental illness were seen largely as spiritual phenomena (see Lewis, 1992). Psychosis, for example, might be attributed to possession by a malevolent spirit. Alternatively, some societies created special roles for the mentally ill as visionaries or shamans. These various explanations often resulted in social support for people who had illnesses for which, at the time, there was no specific treatment.

With the advent of modern medicine, medical explanations were developed for mental illness. Medical explanations often emphasized eradicating diseases in order to restore the individual to health. An inflamed appendix could be surgically removed; antibiotics could eliminate disease-causing bacteria from the body. Freud, who was originally a neurologist, developed theories of mental illness using this medical principle (Freud, translated by Richards, 1973). His methods were designed to discover unconscious conflicts, bring them into consciousness, and thus eliminate the troublesome symptoms related to these conflicts. Remove the inflamed appendix and the individual is restored to physical health; remove the unconscious conflict and the individual is restored to psychological health, or so his theories suggested. A host of subsequent theorists disputed his descriptions of the nature of mental health problems, but the medical principle remained: eradicate the problem, and the individual is restored to psychological health.

In recent decades, however, mental health practitioners have started to question this principle. First, human beings are complex, so psychological health can be difficult to define. For example, if we define it as a personal sense of well-being, then people with personality disorders, who are often not distressed by their symptoms, would be considered psychologically healthy. However, many with severe personality disorders end up in prison, an outcome that is not consistent with psychological health. Second, treating mental health problems does not always result in complete psychological health. For instance, an anxious person may learn to face their fears and thus recover from their anxiety disorder but still struggle with setting goals for the future or some other important life challenge. Third, when treatment is prolonged or has side effects, some people experience a deterioration in their day to day functioning in the course of that treatment. Thus, focusing on symptom elimination is not always in the patient's best interest. Fourth, some people experience improved psychological well-being despite their symptoms. For example, they may take up a new hobby that engages them so completely that they are able to ignore symptoms for long periods of time, or they may find community support that enhances well-being and reduces the impact of their symptoms on daily life. One type of therapy (Acceptance Commitment Therapy; Ruiz, 2010) is even dedicated to this idea, helping clients accept their symptoms and commit to important ideals and goals anyways.

For all of these reasons, recent conceptualizations of mental health have moved away from an exclusive focus on problems and toward broader conceptualizations that include individual strengths. Practitioners have started looking across diagnoses for interventions that are helpful for people with many different afflictions (see Ehrenreich-May and Chu, 2014), and often build upon strengths. Practitioners have also started looking across therapies for common therapeutic elements or outcomes (see Allen and Fonagy, 2008; Wells, Fisher, Myers, Wheatley, Patel, and Brewin, 2009). For example, the ability to examine one's own thoughts and feelings from a somewhat detached perspective has been lauded as a positive outcome in many therapies. Similar descriptions of this phenomenon are provided by many authors using different terminology, which includes metacognition (Wells et al., 2009), self-reflection (Lysaker, Buck, Carcione, Procacci, Salvatore, Nicolo, and Dimaggio, 2011), de-reflection (Frankl, 1978), mentalization (see Allen and Fonagy, 2008), and mindfulness (see Kabat-Zinn, 1994). Positive psychology (Seligman and Csikszentmihalyi, 2000; see Chapter 1) has developed into a prominent movement that studies and emphasizes mental strengths to be developed in order to increase overall well-being, socially adaptive behavior, and other desirable outcomes including empathy.

With respect to empathy specifically, one could say that mental suffering of all types increases the focus on oneself and thus adversely affects empathy in relationships. Conversely, there is the potential for all successful mental health treatments to do the opposite. However, consistent with positive psychology, empathy can also be conceptualized as a valid, strength-focused, desirable outcome of psychological treatment in its own right. To increase the likelihood of this outcome, a closer look at the component processes of empathy in relation to various mental health challenges is needed. These component processes were originally described in Chapter 1 and illustrated in Figure 1.1. They are now briefly reviewed, before examining each in relation to mental health.

Components of Empathy and Mental Health

One important component of empathy is the ability to transcend a focus on ourselves and our own survival. Attention to one's own distress or to threats to oneself, whether real or imagined, triggers the fight or flight reaction, which is usually incompatible with empathy. Once this reaction subsides, attention can shift outside one's own interests. Directing this attentional shift towards others, rather than other pleasant or interesting aspects of our environment, is the second component of empathy. The third component involves trying to take another person's perspective mentally and emotionally. Cognitive factors can make mental perspective-taking difficult for some people, while other people struggle with relating to others emotionally. As Coplan (2011) has described, failure to maintain clear psychological boundaries can be a further factor that interferes with taking someone else's perspective. Lastly, empathy includes effective communication of how we understand the other person's experience, in the hope that he or she will feel validated in that experience.

The number of mental health challenges people can face is vast (see American Psychiatric Association, 2013), and some people simply defy categorization by any diagnostic system. Nevertheless, I will attempt to relate some common mental health challenges to the empathy components described above. Given the scope of this chapter, I have not included all mental health challenges. I also recognize that some challenges affect more than one aspect

76 Nurturing Empathy

Table 5.1 Components of Empathy and Mental Health Conditions

Component of Empathy	Conditions That Could Affect This Component
Preoccupation with oneself/survival	Anxiety disorders Intermittent Explosive Disorder Post-Traumatic Stress Disorder Obsessive Compulsive Disorder Depression Eating disorders
Motivation to attend to another person	Addictions Coping styles Most personality disorders Beliefs/philosophies of life (see Chapter 8)
Cognitive perspective-taking	Autism/other neurodevelopmental conditions Psychosis
Relating to another person emotionally	Psychopathy/Antisocial Personality Disorder
Psychological boundaries	Borderline Personality Disorder
Communicating empathy	Learning disabilities Cognitive biases Lack of education

of empathy, and some empathetic difficulties cross diagnostic categories. However, Table 5.1 shows common conditions where each component of empathy may be affected, recognizing that overlap exists. Subsequent sections of this chapter discuss difficulties people can experience with each component of empathy. All sections include a case example illustrating the effect of a common mental health condition on empathy. Even if you do not suffer from any particular mental health condition, the examples may apply at certain times in your life. For instance, even though most of the readers of this book may not suffer from clinical depression, everyone encounters low moods from time to time, and their effect on empathy may be similar though less extreme than that of clinical depression.

Preoccupation with Oneself

Juanita

Juanita was the second of two fraternal twin girls. She spent much of her childhood both playing with and competing with her twin sister. Although she was smaller, Juanita was the more agile girl, and became an accomplished gymnast. Her sister did better academically. Juanita was eventually found to have a learning disability. With tutoring she kept up in high school, but her gymnastics career faded after the physical changes of puberty made it difficult to continue this sport. She failed a couple of courses in her final year of school, so had to go back for an extra semester to finish. Her sister, on the other hand, excelled at school and won a scholarship to a prestigious university.

After her sister left for college, Juanita fell apart. She neglected her courses, withdrew from her family, and spent much of her day playing video games. She slept late and began missing some days of school. Within a month, she stopped attending completely. Juanita's parents tried to encourage her to persevere, but Juanita insisted she was "useless" and life had no purpose. She ate only junk food. She reported wishing she could "go to sleep and not wake up".

I decided to treat Juanita with a combination of psychotherapy and antidepressant medication. Her parents were very relieved that something was being done to help their daughter, and were willing to help in whatever way I recommended.

I discussed "behavioral activation" with Juanita and her parents: the idea that most people who are depressed feel better if they gradually increase their activity level. Juanita's mother took time off work to make sure she got out for a walk each day. Juanita reported the walks were "a hassle" and complained about the cold temperature outside. I also discussed the importance of Juanita having a realistic career goal. Juanita's father investigated entry-level positions that might appeal to her, but Juanita insisted she would be "a disappointment" if she pursued one of these positions. Her guidance counselor looked into part-time volunteer work that could get Juanita out of the house and count towards her high school requirements. Juanita's response was "How can I help someone else, when I can't even help myself?" Juanita was so absorbed by her own misery that she rejected people's attempts to be helpful and lacked any interest in reaching out to others.

Progress was gradual in this case. The regular walk, despite complaints, was the only realistic option for the first few months. When it was cold, Juanita's mother made some hot chocolate upon returning to the house. When it was rainy, Juanita preferred a warm bath. These simple sensory experiences became a highlight for the day, and a way of attending to something other than her own negative thoughts. As she improved, Juanita was able to work on an online course she needed for her diploma. She didn't enjoy the course, but the concentration required took her away from her depressive rumination for at least an hour a day. Eventually, she also started the volunteer work her guidance counselor suggested, began feeling more accomplished, and improved further.

As shown in Table 5.1, a number of mental health conditions interfere with empathy by increasing self-absorption. Depression and anxiety disorders are the most common conditions of this group, and the latter are discussed further in Chapter 6. As shown in Juanita's example, however, the self-focused thinking associated with depression can affect every aspect of life and be particularly resistant to change. One of the reasons for encouraging activity in the depressed is to interfere with this type of thinking, which tends to predominate when the depressed person isolates themselves at home. Self-focused rumination tends to make depression worse, and depression in turn increases self-focused rumination in a vicious cycle. Breaking that cycle is important in order to both increase people's well-being and restore their capacity to focus outside themselves and relate to others empathetically.

Similar thinking occurs in most people at times when they become excessively focused on regret, guilt, or personal shortcomings. We often think of remorse and regret as morally noble sentiments, and they can be at times when we are atoning for harm done to others. For example, a violent criminal who provides a sincere apology to the victim and his or her family is often judged more favorably than one who does not. Moreover, even the most law-abiding citizens have regrets about things they have said or done to others, or failed to say or do (so-called "sins of omission"). Only the rare sociopath, who lacks empathy entirely, can get through life without guilt or regret. Saying "sorry" is a part of life, and it is often an important part as it can repair hurt feelings and restore relationships.

However, when we dwell upon feelings of guilt for a long time, we may do more harm than good. Guilt-ridden people tend to withdraw from others, limiting their capacity for empathy. Moreover, when they do interact with people the conversation often revolves around their own psychological burdens, with little attention to the needs of the person with whom they are talking. Prolonged guilt without restorative action increases self-absorption, decreasing empathy.

I recall being in this state myself after making some difficult decisions concerning the end of my husband's life. I now marvel at the patience of my good friends, who listened to my self-focused ramblings on this subject again and again. At the time, I thought I was doing the right thing by analyzing my emotions and behavior in order to become a better person. After all, there is an old saying that those who fail to learn from history are condemned to repeat it (see Santayana, 1905/1998). However, once we have learned what we can from past events, it is important to move on. Forgiving ourselves is not just a nice, self-compassionate thing to do, but also an essential aspect of re-engaging with the rest of the world and regaining our capacity for empathy. Listening to others empathetically is only possible when we are no longer preoccupied with our own emotional burdens. As therapists, for whom empathetic listening skills are essential, we may need to seek our own therapy if overcoming this preoccupation is difficult.

These ideas are particularly important when we are raising children. It has long been known that parents with post-partum depression tend to develop insecure attachment relationships with their infants, which often color the child's expectations of relationships for life (Murray, Cooper, and Fearon, 2014). Depression in a parent can affect children at later stages of development too though. Imagine, for instance, being a ten year old whose parent appears uninterested in any of his or her accomplishments, complains about how tiring it is to look after children, and talks about looking forward to "the hereafter" because there is so little that is positive in life. The parent has no idea how upsetting these statements are to the child, as the self-preoccupation of depression is interfering with empathy. Since children often attribute parental feelings to their own behavior, however, the child in this case might feel unaccomplished, burdensome, and anxious about the possibility of parental suicide. These feelings would put the child's mental health at risk. Therefore, it is important for those working with depressed adults to address the thoughts and feelings parental depression can induce in the children. *Can I Catch It Like a Cold* (see Centre for Addiction and Mental Health, 2009), for example, is a book that explains parental depression from a child's point of view. Also, with professional support, many depressed parents can appreciate the impact of the illness on their children and thus reduce its detrimental effects.

In summary, dealing with emotional states that increase a focus on oneself is important to restoring one's capacity for empathy. Treating depression, self-forgiveness, and awareness of the impact of our emotions on children have been encouraged. As Juanita experienced, getting outside the house, engaging in activities that require concentration, and noticing positive sensory experiences are other aspects of shifting our mental focus beyond ourselves. Mindfulness meditation facilitates this shift as well, and is discussed further in the next chapter. We now discuss how to move one's mental focus toward other people.

Motivation to Attend to Another Person

Adam

Adam was a very accomplished businessman, who was aiming to be promoted to a vice presidency at his bank. His cellular phone was never shut off. He responded to clients, colleagues, and supervisors alike, and never grumbled about the inconvenience. He had an astute understanding of market trends, and as his clients prospered so did his reputation as a financial wizard.

At home Adam's life was a different story. He and his wife often fought, as she felt the burden of raising the children with little support from her husband. One of the children struggled badly at school, and Adam was rarely available for parent-teacher meetings. The school suggested a psychological assessment, but Adam had his wife arrange it as the assessment coincided with an important international deal in which he represented his bank. His wife obtained psychological help for the child and parenting advice for herself and Adam, but Adam participated little in implementing that advice.

As his work stress and marital stress increased Adam began to drink. At the end of a long day, the last thing he needed was to listen to another litany of complaints about how little he did to support the family emotionally, and how frustrated his wife was. "You wouldn't even be able to afford that psychologist without my income!" was his angry retort to his wife. After that, he withdrew to his den and checked the latest market news as he sipped his Scotch. Scotch disrupted his sleep, so he woke up irritable and even less inclined to help out with the children. After a while, he needed an alcoholic "eye-opener" in the mornings to settle his moods. He became more pleasant around his family, but started hiding bottles in his desk at work. His upward trajectory at work continued and, even though he helped little, his wife was reassured that he had the family's best interests at heart. There seemed to be a new equilibrium that kept both his career and his marriage stable for several years.

One day, Adam experienced severe abdominal pain at work. He was rushed to hospital and found to be suffering from pancreatitis, an illness often related to alcohol abuse. His liver function tests were also abnormal. Given his many responsibilities Adam had shied away from doctors, so had no idea how significantly his health had deteriorated. Now, he was told in no uncertain terms that he would have to quit drinking if he wanted to live to see his son graduate from high school. Despite the impact on his ambitions at the bank, Adam agreed to a treatment program. Seeing his wife and children's frightened faces, he realized the distress he had caused them. He felt remorse. He resolved to put his family first, fought his alcoholism, and found a more balanced (albeit less prestigious) approach to work.

Unlike Juanita, Adam is not focused on personal misery, but he nevertheless lacks empathy until the very end of the vignette. For most of the story, he is focused on his career (i.e., an external focus, but not an empathetic one). This focus leaves him oblivious to the impact of his actions on others' feelings, and his attention to others' emotions is dulled further by alcohol. Alcohol also reduces attention to his own feelings, reduces self-compassion, and thus ultimately impacts his physical as well as mental health.

Unfortunately, Adam's pattern of trying to escape negative emotions through substance abuse is not unusual. People who cope this way often have little appreciation of the effect of their substance abuse on others. Furthermore, the emotional instability caused by repeated cycles of intoxication and withdrawal can result in insensitive, sometimes aggressive behavior. To avoid this socially unacceptable behavior, the person may then feel they have no alternative but to use the substance more continuously over the course of the day, resulting in addiction.

Social expectations may further exacerbate this pattern. An executive like Adam is typically evaluated based on results, not the process whereby those results are achieved. The focus on results is future-oriented, whereas interpersonal processes including empathy happen in the here and now. Empathy for oneself and for others happens moment by moment, and is easy to overlook when one is constantly looking ahead. Consequently, random acts of kindness are rare in the business world.

To shift our focus toward others we encounter in our daily lives, empathy must become an important ideal (see Chapter 8) and we must resist the temptation to dull our sensitivity to human suffering with substances and other addictions. Alternative ways of coping with negative emotions are discussed in Chapter 6. Moreover, the empathetic ideal must sometimes be prioritized over future goals. In the long run, empathy and success are not incompatible. For instance, effective leaders are often highly attuned to the emotional needs of their workers, and know how to make people feel like valued members of a team. This feeling often inspires greater productivity and greater cooperation among people, increasing success for all.

Nevertheless, an empathetic person must make a consistent effort to attend to people encountered day by day and moment by moment, whether they are "important" with respect to future goals or not. Without this effort we tend to objectify others, seeing them as useful tools to aid our progress, or obstacles in our way. With this effort we can have meaningful, sometimes delightful encounters with other human beings when least expected. For example, some of my most memorable experiences from working in a large urban hospital for over 20 years came while commuting. I would give directions to a confused-looking stranger, share some candy with a fellow passenger when the train got stuck, or thank someone for letting me borrow their phone to call home when running late. What a wonderful distraction from office politics and burn-out! Beyond the personal benefits, putting forth this effort almost invariably makes us better therapists, parents, leaders, and human beings.

Cognitive Perspective-Taking

Nolton

Nolton was a bright boy, and an avid member of his school's rocketry club. He was diagnosed with high-functioning autism after his second grade teacher pointed out to his parents that he never looked her in the eye.

Nolton seemed good-natured, and loved to explain the physics behind his model rockets to his peers. At other times, however, he seemed distant and uncaring. For example, his parents had told Nolton to use a firm handshake and make eye contact when meeting adults. Therefore, when his grandmother opened her arms to hug him, Nolton used a firm handshake and made eye contact. She burst into tears. Another time, Nolton's parents told him that when a friend is crying you should comfort him or her by offering a cup of cocoa. Nolton forgot his best friend's birthday one year, and the friend yelled at him and started to cry. Nolton reached for the cocoa, and was perplexed as to why his friend did not calm down. A third rule his parents suggested was that if you've talked about a subject that interests you for five minutes, you should stop so someone else can introduce a different subject. Nolton would stop talking mid-sentence exactly at the five-minute mark, leaving an awkward silence.

Despite his sweet nature, Nolton alienated others without meaning to. The basic rules of social discourse provided by his parents were applied rigidly, with no modifications based on the other person's point of view. If told explicitly to take another person's perspective, Nolton could do so with effort. He missed the more subtle aspects of the people's feelings, but could understand if they were happy, mad, sad, or fearful. However, it simply did not occur to Nolton to put himself in the other person's shoes without being asked. Over time, Nolton became increasingly anxious about social situations, as he realized how inept he was at managing them.

The ability to mentally take another person's perspective, termed "theory of mind", is one of the key deficits in individuals with autism. It is particularly obvious in those who, like Nolton, have average or above average intelligence, as it stands in striking contrast to their other abilities. When raised in families where emotions are readily discussed, these children can often learn to take someone else's perspective with effort and instruction. However, they may not take the other person's perspective in ordinary social situations when they have not been told to do so. It simply doesn't "come naturally" in the absence of deliberate effort.

The tendency to ignore others' perspective is not unique to autism. Relatives of autistic individuals, for example, have been described as having a "broader autism phenotype", where they appear like neurologically typical individuals to others most of the time, but can show certain autistic traits. Effective researchers, for instance, are often highly focused on very narrow areas of inquiry that might seem like unusual interests to others. When engrossed in their work, they sometimes dispense with social niceties for the sake of advancing their current projects. Most people have times in their lives when understanding people's various perspectives takes a back seat to other priorities, or when the perspective-taking is imperfect. When our understanding of the other person's point of view is imperfect, we tend to fall back on social rules or conventions, much as Nolton does in the example. Well-intentioned social mishaps often result. A person with many environmental allergies, for example, might find the common practice of bringing flowers to a housewarming distressing, rather than seeing it as a kind gesture. Similarly, Nolton's grandmother found the common gesture of shaking hands distressing, as a close relative often expects a hug. Interactions with others need to be individualized depending on the person and the situation, so no set of social rules can be adequate for dictating behavior in all circumstances.

How can we improve our ability to take another's perspective? In the autistic population, exercises that help people recognize others' thoughts and feelings in a situation have been developed. *Social Stories* (see Gray, 2000), for example, challenge the person to discover appropriate responses to a variety of common social situations, and there are a number of recent "apps" to aid emotion recognition and conversational skills.

Beyond specific exercises, we can all learn from social mishaps or socially awkward situations by asking ourselves "How did my words/actions make this person feel?" and "What could I have done differently to make this person more comfortable?" Accessing films, plays, and literature that include complex characters can also be helpful. Comic books, where heroes and villains are clearly distinguished, may be fun sometimes but we should not limit ourselves to these types of stories. Reading stories with flawed heroes and understandable villains can really challenge us to step into another's shoes. Usually, they also mirror the human condition more accurately.

Relating to Another Person Emotionally

Joel

Joel, age 10, was referred for assessment after giving one of his classmates a "swirly", dunking his head in the toilet and flushing until the boy almost drowned. Joel had been through a series of foster homes ever since his doctor found welts on his back after his step-father physically abused him. Gathering some more information, I was told this was the third in a series of "stepfathers" Joel had lived with before the age of seven, as his mother suffered from a personality disorder that resulted in unstable moods and unstable relationships. Joel's Children's Aid Worker reported that the parents in his last foster home were being investigated, as several other children in that home had reported sexual abuse.

Joel was a pleasant fellow to interview, and told me he enjoyed school and had a number of friends. He didn't mention the fact that he had recently doused his best friend's cat in lighter fluid and set it on fire. When I asked him about his recent foster home experiences, he shrugged "no problem", but there was a vacant stare in his eyes. Joel responded to all of my standard interview questions in a manner that seemed reasonable, but intuitively I doubted his sincerity. Asking my usual questions about mad, sad, and scared feelings (the most common sources of discomfort in children), he responded that he rarely got scared or sad, but people who were weak "sissies" or people who challenged his position at the top of his school's social hierarchy certainly made him mad. The fact that he got into trouble for getting angry did not seem to bother him. "There's nothing the principal can do to me that I haven't gone through before" was Joel's nonchalant response. Joel showed a striking lack of empathy for his victims.

I rarely find interviewing children upsetting, having interviewed several thousand children in my career now. Characters like Joel are the exception: they give me chills. As long as the conversation is light and focused on their interests they seem quite reasonable. As soon as you try to discuss distressing feelings they either deflect your questions or shut down and stare coldly. Sometimes termed "callous and unemotional", they lack any ability to connect with their victims' suffering. The ability to understand the victim's perspective may be there to a degree, but they use this ability to manipulate the situation to their advantage, not to foster empathy. Usually, a combination of genetic predisposition and abusive childhood experiences (Byrd and Manuck, 2014) has left them unable to trust others, and they therefore become adept at using others for their own gains. When antisocial behavior persists, children like Joel often end up in the criminal justice system. A few, usually those with high intelligence, eventually control their violent behaviors but continue to lack empathy. Because they seem reasonable and even charming to others they are often able to attract followers and become quite successful. I can even recall a colleague who fits this description.

Teaching these people skills related to empathy merely improves their ability to manipulate others. For these individuals to become truly empathetic is rare. It is most likely to happen if they are placed with one or more consistently trustworthy, consistently empathetic adults with whom they can eventually form an emotional connection. That process, however, often takes years and our foster care systems rarely facilitate it. A trusting relationship with a spouse or with a Higher Power can sometimes result in a similar process later in life, but unfortunately this process is the exception rather than the rule.

Psychological Boundaries

Keisha

Keisha got knots in her stomach whenever Christmas approached. She was expected to make a list for Santa and dreaded this chore. She had figured out long ago that her mother was really "Santa" and knew she was expected to ask for gifts that met her mother's approval. Whenever they walked through the mall, Keisha listened carefully to her mother's comments. "I would have loved a doll like that", meant this doll should be added to the Christmas list. "How could anyone find such a silly game amusing?" meant this game should definitely come off the list. It didn't really matter what Keisha wanted. It only mattered that she asked for things her mother liked, so that her mother would enjoy giving them to her.

As she got older Keisha started enjoying popular music. One of her friends had a karaoke machine, and the girls loved to sing along and pretend they were pop stars. Keisha's aunt asked if she would like a gift card so she could download some songs onto her iPod. Before she could open her mouth though, Keisha's mother responded "Oh no. That wouldn't interest her. We like classical music."

Keisha's mother often assumed she knew what her daughter wanted, and for years Keisha agreed with her mother. Being agreeable made her mother happy, and sometimes it was unclear whether there was a difference between her mother's likes and dislikes and her own. Now that she was a young teen, however, she protested. She started voicing some opinions that were not her mother's, particularly when it came to clothes and music. Her mother responded by ignoring her, sometimes for days. As long as Keisha's words reflected her mother's opinions, she was a "good daughter" in her mother's eyes. When they did not she seemed to disappear. Keisha's mother had only one way of relating to her daughter: as a psychological extension of herself. This approach seriously compromised her ability to empathize with Keisha's feelings.

This example reminds me of an old truism: beware the person who says "I know exactly how you feel." Usually, they are both wrong and lacking in empathy. No person can know exactly how another person feels. We each have a unique psychological perspective that emerges over time from ongoing interactions between our temperamental predispositions and environmental events (see Chapter 2). Even the most empathetic people we know can only grasp a reasonable approximation of that perspective. Those who claim perfect understanding, especially after knowing you for only a short time, often lack psychological boundaries. On the other hand, people with clear psychological boundaries treat others with respectful curiosity, trying to understand them but recognizing that this understanding will always be incomplete. In short, we can never truly stand in another's shoes, only imagine what it might be like.

Those raised by parents lacking in boundaries, as Keisha was, may struggle with this aspect of empathy. It's not just a matter of distinguishing their own opinions from those of others; it's also a matter of recognizing appropriate and inappropriate degrees of closeness with others and of considering what is likely to be helpful or unhelpful in others' circumstances. Thus, Keisha might think she was being empathetic when echoing a friend's concerns, but really be repeating a relationship pattern from her history with her mother: the pattern of being agreeable in order to preserve closeness in the relationship, regardless of whether or not this is what the other person wants or needs. A true friend sometimes disagrees, for example when the other person is planning to do something foolish. A person lacking boundaries, by contrast, may fear losing the relationship if he or she disagrees. Preserving the connection takes precedence over the other person's well-being, which is not empathetic.

Warning signs for therapists indicating that their patients may have this problem include inappropriate or inappropriately rapid familiarity (e.g., hugging you at the end of the first session; giving you a lavish or very personal gift), inappropriate inquiries (e.g., detailed questions about your family life), inappropriate requests (e.g., asking you to agree with their political views or sign a petition for a cause they believe in), or a patient who seems to idealize you or never question what you say. Trust and mutual understanding usually develop gradually in human relationships. The progression from stranger, to acquaintance, to friend, and (sometimes) to intimate friend takes time. In professional circumstances, that progression should probably remain near the "acquaintance" level to ensure that a respectful distance is maintained, reducing the chances of an inappropriately close relationship between therapist and patient. If it is difficult to establish that respectful distance, consider the possibility that the patient lacks psychological boundaries. Caution is indicated with these patients, as their idealization of therapists can quickly turn into resentment and even hatred if they don't feel their emotional needs are met. Like spurned lovers, they may seek revenge upon the former object of their affections, and if you're their therapist, that's you!

Communicating Empathy

Marco

Marco and I were students in the same psychiatric interviewing course. Marco was a gregarious fellow whose encouraging, positive manner was appreciated in our study group. He regaled everyone with amusing stories of his weekend activities, did well on tests with minimal review of his notes, and generally exuded confidence and good humour.

By contrast, I was an anxious introvert who often "burned the midnight oil" and was convinced I would fail if I neglected to do so. I was sometimes irritated by Marco's incessantly jovial manner, probably because it was so different from my own. I've always appreciated the emotional contrasts of life: the well-acted movie that brings you to tears, the beautiful requiem rather than the rousing march, the chocolate that is bittersweet. Ignoring the tragic elements in life, as Marco did, seemed a bit naïve to me.

I had to admit though, that Marco's upbeat attitude worked for him. When I did well, I was thankful that the professor had not made the test too difficult. When Marco did well, he became even more confident in his abilities. When I was given a traffic ticket, I felt guilty and humiliated. When Marco was given one, he laughed "I guess the cop was having a bad day." Marco almost always interpreted events, good or bad, in ways that were favorable to his own self-esteem.

When we started our interviewing course though, something unexpected happened: Marco struggled. On his first practical test, the patient was a middle-aged woman with severe depression. "How's it going?" beamed Marco affably. She burst into tears. "Aw...come on. It can't be that bad", he responded, trying to cheer her up. She launched into an angry defense of why her life was indeed "that bad", and stated that a more mature doctor would understand her plight. Marco apologized for upsetting her and tried to talk about the sunny weather. "They're forecasting rain for tomorrow", she glared. The conversation deteriorated from there.

After failing Marco protested "But I tried to be empathetic!" The examiner suggested he needed remedial work. "It's just an off day. I'll ace it next time", Marco reassured himself. Unfortunately, the next time he had to interview a very shy, withdrawn patient. Marco's exuberance resulted in more withdrawal by the patient. Eventually, they sat in silence. Marco labelled the patient "uncooperative". It soon became clear that only patients with outgoing personalities who had recovered from most of their distressing symptoms liked to talk to Marco. The rest found him annoying and apparently lacking in empathy.

Interestingly, Marco was not an unkind young man. He enjoyed helping others in our group and even did volunteer work on weekends. However, his kind nature didn't come across when he tried to communicate with patients who were anxious or depressed. His exuberant personality seemed to interfere with empathetic communication.

Marco didn't suffer from any particular psychiatric disorder, but rather showed the slightly biased thinking styles associated with good mental health. These include the attributional bias: attributing positive outcomes to our own efforts and negative outcomes to others or to circumstances (Abramson, Seligman, and Teasdale, 1978). Marco's optimism and tendency to minimize his own weaknesses were also healthy, except when they stood in stark contrast to a pessimistic, vulnerable patient in front of him. Over time, Marco learned a more subdued interviewing approach with patients like this. He developed the flexibility to respond to a range of people with a range of emotions in a manner appropriate to the situation. This flexible approach to communicating with others is an important aspect of empathy.

A number of cognitive biases can interfere with this flexibility, in addition to those shown by Marco. People who are always fatalistic (called an "external locus of control"), for example, have difficulty relating to self-starters (called an "internal locus of control"), and vice versa. People who focus excessively on potential threats tend to have difficulty relating to those with a less anxious view of the world. People who consistently anticipate hostility in others tend to be overly guarded, interfering with empathy. Awareness of our own biases can help develop the flexibility needed to respond to those who seem psychologically different or "out of touch" with our perspectives.

Communicating empathetically also requires experience. Finding the words that help someone feel understood is not always easy. For example, one of the most insensitive things to say to someone in distress might be "I know exactly how you're feeling." Almost invariably, this results in the painful cry "You have no idea how I'm feeling!" as the distressed person feels their torment is being minimized by this phrase. There are some common, more helpful phrases such as "that must be very difficult for you", but they sound trite and rehearsed when used excessively. Mirroring the other person's body language can also communicate empathy, but this too may take practice. When in doubt, listening attentively is usually best. We must humbly acknowledge that we never know *exactly* how someone is feeling, but with patience and respectful attention to them we can sometimes come close to understanding.

Summary

- We must address emotional states that increase self-preoccupation (e.g., depression, excessive guilt) in order to restore the capacity for empathy.
- We must become aware of the impact of our emotions on our children.

- We can engage in activities that reduce self-preoccupation (e.g., outdoor activities, activities requiring concentration, positive sensory experiences, mindfulness meditation).
- Empathy must be honored as an important, daily ideal that is sometimes prioritized over future goals or other distractions.
- To maintain sensitivity to others' feelings, we must resist the temptation to escape distress with addictive behaviors and find other coping strategies.
- We can all improve our social perspective-taking by learning from social mishaps: asking ourselves "How did my words/actions make this person feel?" and "What could I have done differently to make the person more comfortable?"
- Trying to understand complex characters in film, theatre, or literature can also improve social perspective-taking.
- At least one long-term, close, trusting relationship is needed in order to develop the emotional ability to relate to others' suffering.
- Recognizing that our understanding of others is imperfect is important in order to maintain respectful psychological boundaries.
- Recognizing our own cognitive biases can help us communicate more empathetically.

Reflective Questions

1. Which component of empathy poses the most challenges for you? How could you improve in this area?
2. Think of someone you see often who appears to lack one or more of the components of empathy discussed in this chapter. How can you improve your relationship with this person based on what you have read?

Questions for Therapists

1. Can you think of an example where getting overly focused on the problem (versus the human being in front of you) was not helpful in therapy? What helped in this case?
2. Which type of patient or personality mentioned in this chapter do you find most challenging? Do you plan to do anything different in relation to these people, based on what you have read?

References

Abramson, L.Y., Seligman, M.E., and Teasdale, J.D. (1978). Learned helplessness in humans: critique and reformulation. *Journal of Abnormal Psychology*, 87, 49–74.

Allen, J.P. and Fonagy, P. (Eds.) (2008). *Handbook of Mentalization-Based Treatment*. Chichester, UK: John Wiley & Sons.

American Psychiatric Association (2013). *Diagnostic and Statistical Manual of Mental Disorders, (DSM 5)* 5th Edition. Washington, DC: American Psychiatric Association.

Bonhoeffer, D. (1997) (Ed. Bethge, E.). *Letters and Papers from Prison*. New York: Simon & Schuster.
Byrd, A.L. and Manuck, S.B. (2014). MAOA, child maltreatment, and antisocial behavior: meta-analysis of a gene-environment interaction. *Biological Psychiatry*, 75, 9–17.
Centre for Addiction & Mental Health (2009). *Can I Catch It Like a Cold?* Toronto: Tundra Books.
Coplan, A. (2011). Understanding empathy: its features and effects. In Coplan, A. and Goldie, P. (Eds.) *Empathy: Philosophical and Psychological Perspectives*. New York: Oxford University Press, pp. 3–18.
Ehrenreich-May, J. and Chu, B.C. (2014). *Transdiagnostic Treatments for Children and Adolescents*. New York: Guilford Press.
Frankl, V.E. (1978). *The Unheard Cry for Meaning*. New York: Simon & Schuster, pp. 171–184.
Freud, S. (1973) (translation by Richards, A.). *Introductory Lectures on Psychoanalysis*. London: Pelican Books, pp. 404–424.
Gray, C. (2000). *The New Social Story Book: Illustrated Edition: Teaching Social Skills to Children and Adults with Autism, Asperger's Syndrome, and Other Autism Spectrum Disorders*. Arlington, TX: Future Horizons, Inc.
Kabat-Zinn, J. (1994) *Wherever You Go, There You Are: Mindfulness Meditation in Everyday Life*. New York: Hyperion Books.
Lewis, D. (1992). *Millennium: Tribal Wisdom and the Modern World*. Toronto: Viking Canada.
Lysaker, P.H., Buck, K.D., Carcione, A., Procacci, M., Salvatore, G., Nicolò, G., and Dimaggio, G. (2011). Addressing metacognitive capacity for self-reflection in the psychotherapy for schizophrenia: a conceptual model of the key tasks and processes. *Psychology and Psychotherapy: Theory, Research and Practice*, 84, 58–69.
Murray, L., Cooper, P., and Fearon, P. (2014). Parenting difficulties and postnatal depression: implications for primary healthcare assessment and intervention. *Community Practice*, 87, 34–38.
Ruiz, F.J. (2010). A review of Acceptance and Commitment Therapy (ACT) empirical evidence: correlational, experimental psychopathology, component and outcome studies . *International Journal of Psychology and Psychological Therapy*, 10, 125–162.
Santayana, G. (1905/1998). *The Life of Reason*. New York: Prometheus Books.
Seligman, M.E.P. and Csikszentmihalyi, M. (2000). Positive psychology: an introduction. *American Psychologist*, 55, 5–14.
Vaillant, G.E. (1993). *The Wisdom of the Ego*. Cambridge, MA: Harvard University Press.
Wells, A., Fisher, P., Myers, S., Wheatley, J., Patel, T., and Brewin, C.R. (2009). Metacognitive therapy in recurrent and persistent depression: a multiple-baseline study of a new treatment. *Cognitive Therapy and Research*, 33, 291–300.

6 Taming the Fight or Flight Response

> Let nothing disturb you, let nothing frighten you...
> Theresa of Avila (1515–1582)

As discussed in Chapter 2, illness, cognitive biases related to threat or hostility, a history of maltreatment in childhood, and perceived scarcity of time, money, or other resources can increase our predisposition to develop fight or flight responses. These responses put our bodies and minds into survival mode: we channel our blood supply and physical resources toward large muscles that help us confront or flee from danger; we narrow our mental focus to help solve or escape the problem before us. In doing so, we often neglect the "big picture", including the welfare of others.

This may be one reason that the saints, including Theresa, have urged us to not be disturbed: we can only attend to others when we are not upset ourselves. I found her wisdom on a bookmark that I purchased in a small shop in the town bearing her name (Musixmatch.com). I was in Spain to speak at a major international conference and took in many of the highlights of Madrid and the surrounding countryside, yet that bookmark was the most meaningful memory I brought back from the trip.

This chapter goes into detail regarding psychological aspects of "fight or flight" reactions. Then, it explores effective coping strategies that can sometimes tame them and lead us toward more rather than less empathetic behavior. Finally, ideas about helping children with these reactions are discussed.

Fear and Anger: Two Sides of the Same Coin

About a year ago, my life was quite tightly scheduled for several months. My son was attending a small college in a neighboring town half an hour's drive away, and there was no reliable public transportation to the college. Therefore, I was transporting him there in the mornings, returning to my home office to see several patients, then picking him up in the early afternoon, and returning to my office to see my remaining patients for the day. Although it was a bit hectic, the routine seemed to work.

One day, the inevitable happened: the car unexpectedly broke down. It was the middle of the day, so without a drive my son would be stranded in the neighboring town. If I tried to get the car fixed, I would have my afternoon patients arriving at the door with nobody to see them. It was a terrible dilemma, and my initial reaction was panic.

After taking a few deep breaths though, I was able to focus on how to manage the situation. Prioritizing my son's welfare, I called the college to reassure him and make sure he could remain there for a few hours without difficulty. Next, I spent a few minutes perusing the car's owner's manual to make sure I had not missed any simple solution to the problem. When I realized I hadn't missed anything, I started making telephone calls both to friends who might be able to pick up my son and to various car repair shops. All were on voicemail. I thought of the patients who would be arriving soon and made a sign regarding my "family emergency" so they would know what was happening.

Finally, it occurred to me to go to my retired next-door neighbors and see if they could help. Thankfully, they were home and were willing to lend me their car to pick up my son. Although I'm usually very anxious about driving an unfamiliar vehicle, I did it without hesitation that day. I safely retrieved my son, and arrived to find my first afternoon patient waiting. I explained the situation, and apologized for the delay. I called one more car repair service, reached them, arranged for them to come to my house later that afternoon, and began the afternoon sessions. I remained professional with my patients and tried to be empathetic with them, despite the circumstances. One session was interrupted by the car repair, but the family was very understanding. By the end of the day, my son was home safely, the car was fixed, and the patients had all been seen and looked after reasonably well.

I provide this example not to boast about my problem-solving abilities, which were only needed because I hadn't planned ahead for this possibility, but rather to illustrate the constructive side of the fight or flight response. Both fear and anger involve high physiological arousal and a rush of adrenaline and other stress hormones, explaining why they are so closely linked. As soon as the panic associated with an overwhelming adrenaline rush settles, the person in this high arousal state often becomes stronger, more clear-thinking, and more adept at doing what is necessary than one would expect based on past history. He or she may lift a heavy weight to free a child trapped beneath it, find a solution to a life-threatening problem in record time, or (as I did) prioritize multiple responsibilities so that all are addressed effectively. If anger predominates, the person may defend the vulnerable or speak out courageously regarding an injustice, even if some personal risk is involved. Like a charioteer in control of two powerful, spirited horses, the person who channels fear and anger effectively can often produce inspiring results.

Managed poorly, however, these same feelings can have very negative effects on empathy. Moreover, some situations can trigger both emotions, amplifying our negative reactions. For example, when a person feels unjustly accused, he or she experiences a fear of humiliation in conjunction with anger at their accuser who is perceived as being unfair and hostile. This combination of fear and anger can result in extremes of either panic or rage. As people are unable to think clearly in these states, it is important not to take any immediate action in these situations and respond only when emotion is no longer intense. In many situations, however, either fear or anger predominates. Therefore, we now examine each emotion in turn, and how responses to it can affect the capacity for empathy.

Anxiety and Empathy

Richard

Richard was a sickly boy born in December, so he was always the smallest in his class and a bit behind his peers academically. In the early grades his teachers were quite protective of him, but as a result he developed a reputation as a "teacher's pet". The other boys used this term to justify ridiculing and bullying him. Soon Richard had stomach pain every morning before school.

In his teens, Richard's only friend was a boy on the autistic spectrum who shared his love of a particular video game. Richard spent increasing amounts of time online playing the game with his friend. As his fear of school and love of the game both increased, he played late into the night and became impossible to waken in the mornings for school.

Richard's parents took him to a sleep specialist who prescribed a medication to increase daytime alertness, but Richard had to be awake to take it in the mornings, and he rarely was. Next, they tried keeping him awake for 36 hours to re-establish a normal sleep pattern. It worked for about a week, and then Richard reverted to his usual behavior. Richard's mother quit her job in an effort to get him to school more consistently, but he rarely got out of bed before noon. She took him to a psychotherapist, but Richard reported feeling "fine" and had nothing to talk about. Richard's lengthy school absences came to the attention of the school authorities, who threatened to involve child welfare services. Richard's mother was frantic, "Doesn't he realize what this is doing to his family?" she cried in exasperation.

Richard's story illustrates how anxiety can make many people appear selfish, lacking in empathy, and stubborn. Although he may claim to feel "fine", Richard's school avoidance began as a result of a highly anxiety-provoking situation: being bullied. Most anxiety relates to a fear of being either physically harmed or humiliated, and bullying often entails both. Once people are anxious, thinking becomes future-oriented and self-focused. The anticipation of harm or unfavorable evaluation takes centre stage, leaving few mental resources for attention to current tasks and even fewer for attention to others. No wonder Richard has no appreciation of what he is doing to his family!

Moreover, the most common unhealthy response to anxiety is avoidance of the situation that one finds anxiety-provoking. This strategy is considered unhealthy because it interferes with facing one's fears (known as "exposure"), and exposure reduces anxiety in the long run (Deacon and Abramowitz, 2004). Relevant to empathy, avoidance of feared situations also results in behavior that appears stubborn and inconsiderate of others' needs. In Richard's case, his prolonged school avoidance was having serious consequences for his parents, but he seemed oblivious to their distress.

Richard's story underscores the need to contain our anxiety if we are to become more aware of others' feelings and therefore more capable of empathy. To do so, we need to address the behavioral, physical, and cognitive effects of anxiety on our lives. Treatments for people with clinically significant anxiety have been developed based on these principles (Deacon and Abramowitz, 2004), and the principles are worth reviewing as everyone becomes anxious on occasion.

As discussed in the example, the behavioral tendency to avoid what is feared must be challenged through exposure, since our avoidance often affects others negatively. This can be done through repeated practice facing gradual approximations of what we fear (termed "desensitization") or by bravely entering the feared situation and remaining there until the fear subsides (termed "flooding"). Overcoming avoidance frees us to relate to others empathetically in a greater variety of situations.

Relaxing practices such as breathing techniques, yoga, or meditation (see later in this chapter) as well as regular aerobic exercise are all helpful in reducing our vulnerability to both physical fight or flight states and tension-related symptoms (e.g., tension headache, anxiety-related stomach pain). Preoccupation with such states or symptoms can undermine empathy. If extreme physical anxiety occurs, as in hyperventilation or panic attacks, it is often helpful to remember that these experiences are time-limited, as the body eventually returns to its resting state, and are usually not dangerous. Nobody would expect people in such extreme states to behave empathetically, though they often elicit empathy from others.

Cognitive strategies for anxiety involve recognizing unrealistically anxious thinking, challenging it with more adaptive thinking, problem-solving situations that make us anxious, and rewarding ourselves for making the effort to do these things. For instance, if a student is anxious about an upcoming test, the student may think "I may fail this thing, and that would ruin my whole year!" When anxious, we tend to overestimate risk and underestimate our own abilities. Thus, the student is likely overestimating the importance of the test (no one test typically makes or breaks one's grade for the year) and underestimating personal ability (anxious people tend to prepare more than the average for tests, so failure is unlikely even if the test is difficult). Some newer treatments also claim to train the brain to attend less to threatening stimuli, reducing the biased thinking that often fuels anxiety (Hakamata, Lissek, Bar-Haim, Britton, Fox, Leibenluft, et al., 2010). Once he has studied and become less preoccupied with the test, the student may realize he has forgotten his father's birthday or hasn't called his girlfriend in several days. Addressing these empathetic failures now becomes possible, as anxiety has been contained.

Interestingly, there is no guarantee that the test will be passed, as the future in inherently uncertain. However, our ability to live with this uncertainty usually improves once we satisfy ourselves that we have done what we can to mitigate foreseeable risks. As some risks are unforeseeable, we may also need to trust ourselves to deal with future possibilities, whatever they may be. Whether this trust comes from self-confidence, a good support network, or trust in a Higher Power varies from one person to another. However, one way or another we need to shift away from thoughts that attempt to control or predict what is to come. Then, as our minds let go of dire future possibilities, we can focus on our present surroundings, including the people we relate to. This present-day focus is necessary in order to behave empathetically.

Anger and Empathy

Aneesha

"Aneesha!" shouted her mother, "Hurry up! You're going to be late for school." Aneesha, a young teen, responded weakly, "OK…coming in a minute." Five minutes later, the exchange was repeated. Five minutes after that, the school bell rang and sure enough Aneesha had to collect another pink slip at the office for being late. It was her third one that week.

Aneesha was the middle of three children, born to unhappily married parents who stayed together mainly for financial reasons. She had a younger brother with special needs who took up much of their time. By the time she started school, her father was a distant figure who showed up briefly on weekends if he wasn't out of town driving his truck. Her mother was irritable, stressed, and rarely had a kind word to say to Aneesha. She resented the fact that Aneesha, who had no particular disabilities, could not behave more independently. She often compared her to other children her age who, she claimed, did their own laundry, prepared some of their own meals, did their homework without reminders, and even helped their parents on occasion.

Aneesha, on the other hand, was a temperamentally placid girl who liked to draw and daydream. Before her brother was born, she developed age-appropriate skills with the encouragement of her mother, and the occasional reward of extra art supplies. Now there were no rewards and encouragement, only nagging. Aneesha resented her mother for spending so much time with her disabled brother and so little with her. It seemed the only time they interacted was around her morning tardiness, and this was an unpleasant interaction, fueling further resentment. Yet, talking with Aneesha, she seemed unaware of these feelings. "I've always been slow and lazy. That's what my mother says, anyways", was her sad explanation of the pattern.

At first glance, Aneesha seems depressed rather than angry. However, her resentment of her mother's nagging and emotional neglect clearly preceded the sad, self-critical demeanor she shows today. Aneesha is angry, even if it is not entirely obvious. Anger is an emotion that is sometimes considered socially unacceptable, particularly toward authority figures like parents or bosses, so one way to express it is to comply with requests in slow or ineffectual ways. Termed "passive-aggressive", this type of behavior is sometimes as upsetting to the object of one's anger than more obvious forms of aggression (Vaillant, 1993, pp. 50–52). It is certainly not empathetic.

Like anxiety, anger has behavioral, physiological, and cognitive components. Behaviorally, the angry person can lash out physically or verbally, or adopt passive-aggressive behaviors as Aneesha did. People prone to angry outbursts are considered "quick-tempered", and this is an apt term as angry responses can occur in fractions of a second. Once they occur, the angry person may regret their actions, as these are often harmful to others, but they cannot reverse those actions. Being aware of this risk in order to prevent harm to others is an important aspect of living empathetically.

Physiologically, anger releases the same stress hormones as anxiety. If the situation calls for physical aggression as when, for example, playing a contact sport or going into battle, these hormones help the person fight effectively. More often in modern life, however, the situation causing anger does not call for physical violence. Then, the effects of stress hormones become detrimental to our health. High blood pressure, high cholesterol, and other cardiovascular risk factors have been linked to this chronic, unnecessary release of stress hormones with anger (Williams, Paton, Siegler, Eigenbrodt, Nieto, and Tyroler, 2000). Managing anger calmly is therefore an important aspect of compassion for ourselves (a topic discussed in Chapter 4).

Cognitively, anger is associated with a bias towards seeing others as hostile rather than neutral (Hawkins and Cougle, 2013). The person one is angry toward is regarded as a threat to one's safety or esteem, not as a complex human being with both likeable and unlikeable qualities. When we regard others as a threat, we often focus on their negative behavior toward us in the past, ignoring their positive actions, to justify a desire for revenge. We also tend to blame them for adverse outcomes, envy them for privileges they have which we lack, and, in extreme cases, dehumanize them to the point of seeing their lives as lacking in value.

In each case, there are alternative thoughts and actions which could reduce our anger, allowing for greater empathy. For instance, if a patient ties me up on the telephone for a half hour, which I am not paid for, I could blame the patient for abusing my time. On the other hand, I could accept the fact that I did not assertively interrupt the call to shorten the conversation and book an appointment, which I am paid for. Interestingly, assertive responses often include empathetic statements as well as firm statements of one's position. For instance, in this case I could say "I'm sorry to interrupt you at such an emotional time (empathetic) but I have another commitment so we'll need to talk about this further at the next appointment" (my position, stated as a "need" which is firm). Another alternative: I could post a notice for all of my patients indicating that they will be charged for lengthy telephone calls, thus reducing the risk of a similar event in the future, and reducing the risk of future aggravation.

Envy occurs when we compare our own joys and fortunes with those of others. The comparison becomes tinged with anger when we feel they are undeserving of what they have, or perhaps we would be more deserving. "It seems unfair" is one of the most common exclamations of envious, angry people. The feeling readily dissipates, however, when we recognize that those whose fortunes exceed our own in one aspect of life may suffer in other domains. The person whose beautiful home we envy may have a terrible marriage; the person who won the award we felt we deserved may be in failing health. When we learn more about the life story of our competitors, we almost never want to walk in their shoes.

Dehumanization of others represents a severe lack of empathy. When anger and violence are commonplace, our sense of dismay at the suffering of others may be dulled with repeated exposure. It has been suggested that violent media and violent games may have a similar effect (Funk, Baldacci, Pasold, and Baumgardner, 2004). Hateful ideologies, discussed further in Chapter 8, often fuel this source of anger as well. Whole groups of people may be depicted as being threatening and less than human, reducing prohibitions about harming or even killing them. The genocides of the twentieth century attest to the ease with which people can be seduced by such ideologies. Yet people who have even one friend in the vilified group usually hesitate to participate in such atrocities: their empathy overrides ideology (American Psychological Association, 2012). Thus, one of the best ways to encourage humane, empathetic treatment among people seems to involve tearing down walls and other barriers between ethnic and racial groups so that people can see each other as they truly are, person to person.

Sometimes these ideas raise an interesting question: can we avoid hating the haters? In other words, isn't it fair to dehumanize a demagogue who kills thousands? The answer may lie in understanding the basis of all hatred: feeling threatened. Every cruel tyrant starts life as a helpless, frightened child who desperately wants to control those who are causing the fear and humiliation he experiences. Over time, this need for control becomes a need for power, and the torments of the past become attributed to a current enemy or group. When we understand this process, we can neither hate nor admire this leader, as he is motivated by fear. Great leaders lack this fear: they speak of reassurance, of hope, and of unity rather than threat and division. Thus, they model and inspire empathy and cooperation in their followers.

Perceived Scarcity, Daily Hassles, and Burnout

In addition to the intense emotions of anxiety and anger, daily stresses and strains can also affect our capacity for empathy. One of these is perceived scarcity, mentioned in Chapter 2. When we feel chronically short of time, money, or energy for doing all the tasks we are committed to doing, we are easily angered by those who ask for a little bit more of these resources, even if the request is reasonable. Our reaction to such requests is invariably not empathetic. There is something to be said for building reserves of time, money, and other resources to allow for unexpected requests, or unexpected opportunities to give or to enjoy. Why not allow for time to unclutter a room, enjoy a sunset, or volunteer to serve a holiday meal to the less fortunate? If you are tired and can afford to, hire someone to do the chores you really dislike. It frees up time and energy, and also creates work for someone who needs and values it. Similarly, keeping a bit of money that is not budgeted but saved "in case of the unexpected" (good or bad) can be tremendously stress-relieving. Without the stresses of perceived scarcity, we have a better chance of staying in the moment, and our capacity for empathy has a better opportunity to grow.

Even with good management of time and money, the cumulative effect of multiple small annoyances or "daily hassles" can affect our capacity for empathy. In fact, these influences have been judged more pernicious than significant life events in some studies (Kanner, Coyne, Schaeffer, and Lazarus, 1981). For example, a person may plan to spend an afternoon doing a highly meaningful piece of work and instead be faced with an incorrect utility bill that will cost substantial money if not addressed, a need to book an emissions test for the car, a request for further information to substantiate a tax deduction, and a teen who suddenly needs a ride to a friend's house to complete a group project. All require attention within a day or so in order to avoid serious consequences. All seem like meaningless drudgery. The stress of addressing these multiple minor problems is compounded by the disappointment of having to delay work that seems more meaningful. The person snaps at their teen as they leave, with no empathy for the teen's stress about finishing the project. At the end of the afternoon, tired and demoralized, collapsing in front of the television seems the only option. If the scene repeats day after day, he or she will eventually gravitate toward the television, or a glass of wine, or some other unhealthy coping strategy more quickly than before. As pessimism about the possibility of doing anything meaningful grows, the person becomes increasingly irritable and lacking in empathy toward others.

The term "burnout" has been used to describe this feeling of being permanently stuck in drudgery. It is as if the flame of enthusiasm for what we value in life is being starved of oxygen by less valuable competing demands, until it is extinguished. How do we prevent this process? Limiting the "hassles" by simplifying one's lifestyle may help, but some problems will persist. Therefore, in addition, most people need some time to recharge and reconnect with the people and the ideals they hold dear. They need to replenish the oxygen that feeds their flame, whether by taking time to reflect on what really matters to them, or by relating to understanding people who share their values and put them in a different frame of mind. Empathetic connections with others can often provide a renewed sense of meaning at times when much of the day seems consumed by the mundane.

Coping Well with Strong Emotions

We all engage in habitual ways of coping with intense emotions that we may or may not be aware of. Some of these habits interfere with empathy, as in the examples earlier in this chapter. However, others may enhance our capacity for empathy and for healthy relationships. Depending on theoretical orientation, these have been referred to as either "mature defence mechanisms" (a term originally used by Freud) or "adaptive coping" (a term more commonly used in modern psychology).

George Vaillant (see Vaillant, 1993) conducted and described a landmark longitudinal study of college men (with subsequent studies of women as well), where mental health and various other life outcomes were related to the habitual use of either mature or immature defence mechanisms. Not surprisingly, individuals who used mature defence mechanisms fared better. However, many of these mechanisms also resulted in healthier relationships with others and a greater capacity for empathy. These included: altruism, sublimation, suppression, anticipation, and humor.

By examining each of these in turn, we can elucidate how use of these mechanisms may enhance empathy. In altruism, the mechanism most obviously linked to empathy, a negative feeling such as anger is channeled into an activity that is helpful to others. Someone who is angry about social inequality, for example, may work to increase affordable housing or access to nutritious food for poor families. In the political arena, altruists often defend the marginalized in society and inspire others to do the same. Leaders of the civil rights movement such as Martin Luther King Jr. are stellar examples of this behavior. In the example of Aneesha earlier in this chapter, directing her anger toward her mother into volunteer work helping the less fortunate would be an example of altruism.

Sublimation occurs when strong feelings are expressed in a creative endeavor. Beethoven, for instance, composed some of his greatest symphonies late in life when he was frustrated by progressive deafness. Aneesha might paint in vivid colours to express some of her angry feelings. Writing mental health-related books is sometimes my own form of sublimation, helping me deal with troubling aspects of the past. Although none of these pursuits are deliberately empathetic, people often benefit from relating works of art to their own emotional experience. It is as if the tortured soul who wrote the symphony understands our suffering, so we no longer feel alone in our torment; it is as if the artist who paints bright orange flames knows the intensity with which our anger burns, making it easier to bear.

Suppression and anticipation allow us to preserve relationships despite our negative feelings. When we suppress strong emotion, we acknowledge it but choose not to act upon it, at least not immediately. Then, when the intensity of fight or flight settles, we can calmly think about how to best address the situation. In Aneesha's case, she would admit to herself the anger she feels towards her mother but comply with her mother's requests promptly regardless and, at a later time, formulate an assertive response to her mother's nagging. This is kinder than letting Aneesha's mother get upset repeatedly by her tardiness. When we use anticipation, we plan ahead for situations where negative emotions are likely to arise so these are handled well. In Aneesha's situation, she could plan an assertive phrase to use each time her mother reminds her to speed up (e.g., "Thank you for the reminder, but I have heard you already"), so that she is less likely to behave either aggressively or passive-aggressively.

Finally, one of the most enjoyable and potentially empathetic mature defences is humor. When used to poke fun at our own foibles and challenges, humor connects us with people struggling with similar circumstances. The comic writer Erma Bombeck, for example, encountered infertility, chronic kidney disease, and a number of other distressing life events, but focused her humor on the ordinary stresses of being a mother and homemaker (see Bombeck, 1978). Women in similar circumstances felt validated, and perhaps a little less burdened by their plight. Unfortunately, humor can also be used to belittle and hurt others, and in this context it is not considered a mature defence. When we enjoy mature humor we are always, at least in part, laughing at ourselves.

Current ideas about coping strategies distinguish between emotion-focused coping (changing one's emotional reaction to the problem or stress), appraisal-focus coping (challenging one's own assumptions about the situation), and problem-focused coping (doing something to eliminate the stressor) (Folkman, Lazarus, Gruen, and DeLongis, 1986). Strategies are usually not judged as being mature, immature, good, or bad. Rather, strategies are considered more or less adaptive depending upon the circumstances, as described below.

Emotion-focused coping is considered most adaptive when dealing with situations where one has little control and thus cannot eliminate the stressor. People who have little power (e.g., young children, the elderly when health is failing, or the marginalized) often adapt best when using emotion-focused coping. Healthy forms of emotion-focused coping overlap with mature defence mechanisms, with one interesting addition: seeking the support of others. When we share our distress, it is often lessened as suggested by the old adage "Misery loves company". When we share distress with others in similar circumstances, this behavior can also be empathetic as members of the group comfort each other. In Aneesha's case, for example, telling one or more friends about her mother's behavior could be a way of both finding and giving support.

Appraisal-focused coping involves thinking differently about the stressful situation. For example, Aneesha could tell herself "Mom's just having a bad day. I shouldn't take this so seriously." When reappraisal reduces the negativity in relationships, as in this case, it can help restore empathy. Similarly, Richard (the anxious boy who avoided school described earlier in the chapter) could tell himself "I won't let the bullies keep me from getting my education. I'll succeed in spite of them!" Although this is not an empathetic attitude, it does result in improved school attendance for Richard, which relieves stress for his family. Cognitive strategies for anxiety and anger, discussed earlier in the chapter, usually include reappraisal.

Problem-focused coping involves thinking about alternative behavioral responses to the situation, evaluating them, and then choosing one response to implement. In Aneesha's case, she could consider the pros and cons of, among other options, responding to her mother by having a tantrum, refusing to leave her room, behaving passive-aggressively (as she did), responding assertively, or complying and talking about the issue at a time when her mother is calm and less rushed. Problem-focused coping is most adaptive when the person has at least some control in the situation. It may or may not result in greater empathy, depending on what factors are considered most salient in choosing a response. For example, Aneesha could decide that refusing to leave her room would be the best way to express her anger, as it would give her mother no option but to eventually give up the nagging and leave for work, despite the unhappy state of affairs at home. In the long run, however, it would damage the mother-daughter relationship. A more empathetic solution would include consideration of her mother's feelings and of the relationship with her mother in the long term. Many empathetic solutions include long-term as well as short-term considerations, often prioritizing long-term relationship preservation over short-term personal gain.

Mindfulness

Mindfulness can be thought of as a particular form of emotion-focused coping. It is a practice that involves developing a focus on the present moment and, in order to do so, cultivating the ability to detach from certain physical and mental phenomena. Thus, thoughts, emotions, and physical sensations are all observed without judgment. No attempt is made to change them. Instead, the practitioner becomes aware of them, allows them to be, and then shifts awareness back to a particular focus. That focus might be the breath (commonly used), a particular bodily sensation or action (e.g., walking), or a specific word or short phrase. This practice is used in a number of different mental health interventions, with positive effects shown for depression, anxiety, and chronic pain (see Kabat-Zinn, 1994). Detailed exercises go beyond the scope of this book, so the interested reader may wish to peruse *The Mindful Way Workbook* (see Teasdale, Williams, and Segal, 2014) or a similar volume.

Meditative states are also induced by a number of spiritual practices, not limited to any particular religion. The key term is "practice", as mindfulness is not based on any particular theory or belief but rather on a willingness to practice daily. For example, I enjoy walking labyrinths which are often found in or near churches. Unlike a maze, a labyrinth has only one route to follow to the centre and back out again. I see this as a metaphor for life: we cannot always choose our path, but we can choose how to walk it. The attention to walking entailed in this practice is a form of mindfulness.

One reason mindfulness practices are not used by more people more consistently is the perception that they take up time, and we have too much on our to-do list already to make room for another "add-on". This concern may be misplaced, however, as short mindfulness exercises can be incorporated into what we are already doing and the mental refreshment they provide may actually make us more efficient and energized in tackling the "to-dos". Taking a few mindful breaths before a meeting, walking mindfully from place to place, or eating mindfully at lunch can all enrich and enliven our daily experience by connecting us to the moment. One can even use the potentially annoying experience of waiting in line as an opportunity for a "mindfulness break". Alternatively, having a conversation with someone else in line can create an opportunity for empathy as we begin to see the person as a worthy, interesting human being rather than an obstacle delaying our progress to the next task.

By calming the mind and improving the ability to attend to experience, including interpersonal experience, mindfulness may provide a helpful starting point for developing empathy. However, mindfulness alone is unlikely to be sufficient for developing empathy. As discussed in Chapter 5 and outlined in Table 5.1, there are a number of psychological component processes that comprise empathy. Mindfulness is likely to reduce unhealthy self-preoccupation (as one develops the capacity for self-observation) and perhaps to increase motivation to attend to others (as one's attention becomes rooted in the present moment), but additional component processes are needed. Nevertheless, if you or your clients who struggle with strong emotion have never engaged in this form of mental discipline, it is worth trying.

Helping Our Children Manage Strong Emotions

Helping children develop empathy is described in detail in Chapter 10, but as inability to manage strong emotions can interfere with empathy in people of all ages, this topic is considered here. To begin, let's consider two eight-year-old boys I saw in my practice: Ken and Kyle. Both showed a combination of anxiety and frequent aggressive outbursts, indicating difficulty regulating strong emotions.

Ken

Ken was the only son of an emotionally stable, financially secure older couple. His parents listened attentively to my suggestions. I instructed them on how to provide Ken with empathetic encouragement to face his fears (e.g., saying "I know this seems hard, but you can do it"), starting with situations that were only mildly anxiety-provoking, and then charting and rewarding his successes. They were pleased to see Ken develop confidence as he worked towards rewards by facing increasingly challenging situations. I also referred Ken's parents to a common time-out system for negative behavior that provides the child with brief, matter-of-fact warnings at the first sign of trouble. They worked together to implement this approach consistently and calmly. After several weeks, Ken learned to contain his negative feelings and behaviors after one or two warnings, the number of aggressive outbursts he experienced diminished, and outbursts that occurred were shorter and less intense than before. Only three monthly parenting sessions were needed before Ken showed marked improvement in managing both his anxiety and his anger. Moreover, Ken's parents were able to make a plan to ensure that gains were maintained: they regularly used part of their weekly "date night" to fine tune their approach to Ken's difficulties. I agreed to remain available in case they got "stuck", but have not heard from them in over a year.

Kyle

Kyle, on the other hand, was the fourth of five children born to a young single mother. She had a history of being abused as a child. The children had three different fathers, but none paid child support so the family lived on social assistance and used food banks. I initially tried using a similar approach with Kyle's mother as I had with Ken's parents, but she was too overwhelmed with financial problems and with the needs of her other children to attend appointments consistently, let alone focus on Kyle's difficulties. Kyle's behavior deteriorated. Given his mother's difficulty keeping appointments, I arranged for a school psychologist and school social worker to become involved in Kyle's care. The social worker provided some coping strategies for anxiety and the psychologist outlined behavior management strategies for Kyle's teacher. There were modest improvements in Kyle's behavior at school, but none at home. Social services eventually became involved after Kyle threatened his younger sibling with a knife. I began prescribing psychiatric medications for anxiety and aggression. Kyle improved when these were started, but deteriorated further after his mother's new boyfriend moved into the home. Although Kyle's treatment spanned years and included multiple agencies and multiple mental health professionals, he did not show any consistent improvements and had to attend a special behavioral class for most of his school career.

Some might argue that Ken and Kyle, despite their similar symptoms, could have had different genetic risks that resulted in different outcomes. Although this is possible, the stark differences in their family experiences almost certainly contributed to their different outcomes too. Ken's parents consistently provided kind but firm encouragement of the behaviors needed to manage both his anxiety and his anger. They showed empathy for his distress while recognizing the need to guide him toward the ability to regulate it for himself. In the long run, people who can regulate distressing feelings feel better about themselves even though learning to do so may be difficult at first. An empathetic parent may find it hard to see their child suffer during this learning process, but knows the child will be happier in the end. In short, Ken got the message "I can cope with things in spite of my feelings, and my parents will make sure I do because they care about me."

By contrast, Kyle's mother is far too overwhelmed with her children, her finances, and possibly her own past history to focus on Kyle's needs empathetically. She is in survival mode. Furthermore, her unstable relationship pattern, likely a product of her traumatic background, creates an unpredictable environment for the children. Kyle gets the message "I need to look out for myself, because I never know what's coming next." Like his mother, he is often in "fight or flight" mode, regardless of what mental health treatments are offered.

These contrasting examples highlight some of the factors needed to help children regulate strong emotions. These factors go beyond the specific skills I discussed with Ken's parents, which are described in numerous parenting books (e.g., see Manassis, 2015; Phelan, 2016).

A stable, predictable home environment is an obvious factor. Unpredictable circumstances exacerbate anxiety, particularly when the adult(s) in the home are not consistently reassuring. Providing such an environment is not always easy though, as the example of Kyle's family shows. I don't mean to imply that single parents always fail in this area, only that they have to work harder as they cannot consistently share the work with a partner. Combining parenting with full responsibility for supporting the family and managing the household is a daunting task for anyone. As the number of children increases, it becomes even more difficult. All children face some changes in home environment, for example a move of house due to a parent finding work in a different town. However, a thoughtful parent recognizes change as a potential stress for the child, limits the number of changes, and prepares him or her as well as possible when change is about to occur.

A second factor needed for children to regulate strong emotions is secure attachment to at least one consistently available adult. As discussed in Chapter 2, such security is associated with a number of positive developmental outcomes. People with a history of early trauma like Kyle's mother often lack the ability to form secure attachment relationships with their children. The children often respond to this insecurity with anxiety or anger. In this case, the child's anger represents an attempt to control the environment in order to feel safe.

A third factor is the parent's ability to model healthy coping with strong emotions. People who are traumatized and overwhelmed as Kyle's mother was can rarely do this. Ken's parents, on the other hand, probably modeled healthy coping to a degree. Parents are almost never in total agreement on how to manage their children's behaviors, so conflict around this issue is frequent. However, when parents are able to discuss their differences and develop an approach that is acceptable to both, they become more consistent and more effective in helping their children. The fact that Ken's parents elected to do this regularly on "date night" suggests that they have learned how to air their differences and resolve conflict, modeling healthy coping.

Fourth, it is important not to unnecessarily increase anxiety or anger in children. One common example is a family that creates a competitive atmosphere among children, where siblings get the message that they are valued for their achievements rather than who they are as individuals. As a result, children who are less successful (by parental definition) resent those who are more successful and become anxious about their place in the family. Increasingly focused on their own inability to live up to parental expectations, they become vulnerable to either depression or to aggressive, non-empathetic behavior designed to alter their status in the family. Similar behavior can result when parents model the biases associated with anger, seeing others as hostile, blameworthy, or (in extreme cases) less than human.

A final factor in children's emotion regulation is protection from traumatic experience. As mentioned in Chapter 2, repeated exposure to early traumatic events alters the body's stress response mechanisms (Bremner, 2005; Matthews, 2002). This change in physiology leaves people vulnerable to chronic dysregulation of emotions. It is particularly evident in children whose trauma precedes the development of language. These children may present with inattention, anxiety, mood instability, impulsive anger, and often self-harm or other destructive behaviors aimed at regulating emotion, but they have no clear understanding of how these symptoms are linked to their early history. Sometimes, a secure attachment relationship with a caring adult can gradually reduce these symptoms over several years, but it is a slow process once children are past the early years when their psychological models for human relationships typically develop.

In conclusion, it takes more than a few parenting tips to help children regulate strong emotions to the point where they can be freed to look beyond themselves empathetically toward other human beings in their surroundings. Rather, it takes a childhood marked by caring, stable, predictable parenting, and free from trauma and unnecessary stress or competition. If parents can also role model healthy coping with emotion and the kind of interpersonal behavior they would like to see in their children, empathy is even more likely to develop.

Summary

- Anxiety and anger can both interfere with empathy by increasing our focus on ourselves.
- Anxious thinking is future-oriented, interfering with attention to the present including attention to others; anxious behavior is avoidant, often with negative consequences for others that we may not be aware of.

- Physical relaxation, challenging anxious thinking, and overcoming avoidance all contribute to empathy.
- Anger can arise quickly, resulting in actions we later regret, and empathetic people must be aware of this risk; action should be deferred until the person is no longer gripped by intense negative emotion.
- Angry thinking is focused on perceived hostility in others, blaming others, unfavorable comparisons with others, past slights, and sometimes dehumanization, all of which interfere with empathy and therefore need to be challenged.
- Building reserves of time and money into our schedules and budgets is needed to avoid becoming grumpy and non-empathetic due to daily hassles.
- Time to connect with people who share our values is important if we are to avoid succumbing to a sense of meaninglessness and "burnout".
- Adaptive ways of coping with strong emotions can often contribute to empathy. These include: altruism, sublimation, suppression, anticipation, humor, support-seeking, positive reappraisal of stressful situations, problem-solving that takes a long-term view and prioritizes preserving relationships, and mindfulness practices.
- Helping children cope effectively with strong emotions requires a stable, predictable home environment, secure attachment, freedom from trauma or excessive stress, and parents who can model healthy coping strategies.

Reflective Questions

1 Do you tend to struggle more with "fighting" (i.e., having a quick temper) or "fleeing" (i.e., avoiding stressful situations)? What could you do to address this issue?
2 What is a practice that you find relaxing and that centers you in the present moment? How could you fit this practice into your routine more consistently?
3 Think of a situation where anxiety affects your capacity for empathy. Is there a different perspective that might help in this situation? Is there a coping strategy that might help?
4 Think of a situation where anger affects your capacity for empathy. Is there a different perspective that might help in this situation? Is there a coping strategy that might help?
5 If you have children, how could you help them regulate strong emotions better?

Questions for Therapists

1 Think about a recent client who has difficulty regulating anxiety, anger, or both.

2　Based on the ideas in this chapter, what additional strategies or interventions might be helpful for this client?
3　If this client manages anxiety and/or anger more effectively, who else would be affected by this change?
4　If the client has children, how would they be affected by this change?
5　How do you help clients regulate strong emotions when they have a history of trauma early in life that has impaired this ability?
6　How can you prevent "daily hassles" and "burnout" from affecting your capacity for empathy with your clients?

References

American Psychological Association (2012). Race, prejudice and stereotypes: APA report on preventing discrimination and promoting diversity. *American Psychological Association Newsletter*, April 2012.

Bombeck, E. (1978). *If Life is a Bowl of Cherries, What Aam I Doing in the Pits?* New York: Fawcett Crest Books.

Bremner, J.D. (2005). Effects of traumatic stress on brain structure and function: relevance to early responses to trauma. *Journal of Trauma and Dissociation*, 6, 51–68.

Deacon, B.J. and Abramowitz, J.S. (2004). Cognitive and behavioral treatments for anxiety disorders: a review of meta-analytic findings. *Journal of Clinical Psychology*, 60, 429–441.

Folkman, S., Lazarus, R.S., Gruen, R.J., and DeLongis, A. (1986). Appraisal, coping, health status, and psychological symptoms. *Journal of Personality and Social Psychology*, 50, 571–579.

Funk, J.B., Baldacci, H.B., Pasold, T., and Baumgardner, J. (2004). Violence exposure in real-life, video games, television, movies, and the internet: is there desensitization? *Journal of Adolescence*, 27, 23–39.

Hakamata, Y., Lissek, S., Bar-Haim, Y., Britton, J.C., Fox, N., Leibenluft, E., Ernst, M., and Pine, D.S. (2010). Attention bias modification treatment: a meta-analysis towards the establishment of novel treatment for anxiety. *Biological Psychiatry*, 68, 982–990.

Hawkins, K.A. and Cougle, J.R. (2013). Effects of interpretation training on hostile attribution bias and reactivity to interpersonal insult. *Behavior Therapy*, 44, 479–488.

Kabat-Zinn, J. (1994) *Wherever You Go, There You Are: Mindfulness Meditation in Everyday Life*. New York: Hyperion Books.

Kanner, A.D., Coyne, J.C., Schaefer, C., and Lazarus, R.S. (1981). Comparison of two modes of stress measurement: daily hassles and uplifts versus major life events. *Journal of Behavioural Medicine*, 4, 1–39.

Manassis, K. (2015). *Keys to Parenting Your Anxious Child* 3rd (Edition). Hauppauge, NY: Barron's Educational Series Inc.

Matthews, S.G. (2002). Early programming of the hypothalamo-pituitary-adrenal axis. *Trends in Endocrinological Metabolism*, 13, 373–380.

Musixmatch.com. *Prayer of St. Theresa*. http://lyricstranslate.com/en/nada-te-turbe-let-nothing-disturb-you.html Retrieved August 30, 2016.

Phelan, T.W. (2016). *1–2-3 Magic: Effective Discipline for Children 2–12* 6th (Edition). Glen Ellyn, IL: Parentmagic Inc.

Teasdale, J., Williams, M., and Segal, Z. (2014). *The Mindful Way Workbook.* New York: Guilford Press.

Vaillant, G.E. (1993). *The Wisdom of the Ego.* Cambridge, MA: Harvard University Press.

Williams, J.E., Paton, C.C., Siegler, I.C., Eigenbrodt, M.L., Nieto, F.J., and Tyroler, H.A. (2000). Anger proneness predicts coronary heart disease risk. *Circulation,* 101, 2023–2039.

7 Relationships and Empathy: Treating the Other Person as a "Thou"

> In the end, it is the reality of personal relationship that saves everything.
>
> Thomas Merton (2015)

This chapter begins to explore the social side of empathy, as introduced in Chapter 3, by placing empathy in the context of human relationships. Different kinds of one to one relationships are examined. Then, various influences toward and away from Buber's empathetic ideal of treating the other person as a "Thou" (i.e., complex human being meriting respect and attention) in these relationships are illustrated. Larger social contexts such as families, groups, and communities are discussed in more detail in Part III in chapters focusing on parents and leaders. However, as Merton's quote implies, many of these contexts are ultimately dependent on strong, person to person relationships.

What Are We Aiming For?

As discussed in Chapter 1, the empathetic relationship is one characterized by inter-subjectivity. This means that each person is interested in the other's unique, subjective experience of life. Rather than judging other people or telling them what they should or should not do, we regard them with benign curiosity, trying to understand their perspective. We consider that perspective valid whether or not it agrees with our own. If we want or need to change that perspective, we do so gently, respecting the dignity of the other person. We also refrain from using our understanding of the other person to take advantage of him or her or to achieve personal gain. Using another person as a means to an end in this way would be cruel and dehumanizing. In summary, we develop a manner of relating to others that is deeply respectful and constitutes (in Martin Buber's (1937/2004) terms) an "I-Thou" relationship, or (in Jean Vanier's (1998) terms) "a relationship of communion", or (in Daniel Stern's (2004) terms) "participating in another's lived story". All describe honoring the person rather than exploiting them, and regarding the other's subjective experience as valid and worthy of interest.

Inter-subjectivity is only possible moment by moment. We cannot maintain this state continuously, as life gets in the way. At some point, we need to stop focusing on the other person and get on with the utilitarian tasks of living. Even new parents completely enthralled with their baby need to eventually change its diaper! Although inter-subjective experiences are often brief, they can still be profoundly meaningful. Participating in another's experience validates and enriches that experience, even when nothing is said. Silently sitting with someone recently bereaved, for example, can be a very moving and caring thing to do, reminding the person of their continuing connection with the human family as they struggle with the loss of a loved one.

Making space for inter-subjective experiences in ongoing relationships can be challenging though. As discussed in previous chapters, everything from unhealthy relationship models from the past, to distraction by daily hassles that prompt fight or flight reactions, to an excessive societal focus on goals and achievement can interfere with finding this space. Furthermore, ongoing relationships seem to follow the law of entropy: they deteriorate when you don't regularly apply energy to maintain and renew them.

Balance and complementarity are also key elements of long-term relationships (Nichols, 1996). For instance, there needs to be a balance between freedom and connection. Each person in the relationship needs to feel free from being controlled by the other person, yet connected enough to care about their well-being. Sometimes this means ensuring healthy psychological boundaries where people do not feel obligated to think or act alike; sometimes it means compromising certain freedoms in order to allow the other person to thrive. What parent hasn't put off a trip to the store to avoid waking a sleeping child that would need to be taken along? On the other hand, what parent hasn't celebrated when that child reached an age where he or she could stay home alone? Then, the freedom/connection balance shifts again in adolescence, as the youth starts to assert his or her independence while still needing parental support. The book title *Get Out of My Life, but First Could You Drive Me and Cheryl to the Mall* (see Wolf, 2002) captures this idea humorously, and reflects the exasperation parents often feel at this stage of family life.

Complementarity is needed in the division of labor in relationships, so there is a sense of "give and take". One person may give more financially, another may contribute more to running the household; one may be better at home repairs, the other may be better at organizing social events. The roles are different but complementary, and may need to evolve over time as people develop and circumstances change. Ideally, partners recognize the value of each other's contributions and so show gratitude for what is given to them and feel motivated to give generously in return. One of the most common sources of conflict in relationships, however, is the feeling that one is doing "more than one's share" relative to the other person. Some people are also compelled to give more than they get, as this may meet certain psychological needs. In both cases, there is an overemphasis on tallying up and comparing individual contributions, and a lack of appreciation of the other person's perspective and of the value of the relationship. In short, healthy relationships are more about gratitude and generosity than accounting.

Various Kinds of Relationships

Empathy toward others can be more difficult to develop in some relationships than others. Many people, for instance, have had the experience of dealing with misbehavior in a child calmly and effectively when babysitting a friend's offspring, but becoming completely irrational when the child is their own. Good behavior is nice in a child one is babysitting, but seems to be more crucial for one's own child and his or her future, so stronger emotions (and often less effective parenting) come into play with one's own child.

As shown in this example, the degree of closeness with the other person or, more accurately, the extent to which the other person's life influences one's own can affect the capacity for empathy. That capacity can vary depending on whether the relationship is a chance encounter with a stranger, an instrumental relationship where each party serves a particular function (e.g., the mail carrier, the clerk at the store, someone in the company who works in a different department), a close colleague or friend where there is an ongoing sharing of experience, a family member (implying a long history together as well as ongoing shared experience), or a spouse (implying commitment to a future together as well as shared history and ongoing shared experience). Each of these relationships can be tinged by predominantly positive or predominantly negative emotion, and each poses different challenges for empathetic behavior.

Figure 7.1 shows different types of one to one relationships as falling on two axes: one to do with emotional valence (positive or negative) and the other to do with the degree of influence people have on one another's lives. Low-influence relationships consist of chance encounters, acquaintances, and instrumental relationships such as those with merchants or public officials. From the therapist's point of view, relationships with patients are also "low influence", and usually relatively positive. In the influential and positive quadrant are relationships characterized by secure attachment (see Chapter 2), and relationships with good friends or collaborative colleagues. Ideally, spousal relationships should also fall into this quadrant. In the influential and negative quadrant are relationships characterized by insecure attachment as well as those among competitors or people who consider each other enemies. High-influence relationships are usually more emotionally complicated than those with people who have limited influence on our lives, so are discussed in more detail later in the chapter.

Relationships and Empathy 111

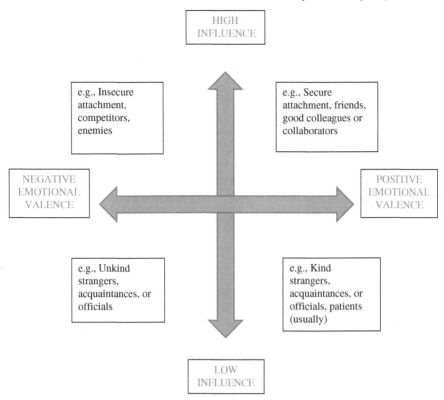

Figure 7.1 Relationship Types by Closeness and Emotional Valence

Low-Influence Relationships

Low-influence relationships often present opportunities for empathy, whether or not we recognize them. For example, many of the people we deal with in instrumental ways are trying to do a good job but may be struggling with overwork, disgruntled customers, or distraction by personal concerns. A smile or kind word at the checkout counter can make all the difference to an exhausted cashier. A friendly conversation with someone while waiting in line is another opportunity for empathy that is often overlooked.

Some people actually *create* opportunities for connection and empathy with others they barely know. I recall an elderly couple living on our street who clearly remembered what it was like to be a parent on Halloween. In our town the weather on this holiday is usually nasty, with rain and biting wind. Dragging around small children outdoors in the dark for "trick or treat" is certainly no treat for parents! This couple, however, invariably greeted the children in elaborate but not-too-scary costumes, provided them with candy, and then offered each parent a small glass of sherry. It wasn't enough to get intoxicated, as the children still needed to be escorted safely down the street, but it was just enough to warm you up inside and remind you that somebody cared.

Low-influence relationships challenge our capacity for empathy when the people we are dealing with treat us in inconsiderate ways. The stranger who cuts us off in traffic is one of the most obvious examples. Rather than taking this sort of event personally, it is usually more helpful to see it as a thoughtless act by someone who was preoccupied with their own anxiety about arriving at a particular place on time, and commit to not acting this way ourselves. The neighbor who digs a trench on or slightly over the property line without discussing the matter first is another example of someone whose behavior is annoying, but of little consequence. It's probably wise to speak up assertively in this situation in order to avoid encouraging further liberties, but it is not a disastrous event. Finding out the reasons for the trench, trying to empathize, and then firmly asking to be notified of any further projects would preserve both one's self-respect and the future of the neighborly relationship.

People we interact with who have very different styles from our own can also be challenging. A new friend or acquaintance who constantly changes plans at the last minute, for example, may be infuriating for someone who is used to a very predictably scheduled lifestyle. If the friendship lasts, however, the scheduler may come to realize that this person brings a more flexible, spontaneous approach to social events that can actually be fun. Conversely, the "free spirit" may come to realize that some planning (e.g., purchasing tickets to events ahead of time) increases the chances of an enjoyable evening. Friendships among people with contrasting styles sometimes challenge both parties to become less extreme or to enhance underdeveloped parts of themselves.

Unkind officials can be particularly difficult to view with empathetic eyes. These might include the police officer who goes out of his way to humiliate you after a minor traffic infraction, or the bank teller who shuts her window exactly at closing time when you are the last person in line and have been waiting for half an hour for service. In each case the official enforces the rules at your expense, so you have no right to complain. You may protest that you are being "treated like a number" or that the official "has no heart", but you are unlikely to get anywhere with your protest. Yet, if you regarded those officials as human beings, even though they are unlikely to do the same, you might find that the need to assert power by hiding behind rigid rules usually relates to a sense of powerlessness in other aspects of life. The police officer, for example, may have been taunted about not doing as well as his peers in training or may be henpecked by his wife, prompting his need to assert power on the road. The bank teller may be paid a low wage and see her behavior as a passive-aggressive way of getting back at those with money to spare. Even if we don't know the story behind the unkindness, it is important to remind ourselves that there usually is a story. Those who prioritize rules over people are often feeling devalued or dehumanized themselves.

The coffee server described at the start of this book is a quintessential example of the "kind stranger" who has little overt influence on our lives but is nevertheless positive. The neighbor who helps one out of a difficult situation, as in my example of borrowing a car in Chapter 6, is a similar positive influence. These people are not difficult to regard with empathy, and may actually inspire greater empathy in those they touch.

It is, however, sometimes easy to forget to show empathy when we are not prompted to do so. As mental health providers, our training prompts us to behave empathetically toward patients and, for the most part, we strive to do so. When we hear of famines, earthquakes, forest fires, or other natural disasters we may similarly become concerned for the people affected, often prompting empathetic behavior. When people are not obvious victims of either psychological or physical distress, however, we may not think to behave empathetically. When someone starts to talk about the weather on the train, for example, a friendly response may open the door for that person to connect with you on a human level. Responding to your email can wait. When someone asks if you know when the store is opening and they have a cranky child in tow, a funny gesture that distracts the child for a moment may make all the difference to her day. Taking a minute to do this won't hurt, and you'll still get your shopping done. When you are in an official position, remember how it feels to use your power to benefit those you meet rather than wielding it indiscriminately just because you can.

In some languages the word for stranger is the same as the word for guest (Belfiore, 1993), showing how deeply these cultures value hospitality. May we treat all strangers as honored guests, whether they reciprocate or not. The results may reach further than we can imagine (described further in Part III).

High-Influence Relationships

Close colleagues, good friends, members of one's immediate family, and spouses or romantic partners have an ongoing influence on our emotional well-being, and so constitute high-influence relationships. In addition, people in authority such as a courtroom judge or a therapist can be "high-influence" even though we may only interact with them for short periods of time.

This is true because both people in ongoing relationships and people in positions of power can elicit feelings and patterns of thinking and behaving that resemble our past experiences with parents. Whether labeled "transference" (Freud, 1973), "internal working models" (see Bowlby, 1969), "core conflictual relationship themes" (see Luborsky, 1984), or "relationship schemata" (see Young, Klosko, and Weishaar, 2003), these ghosts from the past seem to impact our relationships, whether we are aware of them or not. We bring certain expectations to relationships that are close or involve a power differential, behave accordingly, and in so doing elicit from the other person patterns of behavior that resemble the behavior of important people from the past. The simplest example is the common observation that some people have "a chip on their shoulder". In other words, they walk into a neutral situation expecting hostility, behave defensively and sometimes rudely, and as a result elicit unkind behavior from others, confirming the initial expectation. Conversely, people who experienced secure, positive relationships in their families tend to walk into situations with either positive expectations or no particular expectations, freeing them to observe those around them and respond in a manner that is appropriate to the situation.

Therapists are aware of this tendency in their patients, and usually also of their own "ghosts" that may result in particularly strong feelings in relation to certain patients (termed "counter-transference"). Awareness is key if one is to avoid inappropriate or unprofessional behavior with patients, whether or not one elects to disclose this awareness to the patient. Awareness allows the therapist to resist entering into patterns of behavior with the patient that replay early history, whether it is the patient's or the therapist's history.

Parents are well-advised to look for this tendency in themselves when raising children. Recall the example of Arjun in Chapter 2. Here, the son represented an unwelcome part of the father's past, impairing empathy in the father-son relationship. Children can also represent influential people from one's past (e.g., parents, siblings) even if this is not immediately obvious. For instance, a mother I counseled wondered why she sometimes found herself competing with her daughter. Eventually, it became clear that the daughter resembled the mother's successful older sister. However, the daughter was a vulnerable child rather than a competitor, and needed her mother's empathetic, nurturing care. This realization had a profoundly positive effect on the mother-daughter relationship.

Transference can also occur in close working relationships, as shown in the example of Selena and Courtney later in this chapter. Leaders are wise to keep this in mind, particularly when discussions among staff become overly heated relative to the issue at hand, or when people in superior/subordinate relationships seem overly close or show a lack of psychological boundaries. In the latter situation there is a high risk of unprofessional behavior, as one party regards the other as either a parent or potential romantic partner or both, without necessarily being aware of these feelings.

When do old patterns complicate current relationships and impair empathy? Most commonly, this occurs in people with histories of insecure attachment (see Chapter 2; Bowlby, 1969). Recall that the insecure attachment patterns involve sub-optimal models of close relationships that may involve minimizing negative emotion/perceived vulnerability resulting in avoidance of intimacy ("avoidant" attachment style); maximizing negative emotion/perceived vulnerability resulting in support-seeking relationships which may lack psychological boundaries ("ambivalent" attachment style); or compulsive caregiving or controlling relationship behavior resulting from disorganized attachment. All of these can limit the capacity for empathy by imposing patterns from one's personal history onto the relationship with one's partner. The example of Mandy and Michael in the next section shows how this may happen. In the case of childhood trauma, physiological changes in stress responses impact empathy further, in addition to the effect of skewed relationship models (Bremner, 2005; Matthews, 2002).

By contrast, people who were fortunate enough to grow up in secure, supportive relationships or who have dealt with painful past experiences in psychotherapy have a less rigid and potentially more empathetic approach to relationships. They do not need their partners to behave in a certain way in order to regulate their own emotions. Rather, they can respond to their partners as called for by the situation. If the other person succeeds, they can share his or her joy without envy. If the other person is unhappy, they can commiserate and so reduce his or her emotional burdens. If the other person is grumpy, they can recognize his or her stress and not take the behavior personally. If there is disagreement, they can listen to the other person's point of view, try to understand it, and respond accordingly. They may not always agree, but they can "agree to disagree" without harming the relationship.

Relationships Defined by Past Patterns or Future Goals

A very common challenge to maintaining empathy in close, largely positive high-influence relationships is adapting to changes in circumstances and developmental changes in the people involved. Relationships defined by certain patterns from the past or by certain goals for the future are particularly vulnerable. Putting too much emphasis on either the past or the future is problematic, as people may change and goals may change too. Some joint planning is needed, of course, to manage the logistics of major life decisions (e.g., buying a home, starting a family), but even this exercise works better when attending to one another empathetically in the present moment. The following two examples illustrate relationships that seem "frozen in time", one due to unmet emotional needs from the past (described in the previous section) and the other due to an overemphasis on common goals and ideals.

Mandy and Michael

Mandy was living a fairy tale life, or so it seemed. After briefly dating a few men, she met Michael: her knight in shining armor. Michael held the door for her, took her to the finest restaurants, and even smiled sweetly at her father's corny jokes. He was the most considerate man she had ever met. He was ambitious too, and shared many of her values. Michael adored Mandy. He saw her as a bright, caring, but not very confident young woman with a hint of naïveté. He loved introducing her to new adventures, defending her against workplace bullies, and planning their future together.

Their first year together was bliss. Mandy loved Michael's attention to her needs, and in his eyes she could do no wrong. The experience was so different from the fickle affections of Mandy's parents, which disappeared when she was disagreeable, when her grades were less than stellar, or when she failed to be grateful for all she had been given. Michael, by contrast, loved to support Mandy and see her grow and develop. He had spent years trying to get his mother to stand up to her abusive husband without success. Mandy was different. He told her "Don't let the bastards at work get you down", and she listened, persevered, and eventually learned to assert herself. He enjoyed seeing her succeed.

The next few years were more challenging. Mandy continued to love Michael, but she felt constrained by his constant need to help her and constant expectations of gratitude. She hoped for more reciprocity. She found birthday gifts tailored to his interests, and he ignored them. She planned a trip to an exotic location neither had visited, and he discouraged the idea because of business commitments. Yet Michael continued to give her lavish gifts and plan trips that he told her would "broaden her horizons".

Finally, she snapped "I'm your wife, not your project!" Michael was taken aback. When he had taught Mandy to assert herself with others, he had not expected her to use those skills in their marriage. He withdrew from her for several days, and Mandy got worried about their relationship. She apologized, and returned to her previous pattern of being agreeable, accepting his gifts, and expressing gratitude, whether it was genuine or not.

Mandy and Michael eventually reached an understanding of their respective roles in the relationship: he was the shining knight, and she the damsel in distress. They kept to themselves any communication that threatened those roles, and appeared to have a very stable relationship. Mandy's friends even envied her for having such a considerate husband. When the children were grown though, Mandy, now a successful businesswoman despite her private "damsel" role, announced that she was leaving Michael. "We haven't had an honest conversation in years, and I don't know who you are anymore", was her sad conclusion.

Mandy and Michael seemed like a nice couple from their friends' perspective, so it may initially seem surprising that their relationship went so horribly awry. Where did they lose their empathetic connection? How could it have been restored?

The answer to the first question clearly relates to the past. Whether they were aware of it or not, Mandy saw Michael as the source of validation that she had never received from her parents and Michael saw Mandy as a surrogate for his abused mother whom he wanted to rescue. Mandy and Michael's unmet emotional needs complemented each other nicely in the early stages of their marriage. However, as Mandy grew more confident and adventurous, she experienced Michael's behavior as stifling and paternalistic. Michael, on the other hand, could not change from his preferred role of "rescuer" and could not adapt to Mandy's emotional development. As a result, their relationship began to deteriorate.

The answer to the second question is not as obvious. Awareness of their relationship pattern, likely with the aid of a therapist, would have given each partner the opportunity to explore aspects of the relationship that did not reflect the pattern. Mandy and Michael likely shared some interests and activities that did not require them to play their "rescuer" and "damsel" roles. They also likely shared positive memories from early in their relationship when each appreciated the other (one benefit of romantic love). It is possible that focusing on the aspects of the relationship that fell outside their unhealthy pattern would have allowed them to modify their habitual behaviors, without feeling too threatened by this change. Sometimes when we understand our own foibles, and recognize that we also have many strengths, we can learn not to take ourselves quite so seriously. As we no longer feel threatened by our imperfections we can become open to new possibilities.

Interestingly, restoring an empathetic connection in this case might have required being somewhat disagreeable, particularly in Mandy's case. Apologizing for her outburst toward Michael was certainly empathetic, but her disingenuous gratitude and agreeable behavior subsequently was not. From Michael's point of view, grumpy honesty from Mandy (which might have prompted some marriage counseling) would have been preferable to a false, superficial appearance of relationship stability. Unfortunately, Mandy's fear of being rejected by Michael as she had been by her parents was simply too great to allow for this approach.

Bob and Bonita

Bob and Bonita were college science students, and ended up being assigned to the same chemistry lab. As lab partners, they divided up tasks, solved problems together, and supported each other to ensure that each experiment was successfully completed. After a month or so, Bonita started noticing Bob's sense of humour and quiet charm. She started becoming attracted to him. Bob had been dating his high school sweetheart for almost two years though, and was honest about the fact that he was in a serious relationship.

Nevertheless, Bob and Bonita got in the habit of having coffee together after class. They commiserated about the challenges of their undergraduate programs, laughed about the quirks of their professors, and talked about how different things would be in an ideal world. As they shared their thoughts on the latter topic it became clear that they had very similar ideals and values. "Think globally; act locally" was Bob's favorite aphorism, and he tried to live accordingly. Bonita admired that. "What a shame", she thought to herself, "that he's already committed to his sweetheart."

She tried to stop thinking about Bob in a romantic way, as she felt it would be unethical to interfere with his existing relationship. The following year, Bonita and Bob got into different professional faculties, and they lost touch.

Six years later, they accidentally ran into each other on the bus. "Hi, Bob!" Bonita exclaimed. "Hullo", he responded weakly. With his hunched shoulders and five o'clock shadow she hardly recognized him. She told him how pleased she was to be working in an area that actually interested her, unlike the chemistry experience they had shared. She was looking forward to advancing further in her field.

Bob, on the other hand, was teaching science to tenth graders in a run-down inner city school. He knew that few of his students would graduate, and fewer still actually cared about what they were learning. When Bonita suggested that he could look for a better position, he shrugged, "Maybe if I didn't have to feed the kids." He had married his sweetheart and they had twin boys, with a third child on the way. He was cynical about his work, his marriage, and life in general. Bonita tried to be empathetic, but they no longer shared the hopes and ideals that drew them together in college.

In this example, two people share some very empathetic moments together over coffee based on the challenges they jointly face in college and the common ideals they espouse. Circumstances change for both, however, and years later they no longer share either common challenges or common ideals. Bonita's final attempt at empathy toward Bob comes more from a sense of pity than a true ability to put herself in his shoes. She is unlikely to feel motivated to continue the relationship, and may even think to herself "I'm glad I didn't pursue that guy!"

As the two examples illustrate, even though our closest relationships may span years or even decades, empathy in these relationships is still a moment by moment experience. Circumstances change and people change, so ongoing empathy for one another must be reinvented day by day if the relationship is to survive. Some would see this as a chore; others as an opportunity for growing in ways that we might not be able to anticipate. What an adventure!

Empathy for One's Enemies?

Returning to Figure 7.1, there is one quadrant yet to be discussed: high-influence relationships with negative emotional valence. These are relationships characterized by insecurity, competition, and in some cases abject hatred. Showing empathy in these relationships is harder than in any other relationship type.

The inability to forgive past hurts often contributes to this difficulty. Sometimes, we can forgive the violent stranger who robs us, shattering our sense of safety and inflicting months of nightmares and flashbacks, yet we cannot forgive the friend or colleague who betrays our trust. When we allow people to become close enough for high-influence relationships, we become vulnerable and expect them not to take advantage of that vulnerability. When they do, we become enraged. Imagine yourself in Selena's shoes in the following example.

Selena and Courtney

Selena was in a middle management position at a large, successful company. She led a team of people that designed and tested new software. She enjoyed her work and was eager to impress her boss, whom she considered a mentor. One day, her boss invited Selena to lunch and introduced her to Courtney. Courtney had a similar resume to Selena's, and had recently moved to town after her husband was offered a job in another department at the same firm. The boss thought Courtney would be an asset to Selena's team, and wanted to know if the two women could work together. Courtney was self-assured, articulate, and witty, and had obviously charmed the boss. Selena felt some discomfort at the lunch, but couldn't quite put her finger on what the problem was. Therefore, rather than trusting her instincts, she went along with her boss's request to "show Courtney the ropes", and tried her best to be welcoming. She even felt some admiration for Courtney's self-assurance and social graces.

Courtney was a quick study, and soon needed little guidance from Selena. She was confident, voicing strong opinions at team meetings, but she was never rude. She quickly gained the respect of other team members. When she made some suggestions about organizing the meetings differently, people listened and wondered if Selena was being "inflexible" when she protested the changes. Selena eventually acquiesced. Junior members of the team began having coffee with Courtney and complaining about some of the company rules. Even though the rules were designed by her superiors Selena was blamed for enforcing them. Gradually, the team split into two factions: one faction allied with Courtney, and the other loyal to Selena.

One day, Courtney decided to challenge Selena to change one of the rules she considered "outdated" at a team meeting, and suggested she go to the boss if she didn't like the idea. Selena did so, not knowing that Courtney had already met with the boss and convinced him of her position. The boss rebuked Selena, and she returned to the team humiliated. Her leadership had been irreparably undermined, and she knew it. Courtney advanced quickly, first to leading the team, and eventually to leading the department.

How would you feel in Selena's position? How would you react if someone you had tried to welcome and support responded with such treachery?

Before continuing Selena's story, let's consider some factors that might affect your reaction. Would your reaction be different if you learned that Courtney's father had been jailed for fraud and her mother had been physically abusive towards her? Recall from Chapter 2 that the combination of genetic predisposition and abuse is one of the best predictors of sociopathic behavior (Byrd and Manuck, 2014). Would it be different if you learned that the boss had offered a prize for the individual best able to modernize company procedures? Perhaps Courtney was merely responding to an incentive provided by her superior. Would it be different if you learned that Courtney was about to divorce after a third failed marriage, as her need to manipulate others left her incapable of intimacy? Perhaps her coping style is more worthy of pity than hatred. Would it be different if you found out that Selena's leadership style had been questioned long before Courtney's arrival? Perhaps Courtney merely accelerated an inevitable reorganization of the team. Finally (although I don't mean to blame the victim), would it be different if you learned that Selena's family history was one marked by insecurity and betrayal, perhaps resulting in a tendency to inadvertently encourage disloyal behavior in others in high-influence relationships?

These ideas raise an interesting question: should we try to empathize with people like Courtney? After all, sociopaths often regard kindness and empathy as signs of weakness. Communicating empathy overtly might thus invite further abusive behavior towards us. To avoid vulnerability and further injury, a cordial but distant relationship might be wiser.

Even if we don't express empathy toward the "Courtneys" of this world though, there may still be value in trying to put ourselves in their shoes. We can understand where they come from (often traumatized, abused, or neglected as children), the conditions that facilitate their behavior (e.g., a corporate culture that superficially encourages teamwork but promotes people based on individual accomplishments), the emotionally limited lives they lead (unable to allow for vulnerability, their relationships often lack depth), and the limits of their influence in the long run. The fame or wealth they achieve quickly passes, whereas the indelible impressions on others left by acts of kindness endure, often for generations (as explored further in Part III). This understanding can motivate us to change the social conditions that help create a "Courtney". It can also help us understand our own dark, manipulative tendencies and resist the temptation to act upon them.

The Rest of Selena's Story

Selena found a job with another company where her talents were appreciated. Although her career flourished, she couldn't get past the memory of Courtney's behavior. If anyone mentioned her name, Selena launched into a tirade about "superficially charming sociopaths". She preferred to work alone, as she suspected colleagues of trying to sabotage her efforts even when they had given her no reason for suspicion. She disparaged the former members of her team as "naïve and easily duped" and lost touch with them. She focused on projects rather than people, indicating she was not interested in "office politics" which (she claimed) benefitted those who used others. In short, Courtney's manipulative behavior provoked paranoid tendencies in Selena that went beyond what one would expect under the circumstances.

As Selena's therapist, I knew that encouraging forgiveness with cognitive exercises or inspiring readings would do little to address her dilemma. Instead, I explored other relationships where Selena had felt used or betrayed. It didn't take long before I heard about her mother.

Selena and her mother had a volatile relationship when she was a teenager. Selena vacillated between trying to please her mother and trying to become independent of her. Her mother was a self-absorbed woman who only attended to Selena when she could put her on public display as her "successful daughter". In private, she rarely had a kind word to say to her.

Not surprisingly, Selena suffered from low self-esteem and frequent bouts of depression. Eventually, she realized that, for the sake of her own emotional stability, she needed to give up on the idea of having a loving relationship with her mother. She found a job in a neighboring town, and interacted with her mother infrequently.

Selena's emotional problems persisted though, so she went into psychotherapy. Her therapist at the time suggested that mending fences with her mother might be helpful, so Selena went back to her mother, and confided in her how she remembered being hurt as a child. She concluded, however, that she was now willing to forgive the past in the hope of a better mother-daughter relationship. "What's to forgive?" was her mother's cold reply. Her mother claimed that the hurtful incidents Selena described had never happened, and that she was "just being a spoiled, ungrateful child".

Selena felt betrayed, humiliated, and more hurt than ever. She didn't sleep for days afterwards, struggling with the raw emotions her mother's reaction had provoked. She eventually drank enough liquor to pass out. After the hangover cleared, she resolved to never allow herself to be emotionally vulnerable in her mother's presence again. To preserve her mental health, she needed to keep her mother at arms-length.

On reflection, however, Selena realized that she had never given up on the dream of pleasing her confident but critical mother. Without realizing it, she had transferred this dream onto the relationship with Courtney. When Courtney betrayed her, her feelings about being betrayed by her mother were rekindled, so her reaction was extreme. After understanding this connection, Selena became less preoccupied with Courtney, and less paranoid. She reminded herself daily that not everyone she worked with was like her mother.

Later, Selena learned that her mother's experiences growing up in a warzone had irreparably damaged not only her relationship with Selena but also those with her other children. Although she never admitted it, it was clear to the siblings that intrusive memories from their mother's traumatic past had left her unable to provide the warm, secure environment young children need.

Selena had very mixed feelings when her mother died, and struggled with the loss for some time. Eventually, she was able to remind herself of what Patty Davis (2016), another child of an ambivalently loved parent, said: "there were moments in our history when all that was going on between us was love. I choose to remember those moments." Perhaps that is as close to forgiveness as we can get when it comes to really difficult parent-child relationships: choosing to remember the loving moments.

When Others Hurt Us Deeply

As mentioned above, an empathetic understanding of influential but hurtful people can motivate us to change the social conditions that help create them, and sometimes provides insight into our own "dark side". The conclusion of the Selena example, however, raises a few additional points.

First, Selena's understanding of how the incident with Courtney related to feelings toward her mother helped her put it in perspective. Selena realized that not everyone in her life was like Courtney or like her mother, her mistrust of those around her subsided, and she was freed to re-engage in human relationships. Thus, insights about the "hurters" can sometimes help us recognize how different they are from the many decent, ordinary people around us.

Second, even the act of stopping to think about the people who hurt us may be beneficial. It interferes with the primal urge, driven by the fight or flight response, to immediately retaliate. Retaliation often results in escalation of conflict and, when done on a large scale, in war. Though the causes of war are complex, its intergenerational effects are undeniable, as the history of Selena's mother illustrates. A traumatized child of war often transmits part of that legacy to his or her own children. Thus, anything we can do to discourage the violent solutions to problems that sometimes lead to war has implications for the overall human capacity for empathy now and in the future.

Third, the conclusion of Selena's story illustrates another unfortunate truth: unresolved hurts in close relationships complicate the grieving process. It is harder to come to terms with the loss of someone ambivalently loved than someone for whom we had unreserved affection. Rather than feeling sad, we may feel ongoing anger about how they treated us, guilt about those times when we overreacted to that ill treatment, and regret about words that were never spoken or issues that were never addressed. Moreover, we may feel that this response to loss is wrong or invalid, as those around us show only tears. In short, too many mixed feelings are involved.

Finally, the idea that hurtful, malevolent people can be permanently removed from society in order to limit the damage they do is probably a fallacy. We all have the capacity for cruelty toward others under certain conditions, so we would have to remove just about everyone if we followed this philosophy. For instance, experiments have shown that when we trust unscrupulous authority figures, treating others inhumanely becomes commonplace (Milgram, 1963). Similarly, when we respond in extreme ways based on transference reactions or other past experience, we are all capable of being hurtful. Thus, developing empathetic relationships may be less about banishing the "hurters" from our lives, and more about better understanding them and ourselves.

Summary

- Empathetic encounters honor the person rather than exploiting them, assume that the person's perspective is valid and worthy of interest, and are experienced in the moment.

- Challenges to experiencing empathy regularly in relationships include unresolved psychological issues, distraction by daily stress, certain ideologies, and a lack of ongoing effort to adapt to changes related to human development and to circumstances.
- Gratitude and generosity are central to empathetic relationships.
- People in distant or instrumental relationships can influence one another positively by responding empathetically in the moment or by deliberately creating opportunities for empathy, rather than attending to other priorities.
- People who are inconsiderate or have different styles from our own can be difficult to regard with empathy, so it is important to not take the behavior personally, to adapt to difference if possible, and to remember that those who prioritize rules over people are often feeling devalued or dehumanized themselves.
- In close relationships or relationships of differential power there is sometimes a tendency to impose patterns from one's personal history onto the relationship, interfering with empathy, so awareness of these patterns is important particularly if they stem from insecure attachment.
- Ongoing empathetic relationships must be nurtured moment by moment, without undue emphasis on either patterns from the past or future goals, as circumstances change and people change and grow.
- When people betray our trust in close relationships this is difficult to forgive, and restoring empathy may or may not be possible as expressing empathy toward these people may invite further abuse.
- Even if not expressed, an empathetic understanding of those who hurt us deeply may be helpful in motivating us to change the social conditions that create them, in avoiding retaliation, in grieving their loss, and in understanding our own hurtful impulses.
- It is important not to allow negative experiences in relation to others to color our entire perception of the human race: there are good people out there!

Reflective Questions

1 What opportunities for empathy present themselves in your encounters with strangers, acquaintances, or people with whom you have instrumental relationships? Is it possible to pursue these opportunities, rather than prioritizing other goals?
2 When you behave inconsiderately in traffic or in other day to day situations, what are the reasons? Could those reasons apply to others who treat you inconsiderately in similar situations?
3 Is there any person with whom you interact regularly who elicits unusually strong negative emotions in you? Does this person remind you of anyone in your past? What would be an appropriate and empathetic

way to relate to this person? If this is not possible, consider discussing the issue with a therapist.
4   Is an overemphasis on the past or the future affecting any of your close relationships? How could you start to develop greater empathy in this relationship?
5   Is there anyone you regard with hatred? If so, what would be the benefits of regarding them with greater empathy? Is this possible?

Questions for Therapists

1   Do you regard most of your patients as being in the "low-influence positive" quadrant? What aspects of your practice or of the patient (e.g., payment issues, tardiness, treatment adherence) might push them into other quadrants? How can you develop greater empathy for those you have difficulty regarding as "low-influence positive"?
2   Are there patients who are becoming "high-influence" in terms of your emotional relationship with them (either positive or negative)? Identify any issues with psychological boundaries that might be affecting these relationships.
3   What patients most regularly elicit negative emotions in you? Do they remind you of anyone in your past?
4   How would you help Mandy and Michael restore empathy in their relationship?
5   How would you help Selena come to terms with the loss of her ambivalently loved mother?

References

Belfiore, E. (1993). Xenia in Sophocles' Philoctetes. *The Classical Journal*, 89, 113–129.

Bowlby, J. (1969). *Attachment. Attachment and Loss: Vol. 1. Loss*. New York: Basic Books.

Bremner, J.D. (2005). Effects of traumatic stress on brain structure and function: relevance to early responses to trauma. *Journal of Trauma and Dissociation*, 6, 51–68.

Buber, M. (1937). *I and Thou*. New York: Charles Scribner's Sons. Reprinted by Continuum International Publishing Group, 2004.

Byrd, A.L. and Manuck, S.B. (2014). MAOA, child maltreatment, and antisocial behavior: meta-analysis of a gene-environment interaction. *Biological Psychiatry*, 75, 9–17.

Davis, P. (March 11, 2016). Patti Davis delivers heart-rending eulogy at her mother Nancy Reagan's star-studded funeral. *New York Daily News*.

Freud, S. (1973) (translation by Richards, A.). *Introductory Lectures on Psychoanalysis*. London: Pelican Books, pp. 404–424.

Luborsky, L. (1984). *Principles of Psychoanalytic Psychotherapy: A Manual for Supportive-expressive Treatment*. New York: Basic Books.

Matthews, S.G. (2002). Early programming of the hypothalamo-pituitary-adrenal axis. *Trends in Endocrinological Metabolism*, 13, 373–380.
Merton, T. (2015). Apostolic work. In: *Letter to a Young Activist*. https://radicaldiscipleship.net/tag/letter-to-a-young-activist/ Retrieved August 30, 2016.
Milgram, S. (1963). Behavioral study of obedience. *Journal of Abnormal and Social Psychology*, 67, 371–378.
Nichols, W.C. (1996). *Treating People in Families: An Integrative Framework*. New York: Guilford Press. p. 155.
Stern, D.N. (2004). *The Present Moment in Psychotherapy and Everyday Life*. New York: W.W. Norton & Co., p. 58.
Vanier, J. (1998). *Becoming Human*. Toronto: Anansi Press Ltd.
Wolf, A.E. (2002). *Get Out of My Life, but First Could You Drive Me and Cheryl to the Mall*. New York: Farrar, Straus & Giroux.
Young, J.E., Klosko, J.S., and Weishaar, M.E. (2003). *Schema Therapy: A Practitioner's Guide*. New York: Guilford Press.

8 Beliefs and Ideals that Motivate Attention to Others' Well-Being

In the novel *What Dreams May Come* (Matheson, 1978) the lead character and his wife die, and he finds it impossible to enjoy heaven without her, preferring to join her in hell. This story has always pointed me to an important personal belief: that individual salvation is rather meaningless when one is alone and separated from loved ones. It speaks to the importance of finding our "heaven" together, whatever we conceive it to be, as witnessing others' suffering is hellish for those who are truly empathetic. It is only one example, however, of the relationship between belief and empathy. Whereas the previous chapter focused on one to one relationships and empathy, this chapter explores empathy in relation to various broader social ideals and beliefs. The effect of those ideals on day to day life and on therapeutic relationships is examined. As we will see, beliefs and ideals can affect not only our capacity for self-transcendence but also our motivation to attend to the well-being of others. Thus, they can impact multiple component processes of empathy. Implications for different social contexts (families, groups, organizations, etc.) are described further in Part III.

Ideologies, Psychological Needs, and Empathy

Ideology is a touchy subject, as it often inflames passions about various political and religious points of view. Too often, we get caught in arguments about which position is "right" without pausing to think about why we hold that position in the first place. Yet there is increasing evidence that we believe what we need to believe for our own psychological well-being. When we feel threatened, for example, we tend to huddle with our closest allies and are often less welcoming toward those outside our main social group than we otherwise would be (see Music, 2014). In this case, empathy toward those within the group increases and empathy toward those outside the group decreases. When we are financially successful, we want to preserve our wealth and so might be less inclined to vote for policies that raise taxes in order to help the less fortunate. Thus, empathy toward the marginalized in society decreases as the gap between rich and poor increases (Wilkinson and Pickett, 2009). Certain religious beliefs also seem related to psychological need. Anthropomorphic gods, versus beliefs emphasizing spiritual forces or spiritual practices, are more popular in times of turmoil and instability (see Armstrong, 1999). One can imagine that these gods would be perceived as comforting, possibly parental figures at such times. Unfortunately, such gods are sometimes exploited in order to rally support for causes that are not empathetic. Holy wars, for instance, are often justified with claims that "God is on our side."

In summary, we gravitate towards beliefs and ideals that help us cope with our circumstances, and some of these are more conducive to empathy than others. Trying to change beliefs and ideals that impede empathy is not always possible, as the result may be a high level of psychological distress for the believer.

When we focus on relationships rather than ideology, however, we may become empathetic despite our beliefs. A single friendship with someone on the other side of a divisive issue often softens one's position and allows understanding to grow. Thus, perhaps the best we can do is remind ourselves regularly to attend empathetically to those around us, whether or not they share our world view. That way, we will be less likely to prioritize lofty ideals over genuine relationships with the human beings we encounter.

Spiritual and social ideals are now examined in more detail, in relation to empathy in daily life and in psychotherapy.

Spirituality and Empathy: Future-Focused, Divisive, or Self-Serving Ideals

Most spiritual traditions aim to enhance empathy, as shown by the fact that all major religions include some version of the Golden Rule "So whatever you wish that others would do to you, do also to them" (Matthew 7:12 English Standard Version). Certain beliefs can interfere with empathy, however, if the believer focuses on them to a degree that excludes attention to people in the present moment, as shown in the example below. Interestingly, many people hold these beliefs but do attend to those around them empathetically. It is not the belief itself that gets people into trouble, but rather its application to exclude and diminish the value of others.

Helen

Helen was raising her children to be devout. Her husband was a "Christmas and Easter" churchgoer who usually stopped at the bar after work, which didn't help his family. He was not violent, but his drinking clearly reduced his ability to provide for the family and participate in raising the children. Helen reminded her children to say their prayers every night "in case the Lord chooses to take you". The youngest wouldn't turn out the light, fearing "the Lord" would get him in the dark.

For the most part, Helen's life was a series of household chores, interrupted from time to time by the cries of her children. However, believing herself to be one of the few local people who were destined for salvation (unlike the majority, whom she considered "unbelievers"), Helen held her head high when she walked into church. The image of God as a judgmental, punitive father and herself as one of his favored children offered her some comfort and, to a degree, maintained her self-esteem. Unfortunately, it also quashed any motivation to make something better of her life on earth (as she was so focused on heaven), and isolated her from others (given her negative view of most other people). She didn't risk new ambitions or new interpersonal relationships, and she used her faith to justify a limited, emotionally guarded approach to life.

Helen confided in Abby, her eldest daughter, sharing her frustration about her husband's behavior. "I worry about your father's path. He's laughing it up with his mates at the tavern now, but wait till judgment day. He'll have to account for all of his sins, and it won't be pretty. I have to put up with him though. It's better to suffer in this life for the sake of the family, and know that I'll have my reward in the next."

Once, her daughter questioned this attitude: "Mother, if Jesus turned the other cheek, wouldn't he be able to forgive Dad?" She was rebuked sharply "Don't you question Divine judgment!" To Abby it seemed more like Helen's judgment than God's, but she knew enough not to say so. Her mother's only comfort was her faith in a future reward, and without it she would fall into despair. Helen found so little enjoyment in her daily life.

In Helen's case, spiritual coping warded off depression but interfered with empathy because it increased self-absorption. Her focus on heaven (a future reward that detracted from attention to the present moment), focus on individual salvation (which excluded others whom she considered nonbelievers), and focus on her beliefs rather than human relationships or spiritual practices all reduced her capacity for empathy. An empathetic person might wonder, for example, how one could enjoy heaven knowing that others (in this belief system) are condemned to eternal suffering. Alternatively, he or she might wonder, as Abby did, how a loving God could condone such suffering.

William James (see James, 2009), who did a detailed analysis of spirituality across traditions, distinguished between people who use spirituality as a means to an end (called "extrinsic" spiritual orientation) and those who value spirituality as an end in itself (called "intrinsic" spiritual orientation). He observed that the latter was more compatible with the reverence for others that is fundamental to humane relationships. Helen's orientation, with its emphasis on individual benefit in the future, was clearly extrinsic.

To reiterate, belief in an anthropomorphic God is not necessarily problematic, but applying this belief in ways that are self-serving, exclude others, and detract from humane interactions in the present moment clearly is. For example, people with limited cognitive abilities who are not capable of abstract reasoning invariably organize their faith around concrete images of the Divine. Many of these people are highly empathetic, kind, and attuned to those around them, regardless of their worship of personified gods. Similarly, most people gravitate toward personified gods for comfort when in life-threatening situations, as suggested by the old aphorism that there are no atheists in fox-holes. This does not necessarily mean these people lack empathy, but rather that it is human nature to find the image of a caring parent comforting when in extreme distress.

However, as therapists we must be aware that people are often attracted to certain types of spiritual coping or beliefs based on their psychological needs. Addressing those needs can sometimes broaden people's range of spiritual coping and tolerance for diverse traditions and diverse points of view, expanding their capacity for empathy. For example, in Helen's case one could treat her depression, medically or psychologically, and then explore how she could find satisfaction in her present-day life. One need not challenge her belief in the hereafter, merely point out ways of finding greater satisfaction in the present. For example, she could leave her alcohol-dependent husband or accept the fact that she is choosing to stay with an incompatible spouse and make the best of it. Then she could find ways of making life enjoyable and productive despite the circumstances. For instance, she could choose to get a job to increase her financial choices or spend more time with other people in her church to feel that she is not merely a slave to her family. Either way she redefines herself as a person who can make a difference in the present, rather than resigning herself to being a victim. Her capacity for empathy would undoubtedly increase.

Occasionally, one encounters people who remain judgmental and negative towards others even when their psychological needs have been met. In this case a concept that may be helpful, especially with people from traditions that are highly focused on anthropomorphic gods, is the idea that humans are the instruments of God. In other words, if we want to convert our spiritual ideals into something real we need to see ourselves as agents of a Higher Power, regardless of whether that results in any particular personal reward or not. Usually that agency involves an empathetic approach to people we encounter in our daily lives. This idea also reduces the human tendency to passively wait around for divine intervention, rather than actively solving problems.

This idea may also be helpful when seeing people whose spiritual focus is primarily on positive feelings rather than empathy toward others, as shown in the next example. Although spirituality can include profoundly moving experiences, the pursuit of spirituality exclusively for the sake of feeling good is another example of James' "extrinsic spiritual motivation".

John

John grew up in a large, Orthodox Christian community and loved attending church. Church services were chanted in ancient languages that few parishioners understood, but the combination of beautiful icons, priestly processions, incense, candles, and familiar refrains was spellbinding. How could these events not be a portal to the Divine?

John's girlfriend, on the other hand, complained that some of the rules of conduct in his community were stifling and made no sense. She also didn't like the marginal role that women played in his church. John's friends also referred to those who did not belong to their faith as "lost", which she found annoying and presumptuous.

Eventually, she invited John to "a spiritual event". To his surprise, he found himself at the food bank where she volunteered. They received donations, packed boxes of food, and handed out the boxes with a smile to those in need. Everyone assumed that those who contributed gave what they could spare, and that only those in need came in. The atmosphere was friendly and informal. When John asked his girlfriend how this activity related to faith or spirituality, she replied "Imagine what those families will do once they're back on their feet! I believe in them. That's my faith."

Sadly, John replied "This is a social service organization. Unless you pray for those families, there is nothing spiritual here."

Before giving up on their relationship though, John and his girlfriend went to a couples' counselor. The counselor helped them understand how their different backgrounds had primed them for certain spiritual beliefs. John had grown up in a strict household where sensory pleasures were discouraged, except in the context of religious services. His girlfriend had grown up in an impoverished family reliant on food banks, until her professional success allowed her to "give back" to others. Nevertheless, both believed strongly in reaching out to those in need: John because it was a way of showing others the love he had experienced from God; his girlfriend because of her view that all people are interconnected and have something valuable to contribute to the human family. As the two young people came to respect one another's perspectives, some of the differences between them seemed less significant than before. Eventually, they developed a satisfying long-term relationship.

Spirituality and Empathy: Present-Focused, Inclusive, Humble Ideals

Although the previous section described a number of spiritually based ideological impediments to empathy, many spiritual practices increase the capacity for empathy. Recall from Chapter 5 that two key components of empathy are the ability to transcend the focus on oneself or survival and the motivation to attend to others' experience in the present moment. Spiritual practices can help people develop each of these components.

Self-Transcendence

Self-transcendence is encouraged in different ways, but often begins with reassuring the believer of safety. Reassurance of safety is clearest in those traditions that depict God in parental form and encourage a relationship with God that mirrors a secure attachment relationship (Belavich and Pargament, 2002). As in secure attachment, the Divine is seen as unconditionally loving, encouraging and strengthening the believer, and available to return to regardless of how far the believer "wanders off track". The story of the Prodigal Son (Luke 15:11–32 English Standard Version), for instance, describes this relationship between the longsuffering Divine and human frailty using the metaphor of a father-son relationship that is broken and then restored. Many people, regardless of personal attachment history, can find solace in their faith in such a "Perfect Attachment Figure".

Such faith can also reduce anxiety about an uncertain future, allowing for greater attention to the present moment. There is a sense that, like a good parent, God will look after the believer whatever comes. The resulting tolerance of uncertainty frees the believer to attend to what is happening in the present, including opportunities for empathy.

Traditions that do not include parentified gods can also promote a sense of safety. The support of a caring spiritual community, for example, can reduce anxiety about both current and future safety. Familiar rituals also promote a sense of comfort and certainty in many traditions. Meditative practices and prayers that root the practitioner in the present also reduce worry and the tendency to get drawn into fight or flight reactions which interfere with empathy.

Spiritual approaches that help people cope with stress in calm ways that preserve empathy have been further described by Pargament (see Pargament, 1997). Benevolent reappraisal, for example, allows the believer to see the stress as beneficial in a spiritual context. He or she might see the stress as part of God's plan or as a means of developing spiritual strength, improving coping and preserving the capacity for empathy. Collaborative religious coping is another spiritual approach to stress. In this case, the believer engages in "problem-solving with God" through prayer or other practices. The resulting solutions are often considerate of others as well as one's own interests, and reduce the tendency to respond with fear or anger. Seeking support from one's religious community or providing support to others in that community obviously involves empathy, and effectively buffers stress for many people of faith.

Another aspect of self-transcendence emphasized by many traditions is an appreciation of the limits of human power and human understanding. When we take our own power too seriously, we lose the capacity to attend to other people's perspectives and to global perspectives on problems. For instance, we think that asserting our own economic interests is more important than "the environment", without recognizing that we are all part of that planetary environment, and by failing to preserve it we only hurt ourselves in the long run. Therefore, many spiritual traditions emphasize reverence for the natural world.

When we assume we know more than we do, we can also become arrogant and dismissive of others' points of view. Therefore, many spiritual traditions emphasize humility regarding the limits of our own knowledge. For instance, the Sacred may be seen as too great to be grasped by limited human minds, and thus ultimately unknowable. Images of the Sacred are prohibited in some traditions for this reason. In the Old Testament, the prophet Micah summarizes faithful living as "to do justice, and to love kindness, and to walk humbly with your God" (Micah 6:8 English Standard Version). Humility is placed right next to kindness (often equated with compassion or empathy), underscoring its importance for people of faith. In some Buddhist practices, the believer is encouraged to struggle with paradoxical riddles called koans with the goal of ultimately recognizing the limits of his or her understanding.

Interestingly, the limits to knowledge have one further implication: if the Sacred is ultimately unknowable, then how can we presume that He/She/It conforms to our own particular creed? Wouldn't the Sacred be greater than anything our human minds could grasp? Acknowledging that there are limits to our understanding implies that there may be other "understandings" that are equally valid. Empathy for people of other traditions becomes easier when we keep this point in mind, and may allow us to celebrate a diversity of traditions that meet different psychological and spiritual needs for different people.

Attending to Others

The motivation to attend to others' experience and respond empathetically is consistent with a number of virtues that cross spiritual traditions. It is also encouraged in most faith communities, both verbally and by engaging members in altruistic activities. The virtues have received renewed attention through Positive Psychology, as described in Chapter 1.

The universality of the Golden Rule was mentioned earlier, but other virtues can contribute to empathy as well. For example, what is gratitude but the ability to focus on the positive parts of our present and past experience, instead of resentments and fear, freeing us to attend to others in the moment? What is forgiveness but the ability to not dwell on negative interpersonal experiences, opening us to new relationships? What is hope but the ability to not worry about the future, knowing that (perhaps with the help of faith) we will respond to it and to others well? What is humility but the acknowledgement that we don't know everything and can't do everything we would like on our own, so we must value others' perspectives and aid?

All of these virtues encourage the believer to seek what benefits everyone rather than focusing on personal gain. All contribute toward the respectful, attentive human relationships Buber characterized as "I-Thou" (see Buber, 1937/2004), where we honor the person rather than what he or she can do for us. All can contribute to what Haidt (2003) described as "elevation": the positive emotion that occurs when people realize they have done something that benefits another person, prompting them to do more good deeds, in a positive cycle of virtue.

The virtues are not fixed attributes of any particular person or any particular faith. Everyone has days where their behavior is far from virtuous! Rather, the virtues remind us of what is important in the midst of our ever-changing, ever-challenging lives. Like lighthouses in the storm, they beckon us toward a better, calmer, more empathetic way of living.

Social Attitudes and Empathy

As described in Chapter 3, empathy is often compromised in societies characterized by a wide gap between rich and poor, emphasis on materialism, and emphasis on obedience to authority. Here, we examine personal social attitudes that can impact the capacity for empathy. Some of these relate to the human tendency toward tribalism, others to a false sense of autonomy that may arise when people place their individual dreams and desires ahead of those of the "tribe" or community. What they have in common is a skewed view of life that denies the interdependence of all people, and perhaps all beings that share this world. Conversely, the appreciation of our interdependence can be a powerful motivator toward empathy.

Tribalism

Tribalism occurs when people sacrifice their intellectual freedom for the sake of belonging to a particular social group (James, 2006). As mentioned in Chapter 2, oxytocin (the chemical that is supposed to promote empathy) actually enhances tribalism. This fact probably reflects our evolutionary history, when it was adaptive for human beings to prioritize the needs of the group above their own. Ostracism from the group would have exposed the individual to a multitude of dangers, reducing the chances of survival. Therefore, allegiance to the group became a highly valued trait. One can imagine that those who possessed this trait, and the high oxytocin levels associated with it, were more likely to survive long enough to reproduce, preserving the trait over time.

Unfortunately, allegiance to one's "tribe" can be associated with excluding or denigrating outsiders. If the "tribe" consists of people of one's own race, it can result in racism; if it consists of people of one's own gender, it can result in sexism; if it consists of people of one's own economic level, it can result in blaming the less affluent for their plight or envying the more affluent; if it consists of people who are able-bodied, it can result in prejudice toward people with disabilities. The list is not complete, as almost everyone considers some people outsiders with respect to their own social group.

To avoid having this attitude impair our capacity for empathy we need to make a concerted effort to understand and respect the "outsiders". Listening to perspectives from outside one's "tribe" is often a first step in this direction. For example, when trying to address historical injustice toward a particular group, allowing members of that group to tell their stories is critically important. It has been a central process in all efforts at Truth and Reconciliation around the globe. Dialogue with "outsiders" is central to ecumenical movements within religions; similarly, giving the poor a voice is central to movements for social justice.

Moreover, we need to recognize that denigrating the "outsider" is unfair, particularly when it comes to those who may appear less accomplished than ourselves. For instance, Diamond's *Guns, Germs, and Steel* (see Diamond, 1999) eloquently describes the multiple geographic influences that have dictated the evolution of civilizations. He describes how the differences between countries in the developed and the developing world have more to do with location than with the attributes of people who live there. Thus, the poverty of Africa relates largely to the physical geography of Africa, rather than Africans. Conversely, those of us living in developed countries have virtually "won the lottery" of prosperity long before we accomplish anything in our individual lives. What a powerful argument against racism!

Individualism

Individualism, on the surface, appears to be the opposite of tribalism. Here, the emphasis is on people's ability to shape their own destiny (Wood, 1972), regardless of those around them. Freedom to think and act independently is celebrated. People may be encouraged to set ambitious goals for themselves and persevere until they achieve them. It is a popular attitude in developed countries, where circumstances often favor advancement up the social hierarchy for hardworking individuals. Dreams of a better future often inspire this progression, and help the dreamer formulate effective ways of reaching personal goals.

Despite its obvious benefits, individualism can impair empathy when taken to the extreme. One issue has already been mentioned: the tendency of successful individuals to develop the "tribal" attitude that less successful individuals are to be denigrated (e.g., thinking the poor are lazy or lacking in ambition). A second attitude that can reduce empathy is the assumption that only money-earners contribute something to society, which can result in dismissing the contributions of those with disabilities or those who focus on the unpaid work of parenting or caregiving. Third, when dreams of future success become a preoccupation, empathetic behavior in the present may suffer. Ambitious people sometimes come to believe that "the end justifies the means", and neglect the impact of their success-oriented behaviors on those around them or on the environment. In a group project, for instance, a leader may prioritize the success of the project over the well-being of the group members who are working together to complete it. In the short term, this lack of empathy may ensure timely and successful achievement of a goal; in the long term, it will likely reduce people's motivation to work further with this leader. Finally, individualism can result in a false assumption: the assumption that the individual's capacity for independent work in some circumstances represents total independence from other human beings. To illustrate this assumption, consider the following example.

Dana

Although raised in a deprived and depressing home environment, Dana was an excellent student. Every August she looked forward to the smells of September. In kindergarten it had been an admixture of crayons and stale apples brought for the teacher. Later, it became the aroma emanating from new textbooks as they were cracked open for the first time. She read voraciously, usually finishing the yearly texts by October and then moving on to more interesting fare at the library.

Desperate for the nurturing relationships she lacked at home, Dana focused on getting high marks to please her teachers. They were usually pleased, but few took a personal interest like her middle school English teacher, who praised her special talent as a writer. Dana lived for that praise, and the ability to earn it from other teachers kept her optimistic and emotionally stable in high school. After high school, university offered the promise of escaping her depressing home environment and, of course, impressing professors. She continued to work hard, excelled academically, and won scholarships.

Shortly after her university graduation, Dana met a slightly older man from a similar background who was less studious but just as goal-oriented. He was working his way up at a major corporation, and admired Dana's self-reliance and focus. He described previous women he had dated as overly clingy and "touchy-feely". With Dana, on the other hand, he could laugh, talk about their respective goals, debate political views, draw up financial plans for their future, enjoy a healthy sexual relationship, and avoid discussing anything he considered "complicated or messy". Dana, for her part, had found a romantic partner who was also someone she admired and sought to impress. It seemed a perfect match.

Dana and her husband were both successful but not always kind people. They had learned to "tune out" the distress of people around them in order to remain focused on their goals. Their political views leaned towards the right, and they assumed that those who were less successful than they were simply didn't work hard enough. The couple supported each other when needed, but this was rare as both Dana and her husband were very self-reliant. Dana sometimes wondered if the relationship was lacking in emotional intimacy, but when she saw how intensely her friends fought with their spouses she was grateful for the peaceful, stable marriage she had.

Inevitably, life's "messiness" eventually intruded: Dana and her husband had a daughter who contracted meningitis and became severely disabled. The need to care for her eventually compromised Dana's career aspirations.

Then, contrary to everything they believed in, Dana and her husband had to apply for government assistance to pay for their daughter's expensive medical and rehabilitative treatments.

As they started telling others about their situation, however, something surprising happened. People they had barely said "hello" to came to the rescue. Colleagues, neighbours, and families whose children had attended the same daycare as their daughter showed up with food, gifts, and offers to help. Often, they stayed for a cup of tea and listened to the couple's concerns. Some even did chores around the house while the young family got back on its feet.

Dana's husband was grateful, but embarrassed about accepting help. Dana, on the other hand, was overwhelmed and perplexed by the response. "I never thought of myself as living in a community," she remarked, "but I obviously live in a very caring one." She realized she was depending on others, and probably always had to a degree. She no longer clung to the myth of self-sufficiency she had previously believed. As she appreciated the kindness of neighbors, she became kinder too. She no longer limited their friends to those who were considered "successful" by conventional standards. She looked for opportunities to give back to those who had been so generous. Her vision had broadened to include those around her, her companions on the journey, and she related to them genuinely and empathetically.

Although we don't all experience calamities as life-altering as Dana's, most people encounter situations which turn their long-term goals and dreams upside down. Broken dreams are part of the human condition. We can respond by becoming cynical, succumbing to depression, developing new dreams, or reflecting on what has happened before going further. If we take the latter approach, broken dreams can be a wake-up call rather than a curse: a chance to re-evaluate ourselves and our priorities in life.

In Dana's case, a devastating family crisis caused her to change her previous philosophy of extreme individualism. That philosophy seemed to make sense when she was young and needed to prioritize success for both emotional stability and career advancement. It persisted as she found and lived with a like-minded partner. When she needed to accept help from others though, she could no longer cling to the belief in her own total independence. She also realized that those "others", though less successful than she was by conventional or monetary standards, were wonderful people who generously shared their time with her and with her child. Her bias against less accomplished people vanished. Furthermore, she realized that her overemphasis on dreams of future glory had diverted her attention away from present-day experiences. As she attended more to those experiences and to the people with whom she interacted, her social attitudes shifted and her capacity for empathy increased.

Interdependence

Social attitudes that acknowledge interdependence among people are often conducive to empathy. These attitudes involve acknowledging that we are sometimes able to help ourselves and help others, but at other times we need help from others. Problems with denying that we need help from others were illustrated in the example of Dana. Denying that we are able to help ourselves or others can also be problematic though. When we deny that we can help ourselves, we may unfairly blame others for our plight and/or become passive in the face of difficulties rather than seeking solutions to them. When we deny that we can help others, we may accept social problems as "inevitable" rather than contributing time or money to help change them. We may also minimize the potential of our own daily interactions with others to make a positive difference. These attitudes are unfortunate, as passivity, blame, and lack of individual or collective effort are clearly obstacles to empathy and to altruistic behavior.

By contrast, attitudes that acknowledge interdependence and actions based upon them have a vast potential impact (see Barabasi, 2003; Travers and Milgram, 1969). This is because all people on the planet are connected to each other by a rather small number of steps (some have theorized, on average six steps). That is, if you say something to a friend, whether encouraging or hurtful, that message or attitude is communicated to another person, then another, then another, and so on, and within about six steps it has reached everyone. Now, of course, many things we say or do are not profound enough to merit further communication to this degree, but some are. Thus, we each have the potential to change the world through one word or one action. This thought can inspire both exhilarating optimism and a frightening sense of responsibility.

Focusing on the optimistic implications, we can see that no small act of kindness is meaningless, as it can contribute directly or indirectly to kindness in the world. No person is without value, as each can add something unique to the whole of humanity. No person is alone, as all are connected to others whether they are aware of it or not. In short, we all belong to one human family. Whether we show empathy toward other members of that family is up to us, but what we do to any one member affects the whole family.

Showing Empathy when We Don't Share the Patient's World View

Therapists often struggle to remain empathetic when facing differences between their own social attitudes or spiritual beliefs and those of the patient, as illustrated in the following example.

Darren

Darren was a successful salesman who suffered from recurrent bouts of depression that were severe enough to result in several hospitalizations in his twenties. They were less dramatic now, as he was approaching retirement, but he still needed monthly follow-up to monitor medication and maintain stable moods. I provided that follow-up.

Darren seemed to enjoy the appointments, though I hardly got in a word. Instead, Darren would tell me at length about various people he blamed for the unhappiness in his life. Anecdotes about his co-workers were followed by disparaging remarks about immigrants taking jobs from North American workers, smelling up the office with foreign foods, and not bothering to learn English. I'm not sure if he knew that I came to North America in infancy, and am thus an immigrant. Stories about Darren's wife would lead to disparaging remarks about women being "gold-diggers" who only used men for monetary gain. He seemed oblivious to the fact that I was a woman raising a family without male financial support.

Challenging Darren's views was pointless, as he would then either withdraw or dismiss my comments as reflecting inexperience (Darren was older than me). Saying nothing about them made me cringe. Yet, Darren seemed compelled to tell me his views in confidence as he knew they were "not politically correct" and could get him into trouble if expressed too openly.

Eventually, I realized that what worked best was to ask Darren questions about the impact of his experiences and his views on his happiness. How did he feel when he dwelled on the anger toward the people he blamed? How did he feel when he focused on other aspects of life? Were there activities he enjoyed when not plagued by resentment? Could he find some peace of mind despite the events he described? Were there positive aspects to some of his relationships, particularly that with his wife? Was it helpful to focus on these aspects?

Although I was never quite able to put myself in Darren's shoes, he seemed to feel understood when I engaged in this concerned questioning about his well-being. Even though I didn't feel very empathetic towards him, I tried to show empathy in my communication with him, and he appreciated it. Gradually, he dwelled less on his hateful opinions and became more contented with life. He still held the same views but they no longer took centre stage, so he became able to attend to his surroundings and started to enjoy simple pleasures again.

The approach I took with Darren is one I sometimes find helpful with delusional patients: I focus on how they can find contentment despite their symptoms, rather than challenging the symptoms directly. Of course, Darren's social opinions are not really "symptoms" but a product of negative interpersonal experiences which resulted in a lack of empathy and a tendency to blame certain segments of the population, mainly immigrants and women. I sometimes found Darren's prejudices infuriating, but I also saw him as a suffering human being, so tried to be helpful rather than excluding him from my practice.

Patients whose spiritual views differ from my own can also pose challenges. Although not as exasperating as Darren, these patients can be confusing, as one struggles to respond to them in a manner that is helpful, appropriate to their spiritual context, and does not offend their sensibilities. Highly stressful events such as bereavement or trauma are often overwhelming, and thus particularly likely to elicit spiritual coping responses that may or may not be adaptive for the patient. When one does not share the patient's spiritual views, it can be difficult to formulate an empathetic response to such events.

For instance, when a patient states "God is punishing me by letting my daughter die", do you respond from within a secular framework (consistent with the training of most mental health professionals), a conservative religious framework (consistent with the patient's world view), or your own spiritual framework? Do you say "That may be your grief talking" (secular world view), "We cannot know God's reasons, but they may not relate to punishment" (patient's world view), or "God isn't like that" (personal view)? Usually, I find it is least empathetic to choose the final option, as disagreeing about spiritual matters is almost never comforting or validating for the patient.

Instead, there may be value in regarding patients' spiritual beliefs and experiences with empathetic curiosity (Bullis, 1996). In this case, one might ask concerned questions about the context of the daughter's passing, aspects of the patient's previous history that are inducing guilt (as implied by the belief he or she is being punished), and past experiences related to spirituality and religion that have shaped his or her view of God. In the course of the discussion, the patient may or may not find a more comforting response to the loss (e.g., focusing on the daughter being with God and therefore well looked-after, regardless of the reasons) but hopefully the presence of another concerned human being assures the patient that their grief will not be borne alone.

A further therapeutic challenge occurs when a patient's behavior violates one's own spiritual or moral beliefs. Showing empathy can be particularly difficult in such cases. For example, I sometimes see single parents who frequently switch live-in boyfriends or live-in girlfriends, exposing their children to an emotionally unstable environment. They then blame the children for misbehaving, even though the lack of consistency at home would (in my opinion) make almost any child act out. Trying to explain this issue to the parents empathetically, without sounding judgmental or sanctimonious, can be a real challenge. Before starting the explanation, I often find it helpful to remind myself of my own limitations as a parent: Have I ever been impatient or inconsistent with my own children? Have I ever favored one child over the other? Have I ever made choices that were not in the children's best interest? No parent provides their children with an ideal childhood, even those of us trained in mental health who should know better. Remembering one's own shortcomings can reduce the tendency to judge others, and open the door to greater empathy.

Occasionally, the patient's world view seems very foreign to the therapist or it is difficult to distinguish spiritual beliefs from psychiatric problems. In this case, it may be helpful to encourage discussion with a leader of his or her faith before trying to work with the patient empathetically. I sometimes encounter this situation with patients who have Obsessive Compulsive Disorder characterized by scrupulosity (a very high moral standard, and rituals that relate to that standard).

For instance, a very scrupulous boy whose faith emphasized reverence for all life became preoccupied with the possibility of having unwittingly stepped on an ant or other small insect. He had to retrace his steps multiple times to reassure himself this had not happened, to the point of becoming unable to walk outside his home. My suggestion to compare this behavior to what was normative among other people of his faith fell on deaf ears. "I wouldn't jump off a cliff if everyone else did", he dryly remarked. I suggested a discussion with an authority figure in his faith. Fortunately, this man recognized the boy's problem and provided some kind, reassuring advice. As a result, the boy was finally able to see that his standard for himself was excessive and that the rituals were part of an illness, rather than part of his faith. Only then did he become amenable to psychiatric treatment.

Thus, developing empathy with patients whose beliefs and social attitudes differ from our own can be particularly challenging, as can developing empathy for those who violate our own moral standards. Further challenges to developing empathy in psychotherapy are discussed in the next chapter.

Summary

- Beliefs and ideals often meet psychological needs, so differences among them may reflect different people's different psychological needs rather than "correct" or "incorrect" world views.
- Prioritizing human relationships in the present is needed to maintain empathy, particularly if one's beliefs include a focus on future reward or judgment.
- Empathetic people have an intrinsic orientation to faith; to paraphrase a famous saying, they more often ask what they can do for their faith than what their faith can do for them.
- Spiritual beliefs and practices can promote self-transcendence and the motivation to attend to others in many different ways, all of which can be conducive to empathy.
- Tribalism and a false sense of autonomy related to extreme individualism are social attitudes that can undermine empathy; listening to perspectives from outside one's social group, recognizing that differences among groups may relate to circumstances, and honoring all people's contributions, whether monetary or not, may modify these attitudes.
- The appreciation of human interdependence can be a powerful motivator toward empathy as we recognize how we impact others directly and indirectly, and also our reliance on other members of the human family.
- Benign curiosity is often a helpful approach when dealing with patients whose spiritual or social attitudes differ from one's own.
- Remembering one's own shortcomings is important in order to develop empathy for patients whose behavior violates one's own moral code.
- When patients' views differ greatly from one's own, consultation with a spiritual leader in their community may be helpful.

Reflective Questions

1 What aspects of your spiritual tradition enhance empathy for others? What aspects (if any) interfere with empathy for others? Which of these aspects do you focus on more consistently?
2 Which of your social attitudes enhance empathy for others? Which of your social attitudes (if any) interfere with empathy for others? Which of these attitudes do you focus on more consistently?

Questions for Therapists

1 Have any of your spiritual beliefs posed challenges in developing therapeutic relationships with clients? How have you addressed those challenges?
2 Have any of your social attitudes posed challenges in developing therapeutic relationships with clients? How have you addressed those challenges?
3 How would you be helpful to "Darren" or another client whose view of society is very different from your own?
4 How would you be helpful to a client whose spiritual or moral views are very different from your own?

References

Armstrong, K. (1999). *A History of God: The 4000 Year Quest of Judaism, Christianity, and Islam.* New York: Vintage Books.
Barabasi, A.L. (2003). *Linked: How Everything Is Connected to Everything Else and What It Means for Business, Science, and Everyday Life.* New York: Plume Publishing.
Bullis, R.K. (1996). *Spirituality in Social Work Practice.* New York: Taylor & Francis. p. 48.
Belavich, T.G. and Pargament, K.I. (2002). The role of attachment in predicting spiritual coping with a loved one in surgery. *Journal of Adult Development*, 9, 13–29.
Buber, M. (1937). *I and Thou.* New York: Charles Scribner's Sons. Reprinted byContinuum International Publishing Group, 2004.
Diamond, J. (1999). *Guns, Germs, and Steel.* New York: W.W. Norton & Company.
Haidt, J. (2003). Elevation and the positive psychology of morality. In C.L.M. Keyes and J. Haidt (Eds.) *Flourishing: Positive Psychology and the Life Well-lived.* Washington, DC: American Psychological Association, pp. 275–289.
James, P. (2006). *Globalism, Nationalism, Tribalism: Bringing Theory Back In.* London: Sage Publications. p. 5.
James, W. (2009). *The Varieties of Religious Experience: A Study in Human Nature.* New York: Seven Treasures Publications.
Luke 15: 11–32; *The Bible: English Standard Version.*
Matheson, R. (1978). *What Dreams May Come.* New York: Tom Doherty Associates.
Matthew 7:12. *The Bible: English Standard Version.*

Micah 6:8. *The Bible: English Standard Version.*
Music, G. (2014). *The Good Life: Well-being and the New Science of Altruism, Selfishness, and Immorality.* New York: Routledge.
Pargament, K.I. (1997). *The Psychology of Religion and Coping: Theory, Research, Practice.* New York: Guilford Press.
Travers, J. and Milgram, S. (1969). An experimental study of the small world problem. *Sociometry,* 32: 425–443.
Wilkinson, R. and Pickett, K. (2009). *The Spirit Level: Why More Equal Societies Almost Always Do Better.* New York: Allen Lane. p. 352.
Wood, E.M. (1972). *Mind and Politics: An Approach to the Meaning of Liberal and Socialist Individualism.* Oakland, CA: University of California Press, p. 6.

Part III

Developing Empathy: Why Bother?

9 Implications for Therapists

> Empathy is in itself a healing agent...it brings even the most frightened client into the human race. If a person is understood, he or she belongs.
>
> Carl Rogers (1986)

In Part III ideas discussed earlier in the book are organized and applied to three specific audiences: therapists, parents, and leaders. Then the final chapter highlights empathy-related ideas that are relevant to all human beings. The quote eloquently highlights the role of empathy as a therapeutic agent, conveying reassurance and inclusion. Before further exploring the role of empathy in psychotherapy though, let me comment on all of the audiences addressed in Part III.

The three specific audiences all represent authority figures of different types. As such, they have additional responsibilities relevant to empathy beyond behaving empathetically in one to one relationships. Authority figures are role models that others often emulate, and so can influence the development of empathy in others through their behavior. Therapists who show self-compassion by not overscheduling their day and who treat their receptionists kindly are role models of empathy, as are parents who show empathy toward spouses, teachers, store clerks or other people they interact with in view of their children. Organizational and political leaders are often in the public spotlight, creating ample opportunities to role model empathy.

Furthermore, authority figures are often in charge of groups of people or of systems that influence multiple individuals. Although this is most obvious in positions of official leadership, parents can be considered leaders of family systems (see Chapter 3) and therapists may be influential in mental health care systems by advocating for policies that support better patient care. Creating groups or systems that foster empathy rather than competition is no easy task, and is discussed in more detail in Chapter 11.

In this chapter, we begin to think about empathy in relation to psychotherapy. Implications relevant to assessment, goals of therapy, process of therapy, and content of therapy emerge. Each will be discussed in turn in a manner that, hopefully, crosses various theoretical orientations. If you have been working through the Questions for Therapists in each chapter, you may have already discovered these or similar ideas. In this case, consider this chapter a helpful review. If not, now may be an opportunity to reflect upon the implications of this book for your practice. Think about whether or not you want to change any aspects of assessment, goal-setting, therapeutic process, or therapeutic content in response to the ideas presented here. Also, if you haven't answered the Questions for Therapists from previous chapters, it might be helpful to do so now.

Chapter 9 concludes by discussing advocacy on behalf of our patients as a part of empathetic psychotherapy. After reading this section, think about any situations where your patients might be disadvantaged by policies or mental health systems issues in your area. How could you begin to address these disadvantages? How would this project impact your usual practice and priorities? To begin, however, let's look at empathy in relation to assessment for psychotherapy.

Assessment

In North America, much of the mental health assessment that precedes psychotherapy focuses on diagnosis of mental illness. In current diagnostic manuals, the hallmark of most mental illnesses is that they cause the individual distress, impairment in his or her adaptive functioning, or both (see American Psychiatric Association, 2013). This is consistent with our culture's individualistic perspective on mental health and mental illness. Few diagnostic criteria mention the impact of the illness on other people with whom the patient may come in contact. The Personality Disorders do so, but mainly in terms of their effect on the patient's relationships rather than the effect on other people per se.

Therefore, our assessments sometimes neglect this important aspect of mental illness: its impact on those around the patient, as well as the impact of those people upon the patient. For instance, suppose that Darren, the salesman with sexist and anti-immigrant views described in the previous chapter, had started to act on some of his hateful ideas. What if he reported vandalizing community centres or places of worship frequented by the immigrants he despised? To what extent should one's empathy for the patient and obligation to maintain doctor-patient confidentiality supersede empathy for the other human beings touched by the patient's actions? In my jurisdiction, confidentiality is only breached when patients pose an imminent danger to themselves or others. I'm not sure spray-painting a place of worship constitutes "imminent danger", so would probably not report Darren's actions. However, his actions could contribute to others' hatred of certain groups of people, potentially causing those groups to face dangerous consequences later. Awareness of the impact of our patients' actions on others and empathy for those people can create some difficult ethical dilemmas for mental health providers.

Not asking about these actions, however, may be even more problematic. When we focus narrowly on symptoms, we may never hear about the people in the patient's environment who could be affected by them. Extreme cases where people are harmed or even killed by those with mental health problems may make headlines, but every patient's illness affects those around them to some extent. As a child psychiatrist, for instance, I often see children whose parents are being treated for mental illness. With the parent's permission, I sometimes communicate with the parental mental health provider. That provider is often astonished to hear how profoundly the patient's symptoms are impacting his or her children. If you see primarily adult patients, please remember to ask if they are parents, and if so how their illness is affecting the children.

Including a biopsychosocial assessment of factors contributing to the patient's symptoms often improves the chances of discovering the effects of symptoms on other people. This assessment always includes questions about how the environment is affecting the patient's symptoms, making it easy to ask, conversely, how the patient's symptoms are affecting those in his or her environment.

Often, factors contributing to symptoms are also relevant to the patient's capacity for empathy. For example, as discussed in Chapter 2, insecure attachment relationships in early childhood place the patient at risk for both psychopathology and impairments in empathy. The same could be said of traumatic experiences. On the other hand, nurturing, encouraging environments that might reduce the risk of anxiety or depression would probably contribute to the development of empathy.

Therefore, a review of biopsychosocial factors relevant to empathy may enrich mental health professionals' understanding of their clients' difficulties beyond that offered by diagnostic assessment. The summary tables in Chapter 2 and Chapter 3 offer a guide to, respectively, developmental factors that may influence empathy positively or negatively and social influences on empathy. Although some of these influences are typically emphasized more in the mental health assessment of children (for example, those related to early development), they can contribute to understanding patients of all ages. I have written a separate book for those interested in a more detailed guide to biopsychosocial formulation with children and youth (see Manassis, 2014).

Moreover, most patients tend to appreciate an assessor who takes an interest in life experiences that are not necessarily symptom-related. Doing so acknowledges that the patient is a complex human being, with positive experiences and strengths as well as difficulties. Thus, it is often experienced as empathetic and encouraging. These additional aspects of the patient's life story can also be built upon in subsequent psychotherapeutic work, whether or not that work is focused on developing greater empathy. Knowing that a patient used to be praised for his or her musical ability by an empathetic teacher, for instance, may suggest that picking up his or her favorite instrument again might be helpful in recovering from depression.

Finally, the experience of assessment should be characterized by empathy, gentleness, and a constructive conclusion whenever possible. Too many patients report being asked detailed, intrusive questions about their worst life experiences during assessment, feeling emotionally devastated, and then being told that the process is over and they are free to leave. The assessor in this case has failed to address the raw emotions uncovered by his or her questions, and has not provided any constructive suggestions to help the patient move forward from this experience. Time constraints are no excuse for this lack of empathy. When a difficult topic is raised, it is the assessor's responsibility to decide if it can be explored and addressed fully during that session or needs to be deferred to another day when there is more time and more opportunity to empathetically support the patient through the discussion.

The Goals of Therapy

Jason

I rarely refuse to provide psychotherapy to a patient because of the risk of side effects, but in Jason's case I did. Jason was a husky 15 year old whose mother brought him in for "insomnia and nerves, just like me". Sure enough, Jason's mother had severe Generalized Anxiety Disorder (a tendency to worry excessively) and had been prescribed several medications for this problem. Jason, on the other hand, nodded obediently when his mother described his symptoms but indicated they were "not that bad" and were common in high school students his age.

When interviewed alone, Jason indicated he had trouble sleeping ever since starting a new school several months earlier. Intrigued, I asked about how the new school differed from the old one. "Same boring classes, same boring teachers," Jason started, "but the people are different." When asked to elaborate, he told me his friends at the new school spent afternoons at the mall. They often dared each other to shoplift small items without getting caught. Recently, their petty crimes had escalated to include stealing from their peers by cornering them in the schoolyard and threatening to cut them with a knife. One of Jason's friends had recently mentioned that his father owned a gun. Jason was a reluctant participant in his new friends' activities, but wanted to fit in with the group. He felt badly about robbing and threatening others. He couldn't fall asleep at night because he worried about the police knocking on his door.

When Jason's mother asked me to provide psychotherapy for her son's worries, I refused. Helping Jason worry less about harming others would have condoned his illegal behavior, potentially contributing to harm to other community members. Jason's worries were preventing him from behaving even worse! Instead, I discussed with Jason the risks and the benefits of continuing to associate with his new friends. After recognizing that these friendships were not worth the risk, Jason was able to tell his mother about the reasons for his worries. Once she called his school about the issue Jason's principal became involved and put a stop to the schoolyard robberies before anyone was seriously hurt.

Jason's case raises a number of interesting therapeutic issues. First, parental reports of children's feelings often need to be taken with a grain of salt. Only the young person can tell you whether or not they are truly anxious or depressed, and what the reasons are for those feelings. As shown in this case, the reasons may or may not relate to a psychiatric disorder. Jason's worries were based on realistic concerns, so treating them involved helping him deal with reality rather than engaging in psychotherapy (for example, Cognitive Behavioral Therapy) that might have minimized their importance.

Second, when the patient poses a potential danger to others, as Jason did to his schoolmates, there are limits to therapist-patient confidentiality. Fortunately, in this case Jason had a secure enough relationship with his mother that he felt comfortable sharing his dilemma with her. If he had not done so, however, I would have had to tell her about the potential dangers he revealed to me anyways. This action might have shown a lack of empathy for Jason, but been consistent with empathy for those whom he might harm. When a patient endangers others, the therapist faces competing loyalties: loyalty to the patient versus loyalty to the greater community. Usually one can remain loyal and empathetic towards the patient, but dangerous situations are the exceptions to this rule.

Finally, and most relevant to this book, Jason's case illustrates that the goals of therapy need to include an empathetic perspective. Engaging in psychotherapy that makes someone feel less anxious or less guilty about harming others is simply not ethical, and shows a profound lack of empathy for those other people. Psychotherapy typically focuses on enhancing individual well-being, but the well-being of those around the patient must also be considered. Moreover, individual well-being is actually enhanced in the long run if others' needs are considered when setting therapeutic goals. We are relational beings, and our well-being is intertwined with that of others. The pleasure of besting others in competition is short-lived, but the joy of contributing to others' success and happiness lasts. Thus, perhaps there are situations where empathy should be an explicit therapeutic goal, rather than a mere by-product of greater personal well-being.

Recall from Chapters 1 and 5 how the goal of symptom reduction is gradually being replaced by a broader ideal of mental health in Positive Psychology. This ideal, abbreviated in the PERMA acronym includes engagement in interesting activity, relationships, and meaning or sense of purpose, as well as the traditional, individualistic goals of positive emotion and accomplishments (Seligman and Csikszentmihalyi, 2000). Similarly, the capacity for self-observation, cited as a common therapeutic outcome by many authors (see Chapter 5), reduces self-absorption and therefore facilitates empathy. As discussed in Part II, therapeutic goals related to better physical health, cognitive and emotional perspective-taking, developing clear psychological boundaries, coming to terms with difficult relationship issues, and taming the "fight or flight" response also contribute to the capacity for empathy indirectly.

The social ideals discussed in Chapter 8 raise a further interesting question: should our therapeutic goals emphasize patient autonomy or an ability to accept and live well with interdependence? The answer probably depends on the patient in question. Patients who are dependent on abusive or addicted partners would clearly benefit from greater autonomy. Such autonomy would improve both personal well-being and empathy for others with the possible exception of the problematic partner. On the other hand, the false sense of independence shown in the example of Dana (Chapter 8) was clearly not healthy, and interfered with her capacity for empathy. In this case, accepting and living well with interdependence was a helpful outcome. It seems that empathy flourishes in relationships where neither extreme prevails: where we are independent enough to speak empathetically but honestly regarding our concerns about one another yet able to humbly acknowledge that we don't have all the answers and that we often need one another's support. I believe this outcome would be ideal for most patients.

The Process of Therapy and the Therapeutic Relationship

The process of therapy includes numerous pragmatic issues such as scheduling, payment, and dealing with tardiness or missed appointments, as well as the actual conversations between therapist and patient. The therapist who works outside a large institution is in the odd position of being both helpful counselor and owner of a small business. These roles often conflict and pose challenges to maintaining empathetic patient-therapist relationships. Nevertheless, we may provide role models of empathy (or not) through the manner in which we conduct the "business" of psychotherapy.

As discussed in Chapter 6, it is important to not allow daily stresses associated with practice or "burnout" to interfere with empathy in relation to our patients. It is often more helpful and empathetic to patients to take a vacation that reduces access to care than to persevere when one is in a very tired, cynical, grumpy, or depleted state. Therapist absences sometimes challenge patients to grow; "going through the motions" of psychotherapy never does. Managing our own stresses well is sometimes important to patient safety too, as the tragic example of Marvin in Chapter 1 illustrated.

Patients who are inconsiderate of the therapist and of other patients pose a particular challenge in psychotherapy. Personally, I find them more difficult to manage than characters like Darren from Chapter 8 whose views I find offensive. Ideology can be more readily understood in relation to a person's psychological needs (see Chapter 8) than actions that show a clear disregard for others. For example, some patients either repeatedly fail to show up for appointments or show up very late, disrupting care for subsequent patients. These patients seem to be oblivious to the impact that their behavior has on the therapist's ability to earn a living and on other patients who may be discussing sensitive issues just as they barge in. Although it may seem harsh, having clear financial consequences for such behavior (commensurate with patient socioeconomic level) is often more empathetic to everyone in the practice than allowing it to continue. Sometimes, this changes the behavior and allows the therapist to explore (among other issues) the psychological reasons for it. If the behavior persists despite these consequences, then referral to a colleague who is either more tolerant or better able to manage such patients may make sense. Patients who repeatedly engender resentment in their therapist are unlikely to be shown much empathy, and are thus unlikely to benefit from treatment by that therapist. It is in their best interest to be referred to someone who can work with them empathetically. On the other hand, being compassionate about sudden patient illness or death of a close family member by *not* charging for missed appointments in these cases can allow the therapist to model humane, empathetic behavior.

Beyond the pragmatics of therapy, most schools of thought agree that the patient-therapist relationship is central to therapeutic change. A key element of most psychotherapies is to connect with the mentally healthy parts of the patient empathetically in order to overcome the unhealthy parts, without letting one's own emotional issues interfere with that process. When this happens, patients feel both validated and strengthened, often facilitating change. When it does not happen, patients may feel the therapist is lecturing them without showing understanding. For instance, if an anorexic patient is asked "Has your doctor been helpful to you?" he or she may reply "No, not helpful at all. She keeps insisting I should eat more." Ironically, the goal of therapy would be to have the patient eat more, but the therapist has obviously not connected with the patient empathetically in this case, resulting in the patient resenting this goal.

The challenge of connecting empathetically with patients is similar to the challenge of establishing a secure attachment relationship as described in Chapter 2: the therapist must neither dismiss the patient's concerns nor become overly involved with those concerns. The anorexic patient, for example, may need to hear from the therapist that he or she appreciates how difficult it is for the patient to accept food when there is a constant dread of seeing a "fat person" in the mirror. To urge eating before this discussion occurs would seem dismissive of the patient's concerns. Recall, however, that empathy is also compromised when people get emotionally caught up in other people's suffering (Batson, 1987). We actually show greater empathy when we strive to understand the other person's experience without simultaneously living that experience than when we do live it. When therapy becomes distressing for the therapist, the instinct to relieve personal distress takes over, often to the patient's detriment. A caring, empathetic therapist is one who listens actively to patient concerns but remains detached enough from those concerns to think about helpful solutions.

If it is difficult to connect with the patient empathetically, consider three possibilities: first, perhaps the patient has very little mental health to build upon, in which case a treatment other than psychotherapy (for example, psychiatric medication) may be needed before he or she is ready to work with you; second, perhaps the type of treatment you provide is not ideally suited to this patient; third, perhaps there are personal issues interfering with your ability to develop empathy for the patient. The first possibility should become clear within a few sessions, and result in prompt referral to a more appropriate treatment. The second possibility may arise if one is using a particular therapeutic approach (for example, a manual-based treatment like Cognitive Behavioral Therapy) in a patient who is averse to this approach. For example, I often see children who have had very negative experiences at school and balk at using a manual because it reminds them of these experiences. In this case, modifying the treatment by using other, less literary ways of illustrating key concepts may be helpful. If the young person still protests that a treatment focused on thoughts is not relevant to their concerns, considering an alternative evidence-based treatment may be helpful.

The third possibility is perhaps the most intriguing, as it has different implications for each therapist. What personal issues typically interfere with your ability to develop empathy for patients? Personally, I struggle with whiners. When I see children who habitually elicit parental sympathy by whining, I have difficulty developing empathy for them. This may relate to the fact that I was never successful at using this strategy myself as a child, whereas my sibling seemed to be more successful at doing so. Thus, whiners rekindle old feelings of anger and sibling rivalry for me, which interferes with my empathy toward them. When seeing these children, I have to remind myself that, objectively, whining is an effective way of getting one's needs met in certain families, but is usually not adaptive in the long run as it may interfere with developing autonomy. When I can help families develop alternative patterns of interaction the whining stops, the child starts to engage in more age-appropriate behavior, and the parent-child interactions often become much more empathetic than previously. However, I don't always do well with whiners in individual psychotherapy unless they are amenable to finding other ways of getting their needs met. Knowing this personal limitation, I often focus on family patterns in these cases, or refer to a colleague who enjoys doing individual work with these children more than I do.

Assuming a somewhat empathetic relationship is established between therapist and patient, ambiguity about therapist intentions can still strain that relationship and pose challenges to empathy. For example, in my personal psychotherapy I once discussed an incident where my colleagues had treated me particularly badly. My therapist's response was "Why do you let them treat you that way?" The therapist's intentions in this case can be interpreted empathetically to mean "You deserve to be treated better", critically to mean "You are quite foolish for letting your colleagues treat you so badly," or objectively "What aspects of your development have predisposed you to this unassertive behavior?" I initially assumed that my therapist was being both critical and objective, so launched into a discussion of old childhood issues that might have contributed to unassertiveness and how I was planning to change this behavior. It took several sessions before I realized that her question was intended empathetically. Recognizing this fact restored my faith in the therapeutic relationship, and also prompted reflection on how I often assume others are being critical until proven otherwise, which can be detrimental to relationships more generally. In short, I learned to give others the benefit of the doubt. Thus, an empathetic "disconnect" in therapy is not necessarily disastrous, and can sometimes lead to important insights.

A further challenge to patient-therapist empathy occurs when change is slow or imperceptible. There are patients who attend sessions faithfully but seem to talk about the same types of problems over and over again. Therapist questions or suggestions are met with the same repetitive responses, and after a while the therapist feels more like a "professional friend" than an agent of change. As most of us are trained in methods designed to facilitate constructive change, this can be a rather frustrating experience. Although it may not seem empathetic, it is often more helpful to identify this issue for the patient than to quietly seethe with resentment. Explain that you would like to develop a therapeutic process that is more likely to meet the patient's goals, rather than just reviewing the same issues each week. Some patients are able to use this discussion to refocus on their goals; others may indicate that their goal is to have friends like the therapist, which can also become a focus for further work; some will negotiate for supportive therapy on a less frequent basis (e.g., monthly rather than weekly); only a few will leave to find a new therapist who is willing to listen to their weekly litany of woe without protest.

The Content of Therapy

Much of the content of therapy helps our patients develop one or more of the components of empathy discussed in Chapter 5. Coping strategies for dealing with stress reduce self-preoccupation. Therapeutic work on relationships often increases motivation to attend to others' perspectives and needs. Improved psychological boundaries and perspective-taking abilities improve cognitive aspects of empathy. Attachment-focused therapies often result in stronger emotional connections with others. Communicating empathy is something we model regularly in therapy, and our patients often emulate it.

Certain types of content may need to be emphasized, however, if we are to optimally support the development of empathy in our patients. Symptom reduction is certainly important, but so is the patient's ability to develop and maintain the calm, centered, outwardly focused frame of mind that allows for authentic, empathetic relationships with others. As detailed in Chapter 6, activities that support this frame of mind include (among others) physical exercise, positive sensory experiences, artistic pursuits, activities that require full concentration, altruistic activities, and mindfulness practices. Encouraging patients to engage in one or more of these activities regularly is likely to deepen their capacity for empathy.

Moreover, it is important not to shy away from discussing spiritual content. As reviewed in Chapter 8, discussions of spirituality are usually perceived as empathetic when the patient's beliefs are approached with respectful, benign curiosity. They are particularly important when patients are struggling to find a sense of purpose in life or are trying to cope with devastating life events that defy rational explanations. In these circumstances, empathy for the patient may require attention to matters outside our usual scientific comfort zone.

For some patients, spiritual or religious beliefs provide a clear sense of purpose. When they do not, however, the desire to find this sense can still be acknowledged and explored in psychotherapy. It has been said that the purpose of life is a life of purpose (Byrne, n.d.). This statement may initially sound facetious, but reflects the observation that purpose is often found in the meaningful actions people engage in day to day rather than in some grand overarching goal. Feeling that one is making a positive difference to others or to one's environment, however small, can be more satisfying than striving for future successes that may or may not materialize. This is not to say that people should stop striving, for commitment to a worthwhile goal often provides them with direction and self-discipline. However, once a goal is set it should no longer take center stage in the mind. Rather, as spiritual sages have emphasized for millennia, it is the moment by moment journey of life that takes the foreground in a life of purpose.

Victor Frankl's meaning-focused therapy, termed logotherapy, has explored this idea in detail (see Frankl, 1984). It emphasizes helping patients choose to respond to circumstances in ways that are consistent with their values. When they do so, life is experienced as having meaning. Frankl uses the metaphor of learning chess: a student might ask "What is the best move in the world?" The answer is "The move the situation calls for." As therapists, we may not all practice logotherapy, but we can certainly borrow from this wisdom.

A similar approach may be helpful when patients are trying to cope with overwhelming traumatic events or apparently pointless suffering. There are many spiritual traditions that ascribe meaning to human suffering, but in the face of catastrophic events these explanations may seem hollow to the sufferer. Psychiatrists don't do much better. Treatments for the traumatized tend to be symptom-focused and don't necessarily address the tough questions concerning why bad things happen, what they mean, and how to make them congruent with the rest of one's life story. Why does this person die and that person live? What is the purpose of an apparently random accident or illness that cuts short a vibrant, productive life? What sort of world do we live in if the basic sense of safety and stability we take for granted can vanish in a heartbeat? The struggle to find meaning in suffering is as old as the biblical Book of Job, yet continues to confound us.

In these cases, Frankl discourages quests for grand explanations for tragic events. Rather, he urges us to find meaning, and help our patients find meaning, in choosing how to respond to such events. Responding in a manner that the person feels is responsible and appropriate to the situation is encouraged. Even in extreme situations people seem to find meaning in responding well to their circumstances.

By contrast, the search for grand, abstract meanings for devastating events can be maddening. People inclined to rumination and self-analysis may be particularly prone to such futile quests to explain inexplicable life events, as I learned when I encountered such events myself several years ago. I share the following, rather personal example in the hope that it may allow you to shorten the course of mental suffering for patients you might see in similar overwhelming circumstances.

An Unexpected Tragedy

It was Victoria Day 2003, a celebration of a former British queen unique to Canada. Our city was gripped by the SARS epidemic so, even as psychiatrists, we had to work in masks and limit our patient contacts to urgent cases. Some people were anxious about this, but I knew the risk in our department was very remote, and so chose to see the reduced workload as a positive turn of events. I welcomed the extra time with my family in the suburbs.

On this day, we all went to the beach to set off fireworks. The men in the neighborhood traditionally competed to see who could create the biggest and best fireworks display over the lake. My husband was no exception. He assembled an arsenal of rockets and explosives that was both impressive and frightening. "Be careful. You're going to blow yourself up!" I shouted, as I huddled with the children at a distance. He knew what he was doing though, and the glorious display went off without a hitch. I had no reason to worry.

Six weeks later, on an ordinary Monday, he drove the children to school. We had organized our commuter lifestyle by having him start work late and finish late so he could do the morning drop-off, and having me start work early and finish early so I could do the afternoon pick-up. Before I left that morning, he wished me a good day. They were the last words I heard him say.

Just as I got home that afternoon, the telephone rang. The person at the other end identified himself as a neurologist on call to the emergency department of a major hospital. He indicated that my husband was being admitted after having a stroke, and seemed to be deteriorating. He encouraged me to come quickly. Due to the epidemic, the children couldn't come, so I first had to find someone to look after them. By the time I arrived at the hospital, my husband was in surgery. Two hours later, the surgeon walked by without a word. The anesthetist stopped when I called out and agreed to answer my questions. My husband had suffered a brain hemorrhage, likely due to undiagnosed hypertension. The surgeon had removed the blood clot, but the brainstem had already been crushed due to pressure, and only a heroic resuscitation attempt had allowed my husband to survive the procedure. When the anesthetist found out the ages of my children, she hugged me and started to cry. I appreciated the hug, but I knew then that this situation would probably not end well.

The next 36 days were surreal. They didn't match anything in my previous life experience. My husband was comatose for the first ten days, then regained consciousness but was in a "locked in" state, unable to speak or move. His vital signs gradually improved, but his functioning never did. I visited daily and read to him. When not at the hospital, I struggled. I slept little and ate almost nothing. I consulted every neurologist and neurosurgeon I knew about my husband's condition, spent nights on the internet gathering more information, hoping that by gathering knowledge I could somehow regain control of an uncontrollable situation. Meantime, I juggled looking after the children, keeping my job, dealing with bankers who had frozen all assets that were in my husband's name, and trying to find out if there was either a medical or financial power of attorney (there wasn't). The medical record indicates that I frequently talked to both medical staff and to the social worker that was eventually assigned to me. The social worker noted that I seemed thoughtful, logical, and caring throughout the ordeal. Personally, I remember being agitated and frequently questioning my sanity. I suppose I behaved more stoically than I felt.

Ultimately, my conversations with my husband's surgeon led me to one inescapable conclusion: his condition was unlikely to change, and based on my knowledge of his character I did not believe he would want to continue living in that condition. This was not an entirely logical conclusion, as I had never actually discussed this type of situation with my husband before it happened. I remember vividly one visit that seemed to confirm it for me though. Despite his paralysis, my husband had been blinking occasionally since regaining consciousness. It was unclear if this was deliberate or a reflex, as it didn't seem to occur consistently in response to yes or no questions. That day, I was informed that the lack of blinking had resulted in severe conjunctivitis. One eye had to be patched shut to treat this, and the other would likely follow in a day or two. The remaining open eye looked grotesquely bloodshot and was oozing pus. It still appears in my nightmares sometimes. The next day, I talked to the surgeon about ensuring comfort but withdrawing life-prolonging treatments. Given his strong vital signs, I was told my husband would likely last a few more days.

The next day, I tied up some loose ends at work, made sure the children were looked after, and went to the hospital, intending to stay till the end. I walked into my husband's room and found a corpse. He was still warm, and nobody had noticed he had died. I screamed. I somehow phoned some friends to get me home and contact the funeral home. I touched his forehead before I left. It was cold. I had to convince myself he was actually gone.

It took years to make this part of my life congruent with the rest. The first month I returned to work, I had panic attacks and flashbacks every time I walked into the hospital. There were constant reminders of my husband's death in this environment. When at work I felt like a fraud. As a cognitive therapist, I often told patients that the things they worried about were improbable, but in the back of my mind was a voice screaming "But there are a thousand horrible things you never thought to worry about that could happen instead!" After all, I had worried about my husband being blown up by fireworks, and never thought to worry about a blood vessel "blowing up" in his brain.

Furthermore, despite my supposedly "thoughtful" approach to my husband's illness, I felt like a killer. The minister who did the funeral service told me "you let nature take its course". Logically, he was correct, but survivor guilt does not follow the rules of logic. I journaled, I questioned my actions and my motivations, I read stories about people in "locked in" states, and I developed a morbid fascination with end of life care. I even wrote a paper about it. I felt sick to my stomach whenever I saw someone in a wheelchair. Even though it was irrational, I couldn't help thinking they were secretly accusing me of killing one of their own. I began attending church regularly, and became convinced that God had forgiven me. Unfortunately, that didn't mean I could forgive myself.

I also struggled with the question "why"? Why would someone in the prime of life with no risk factors apart from a few extra pounds be struck down and forced to suffer such a miserable end? I started to resent morbidly obese people who got to live despite looking far less healthy than my husband did. Every year there was a different attempt to make his death mean something, usually around the anniversary of his passing. One year there was a tree planted in his honor, another year a scholarship dedicated to his field of study, and so on.

Ultimately, I came to the conclusion that meaning was not to be found in another memorial ceremony, or another analysis of my motivations, or another book on traumatic grief. I did find some solace in changing my approach to psychotherapy: I realized it was more about helping anxious people live with the knowledge of an uncertain future than convincing them that the future would probably not be too bad. Thus, I no longer felt like a complete fraud. More importantly though, I realized that the day to day grind of looking after my children and helping them face their developmental challenges provided more than enough reason to keep going with life. The suicidal thoughts of my youth didn't even enter my mind: I had to look after my family. I had no other option. Doing so was meaningful because at that time and in that place it was what I was meant to do. I sometimes wish I had come to that realization sooner.

Advocacy and Mental Health Care Systems

As mentioned earlier in this chapter, therapists are responsible not only for developing empathetic relationships with their patients but also for being role models of empathy and contributing to mental health care systems based on empathy. Most mental health care systems are not based on empathy, but rather on monetary considerations. Wherever we live, we are responsible for providing the most "bang for the buck" in the eyes of governments or insurance companies. In my own jurisdiction, this imperative results in long waiting lists for my own, publicly funded services and short or no waiting lists for privately funded professionals. As I struggled to find services for my developmentally disabled son, for example, I learned quickly to bring along a cheque book. By doing so, he was able to access speech therapy in two weeks instead of two years. The same occurred when he needed occupational therapy. Yet we live in a jurisdiction that, in theory, provides universal, publicly funded access to health care.

Admittedly, public understanding of mental health issues has improved in recent years. The stigma associated with suffering from depression, an anxiety disorder, or another mental health issue has decreased over time, and people suffering from these conditions face less discrimination than they did in the past. Nevertheless, access to mental health care is still difficult in many areas, often leaving affected people outside major metropolitan areas with little assistance.

These conditions result in competing priorities for many conscientious, empathetic therapists: does one spend the entire day providing empathetic, exemplary care for patients or does one spend some working hours on advocacy for better systems of mental health care? The latter is a part of exemplary care for many of us. For example, a few years ago with the advent of tele-health, I chose to use this medium to train mental health providers in the northern, remote regions of our province in Cognitive Behavioral Therapy, an evidence-based treatment for childhood anxiety and depression. Doing so was very satisfying because I encouraged and guided my trainees in training others, so that this evidence-based treatment would become more broadly available in rural areas. However, organizing and implementing this project took considerable time away from the patients I was treating in my own, urban setting. Thus, I made a conscious decision to compromise local patient care for the sake of many others who were (at the time) receiving no effective care.

Similarly, the therapists receiving the training had to make compromises. They had to arrange coverage for their patient-related duties so that they could participate in regular, weekly supervision sessions with me. Some of their patients might have been adversely affected in the short term as a result. However, in the long term their new knowledge allowed for better and more effective care to all of their patients. We talked about these short-term versus long-term trade-offs in our supervision sessions, and I developed the utmost respect for their dedication to the well-being of their communities in this regard. The training therapists' ability to adapt my teachings to their own very different environments and (in the case of Aboriginal communities) very different cultures was equally impressive.

Other aspects of advocacy can include protesting government policies that result in sub-optimal care for people with mental health problems. For instance, our own province recently cut off funding for intensive therapies for autism after the age of five years, arguing that the evidence for dramatic change at older ages was limited. From a parent's point of view, however, *any* change that allows a child to function better is worthwhile. If an intensive therapy allows a young person to use the bus without assistance, for example, that may be a small change but it can have a huge impact on his or her level of independence. Many concerned mental health providers are in disagreement with our government on this policy, and are voicing concerns.

Overall, an empathetic therapist is often caught between competing demands to respond to the needs of individual patients, to the need to improve systems of care for all, and to the needs of his or her own family. Juggling these demands effectively requires a mindful attitude that responds to each person and each presenting concern with calm, empathetic wisdom, moment by moment.

Summary

- If you haven't asked yourself the Questions for Therapists in the earlier chapters, think about them now.
- When assessing, inquire about the impact of the patient's symptoms on other people.
- Consider doing a biopsychosocial formulation as well as a diagnostic assessment.
- The process of assessment should be gentle, empathetic, and lead to a constructive conclusion for the patient.
- When very stressed or "burned out", it is often more empathetic to take a vacation than persevere with providing sub-optimal psychotherapy.
- Penalties may be needed to address patient behaviors that are inconsiderate of the therapist or other patients, to avoid resentment and show empathy toward those patients.
- If empathy is difficult to establish in the psychotherapeutic relationship, consider the need for other treatment first, the need for a different type of therapy, or personal issues that may be interfering with empathy.
- Empathetic "disconnect" as a result of ambiguity can be a learning opportunity in psychotherapy.
- Confront lack of change in therapy empathetically to re-focus on constructive goals.
- In addition to your usual therapeutic content, encourage patients to engage in activities that promote a calm, centred, outwardly focused frame of mind conducive to empathy.
- Do not shy away from spiritual content in psychotherapy, as it is often necessary when responding empathetically to patients who are struggling

with questions of purpose or who are coping with overwhelming life events.
- Encourage responsible, appropriate responses to life events as a way of making them mean something, regardless of whether or not the patient can find an overarching meaning for them.
- Empathetic mental health professionals must sometimes engage in advocacy on behalf of their patients or to help develop better systems of care; doing so can require compromises regarding the needs of individual patients and of one's family.

References

American Psychiatric Association (2013). *Diagnostic and Statistical Manual of Mental Disorders (DSM 5)* , Fifth Edition. Washington, DC: American Psychiatric Association.

Batson, C.D. (1987). Prosocial motivation: is it ever truly altruistic? In L. Berkowitz (Ed.) *Advances in Experimental Social Psychology*. New York: Academic Press, pp. 65–122.

Byrne, R. (n.d.). *BrainyQuote.com*. http://www.brainyquote.com/quotes/quotes/r/robertbyrn101054.html Retrieved June 29, 2016.

Frankl, V.E. (1984). *Man's Search for Meaning* (Revised and updated). New York: Washington Square Press.

Manassis, K. (2014). *Case Formulation with Children and Adolescents*. New York: The Guilford Press.

Rogers, C. (1986). http://cultureofempathy.com/references/Experts/Carl-Rogers-Quotes.htm Retrieved August 31, 2016.

Seligman, M.E.P. and Csikszentmihalyi, M. (2000). Positive psychology: an introduction. *American Psychologist*, 55, 5–14.

10 Implications for Parents

Why Empathy Matters for the Next Generation

> He was our father, and he walked with the Father and with love, always.
> words in a small roadside shrine in Rhodes, Greece

This roughly translated quote has stuck with me over the years, as it exemplifies how many parents, including myself, would hope to be remembered by their children. When we reach our children with empathy, we reach across the generations. It is one of the few aspects of life that transcends death, regardless of one's beliefs. Our empathy is remembered by our children, and those children go on to nurture empathy in others.

Beyond the parental perspective, however, we must consider the benefits to children who experience empathy with a parent. Usually, this occurs in secure attachment relationships (see Chapter 2 and Bowlby, 1969) where parents are sensitively attuned to their child's needs, yet able to encourage gradual independence by functioning as a "secure base" as the child explores the outside world. Having experienced reliable, empathetic responses with their parents, these children have an enhanced ability to develop empathy themselves (Schore, 2001).

Children who have a capacity for empathy show better adjustment at school, less aggression, fewer anxiety and mood problems, and greater resilience in the face of stress than their peers (Schore, 2001; Zimmerman, 1999). These positive outcomes are thought to be due to the development of social/emotional knowledge, increased ability to solve problems non-violently, the increase in self-esteem that comes from altruistic behavior (i.e., feeling good about doing good), as well as to the benefits of an empathetic state of mind. In the empathetic state of mind, people tend to shift their attention outside themselves in order to focus on others, and to stay in the here and now rather than worrying about the future or ruminating about the past. Both of these tendencies reduce depression and anxiety.

Beyond the well-being of the individual child, empathetic interactions often result in greater cooperation among children (e.g., more effective work in groups, less bullying in the school yard), youth interest in social justice and environmental issues, and less prejudice towards people from minority groups. In addition, as all people, including children, become more globally connected though the internet and other technologies, the ripple effects of empathetic interactions are extended more broadly than ever before (see Chapter 12).

On the other hand, children who experience a lack of empathy growing up often seek it in maladaptive ways. For example, youth who feel misunderstood at home sometimes seek a sense of belonging by joining unhealthy "surrogate families" such as street gangs, cults, or extremist groups. Alternatively, they may become vulnerable to unscrupulous adults who abuse their trust. Given the tendency to transfer feelings from close relationships in the past onto current relationships (see Chapter 7), children whose parents don't "get" them empathetically may also seek out partners resembling those parents, often with disastrous results. It is unfair to expect spouses or partners to meet unmet emotional needs from the past, and eventually their inability to do so results in disappointment. Relationships formed with such "surrogate parents" rarely last. It is also difficult for these children to behave empathetically toward others, as they lack mental models of relationships based on empathetic behavior.

For all of these reasons, this chapter focuses on developing empathetic relationships with children, and helping them develop the capacity for empathy themselves. It concludes with a section on developing empathy in children with special needs.

Developing Empathy with Children: A Biopsychosocial Approach

If you google "developing empathy" or "fostering empathy", you will quickly find several websites listing a dozen or so parenting tips that (they claim) address this issue. Some also refer to programs that aim to foster empathy such as the Roots of Empathy approach offered in some schools. As mentioned in Chapter 2, this approach involves bringing a baby and caregiver into the classroom, and inviting children to observe and comment on how the baby might be feeling (see Gordon, 2012). There is some evidence that this experience enhances empathy in participants. What is not clear is whether a pleasant experience with an infant in elementary school translates into an enhanced capacity for empathy in adulthood, given the many other experiences that happen to developing children and youth in the interim. Some anti-bullying programs in schools also offer lessons in empathy, but again it is not clear how much they impact the capacity for empathy in the long run. Not surprisingly, there is even less evidence for the lists of parenting tips.

If there is a shortcoming to the above approaches, it probably relates to a lack of attention to the different components of empathy. Almost all of these programs emphasize perspective-taking abilities but neglect other important components of empathy as outlined in Chapter 5 (e.g., self-transcendence, motivation to attend to others, communication of empathy, etc.). Without these additional components, the chances of helping someone developing consistently empathetic behavior year after year are slim.

If we want to understand how empathy develops longitudinally, a biopsychosocial approach is often helpful. Emphasis on attachment relationships is needed as these form the mental templates for how we relate to others, and have substantial evidence for long-term effects on empathy (Schore, 2001; Zimmerman, 1999). An example of a child's development illustrates some factors related to developing empathy.

Mary and Benny

Mary was a single parent who had suffered repeated bouts of depression. She was socially isolated, rejected by her family for having a relationship with a man from a different ethnic background. Physically abused as a child, Mary was determined not to let her eight-year-old son, Benny, suffer the same fate. Although he was a rambunctious boy, she never spanked him or lost her temper with him. She educated herself about time outs and other non-violent forms of discipline.

Despite these efforts, Benny seemed incorrigible. He stole food from the refrigerator and money from his mother's purse. He swore and often lied. He engaged in dangerous stunts on his skateboard and played violent video games. He blamed others when caught misbehaving, resulting in frequent arguments with Mary. She, in turn, described him as "manipulative" and "spoiled". She wondered if he was behaving badly to punish her, and protested "I don't deserve to be treated this way!" She could not identify any strengths or likeable qualities in Benny. At school, Benny was distractible and often left his seat. However, he responded to his teacher's firm but patient requests to settle down, and tried to do his work. He rarely got into trouble there.

After being assessed by a psychiatrist, Benny as started on medication for ADHD. His schoolwork improved, and his teacher encouraged him to join the baseball team. Benny's coach considered him a talented pitcher, and Benny looked up to him. The coach became an important mentor in Benny's life. As Benny practiced and became more successful, he was encouraged to help younger players. He enjoyed doing this, and became a respected leader on the team. His home life continued to be difficult, but Benny flourished at school and in his athletic program.

Despite the positive conclusion to the vignette, Benny's future remains somewhat uncertain. What happens when he graduates or if his coach moves away? Will he continue to do well in academics and athletics, or become discouraged from a lack of positive feedback at home? Will his expectations of close relationships be based on the experience with his coach, or the experience with his mother? If the latter, how will those expectations affect his interactions with others?

We cannot predict precisely what will happen to Benny. However, we can understand the factors that may increase or decrease his capacity for empathy and all of the positive outcomes associated with it. In order to understand Benny's story, it helps to look at the biological, psychological, and social factors that influenced his development of empathy. Biologically, Benny's skateboarding stunts suggest that he may have the gene associated with thrill-seeking and lack of empathy. The impulsivity associated with ADHD (i.e., the tendency to respond to situations quickly without thinking ahead) could also interfere with empathetic behavior.

Psychologically, Benny almost certainly had an insecure attachment relationship with his mother. His mother's depression, traumatic early history, and lack of spousal or community support (for cultural reasons) would all interfere with her development of a secure relationship with Benny. Also, parents in secure attachment relationships typically do not describe their eight-year-old children as "manipulative", understanding that the child's ability to deliberately and maliciously manipulate an adult is quite limited at this age. Moreover, they can usually name some positive or likeable qualities that they believe their child possesses. The insecure relationship with his mother would prevent Benny from developing an intuitive understanding of empathy that is based on experiencing it with a parent. Learning the component skills of empathy would be difficult for Benny due to ADHD, even if a program teaching such skills were offered to him.

Social influences had mixed effects on Benny's capacity for empathy. The violent video games probably did not help. Even though there is controversy about whether or not such games actually provoke violence, they certainly do not foster empathy. At school, Benny responded positively to a kind but firm teacher and subsequently to his baseball coach, perhaps yearning for a better relationship with an adult than the one he had with his mother. The coach's perception of positive qualities in Benny suggests that Benny was able to experience some empathy in this relationship and thus develop a more empathetic approach to others. The coach's encouragement of empathetic behavior towards younger players likely furthered Benny's development of this approach. The psychiatrist's medical treatment of his ADHD may also have allowed Benny to focus on the consequences of his actions, including their impact on others. This ability may have promoted some additional development of empathy.

Understanding these different factors helps us make sense of Benny's progression from an apparently incorrigible youngster to a responsible, empathetic team leader. Given the ongoing conflict at home, however, it is uncertain whether Benny will maintain an empathetic approach to life beyond his graduation from his positive school environment.

Admittedly, this biopsychosocial approach places a lot of emphasis on the role of parents, which can sometimes seem parent-blaming. When we add to the need for a secure parent-child relationship the value of role modeling empathetic behavior and managing the family system in a way that promotes empathy, empathetic parenting seems daunting indeed! Nobody's perfect though, and doing all of these things consistently may be unrealistic. Rather, each of these parental roles represents an opportunity to help children gravitate toward a more empathetic, less self-absorbed way of life. Some opportunities work out, and others don't. However, we can still seek these opportunities and try to take advantage of them. Let's look at some possibilities.

First, a stable, caring, supportive environment that promotes good health habits will facilitate the biology of empathy. This suggests that as a parent you should try, as best you can, to keep your life orderly, avoid instability in relationships or finances, protect your children from traumatic or abusive experiences, and have only as many children as you can afford to raise. Recall the contrast between Kyle and Ken in Chapter 6, where one boy had a stable home environment and the other did not.

If you can also model good self-care and practices that promote a centred, empathetic approach to life, this is ideal. Modeling empathy includes good personal management of fight or flight reactions, including self-compassion and healthy coping strategies (see Chapters 4 and 6). This management allows you, for the most part, to model treating everyone respectfully and empathetically. Including your children in these healthy coping habits (for example, regular exercise, relaxation, or yoga) can further increase their impact. Espousing values and beliefs that promote empathy and inclusion doesn't hurt either (see Chapter 8).

Next, parents who look after their own psychological health are more likely to develop secure relationships with their children, so personal mental health should be a priority. It is especially important to address any unresolved grief or traumas from the past, as these often result in the least optimal attachment relationships (Raby, Steele, Carlson, and Sroufe, 2015; also see Chapter 2). Other "red flags" for insecure attachment include a need to minimize or disregard the child's feelings, or a need to confide in the child about one's own problems. For example, if Benny had been less rambunctious, his depressed mother might have used him as a sounding board for her troubles, compromising Benny's emotional development. Seeing the child as a means of realizing parental ambitions is another common unhealthy pattern. I recently attended a high school graduation, and couldn't help but notice some tense, even painful expressions on the faces of those marching across the stage as their future goals were read out. The utterly delighted expressions on their parents' faces suggested whose goals were really being announced.

Parent-child relationships that are empathetic and conducive to the development of empathy are characterized by caring, affection, and respectful boundaries. Ideally, the parent is not only unconditionally loving and patient with the child, but also curious about this fascinating young creature entrusted to his or her care. The parent is genuinely interested in the child's world, as he or she sees things the parents might consider commonplace for the very first time. The child's reactions become a source of wonder, and sometimes an opportunity for the parent to relive aspects of his or her own childhood. At the same time, limits are set calmly and consistently when needed, not to assert parental power but rather in the hope of preparing the little one for future challenges. Almost invariably, the parent needs the support of other adults to maintain this composed and caring approach day to day (Dickstein, Seifer, and Albus, 2009), and no parent maintains it perfectly.

For parents raised in homes where attachment was insecure, this approach also implies doing what *does not* come naturally. We tend to relate to our children in ways that our parents related to us unless we become aware of the relationship patterns and consciously try to change them. Without this awareness, history tends to repeat itself. Personal therapy or attachment-focused interventions can reduce the chances of passing along patterns that lack empathy (Bakermans-Kranenburg, van IJzendoorn, and Juffer, 2003). For example, the Circle of Security intervention involves having parents interact with their young children (aged five years or less) and then review videotapes of those interactions with a therapist (see Powell, Cooper, Hoffman, and Marvin, 2013). Identifying places where parent and child are not "in sync" with one another emotionally allows for reflection and development of alternative relationship patterns.

Even when parents are relatively insightful, however, certain child temperaments can pose challenges to the parent-child relationship. My daughter, for example, was an enigma to me early in her life. As a baby, she cried inconsolably for hours at a time, and more loudly when I tried to hold her and offer comfort. When she had to be taken to the hospital for treatment of jaundice, several experienced nurses reported the same. Only her father was able to settle her. He seemed to have an endless variety of strange, funny-looking faces to present to her, making her laugh and forget her distress. This playful approach to dealing with distress seemed to help. I was eventually able to emulate some of the distractions, but never did them quite as well as her Dad. Although she didn't sleep through the night until she was three years old, my daughter eventually turned into a responsible, empathetic, socially astute young woman of whom I am now very proud. I don't think I can take credit for that outcome entirely, but I tried my best.

Children who are temperamentally similar to their parents may present different challenges. In this case, it is tempting to over-identify with the children and assume one knows what they need or think without asking. Doing so can show a lack of empathy. For example, some parents assume they know what their children want for Christmas based on their own childhood memories, and are surprised when the children are unhappy with the result. There is a good reason to have children make "Santa lists", as these often clarify the differences between children's wishes and those of their parents. When children who match their parent's temperament have problems, parents can also experience undue guilt, feeling that they have passed on flaws to the children who seem so similar to themselves. Such experiences can make it difficult to set appropriate limits and engage in constructive problem-solving.

Seeing the child as a separate being, on the other hand, helps the parent support aspects of development that may be lagging without feeling overly responsible for the child's difficulties. If the parent sees the child as representing an unwelcome part of themselves or their past, as in the example of Danny and Arjun (Chapter 2), this perception may also interfere with empathy. Awareness of one's own past struggles can reduce the chances of projecting them onto one's children.

Regardless of temperament, it is also important to remember that children grow and develop, so empathy toward teens is very different from empathy toward younger children. Empathy toward teens may mean asking them how they feel, rather than telling them based on one's observations. The latter is more effective with younger children who have a limited emotional vocabulary. Empathy toward a teen may also mean doing what is helpful to them even if, as they assert their autonomy, they protest against your actions. "My mother won't let me do it", is often a welcome excuse for avoiding situations the teen is uncomfortable with. Relating to the youth empathetically usually includes a mix of respect for different opinions, as one would show an adult, and support when they still need it. Teens are not truly independent as long as they live under your roof, so an empathetic parent only doles out freedom as the teen shows the ability to manage it responsibly. This practice is consistent with authoritative parenting, a style characterized by both caring and guidance, and associated with the development of empathy (Hastings, McShane, Parker, and Ladha, 2007).

Parenting Within a "System"

Beyond their individual relationships with children, many parents find themselves struggling with the "noise" around those individual relationships. Sometimes that "noise" comes in the form of family dynamics; other times in the form of home and school conflicts. Recall the example of Jennifer and her boys in Chapter 3. In this case, sibling conflict makes it difficult for the parent to show empathy toward one boy (Colin) and leaves that child feeling misunderstood and unsupported by his parent. A wise parent realizes that sibling conflict is never entirely one person's fault, and tries to get everyone's side of the story before judging. When in doubt, the best solution is usually to time out both parties so everyone can cool off. Afterwards, it is usually pointless to try and assign blame or figure out "who started it". Rather, the important issue from an empathetic point of view is to ensure that everyone's most important needs are met. In the example in Chapter 3, helping Colin complete his recently destroyed science project, and comforting the younger brother with assurance that his toy will be replaced are key priorities.

Similar difficulties with family dynamics can occur if the child's needs compete with those of a spouse. Here it is important to remember that the spouse can actually be helpful in raising the child if he or she feels supported. For example, if a spouse says "You're grounded", to a child who has committed a minor infraction of the rules, it is tempting to say "Aw...she didn't really mean any harm, let's let it go for this time." However, doing so undermines the spouse's credibility as a co-parent, placing more responsibility on the "soft" parent for managing the child's behavior. Unless the spouse is being abusive, it is usually more helpful to support his or her attempts at setting limits, even if they seem a bit harsh. When this occurs, the parents present a "united front" and child misbehavior generally decreases. Spouses can still discuss the best way of setting future limits afterwards in private, but the important thing is that they support each other in their parenting efforts in front of the child. When parents are able to discuss their differences and develop an approach that is acceptable to both, they become more consistent and more effective in helping their children. Recall how Ken's parents did this regularly on "date night" in Chapter 6. Empathy for the child can still be preserved, as the parents explain how limiting "bad behavior" is different from considering him or her a "bad child".

Supporting one's children in the face of various challenges outside the family is important as well. On the one hand, it is important to advocate for our children's well-being when they are being bullied by other children or by humiliating teachers. No child should be subjected to bullying and be told to "suck it up". Every child deserves to be treated with respect, and when this does not occur a child needs to know that there is at least one adult "in their corner" who will ensure that the bullying does not continue. If it is possible to access a school program such as Roots of Empathy for your child's school, this is ideal (see Gordon, 2012). On the other hand, it is sometimes important to consider teacher perspectives. Empathy for the teacher's point of view can often result in constructive discussions of how to best support the child's school progress, and similar expectations between home and school are very supportive of improvement. Lack of empathy for the teacher's point of view, by contrast, can sometimes result in making excuses for the child's maladaptive school behavior. When parents side with the child against the school, school success invariably suffers.

In summary, systems issues are often challenging for parents in that empathy for the child's feelings may make it difficult to support other adults in the child's life who are being stricter and less empathetic than the parent. Here, the parent must remember that the child's adaptation in the future may depend upon the lessons taught by those adults. Thus, difficult as it may be, we must sometimes allow our children to suffer in the short term to ensure their long-term ability to cope with the challenges of life.

Some experiences outside the parent-child relationship can be conducive to empathy, however. Benny's experience with his coach, for example, supported his development of empathy despite his negative home environment. Another example is involving children in volunteer community activities or activities that focus on protecting the environment. These activities can foster the development of empathy, as they underscore the value of all living beings and the interconnections among them.

Participating in such activities with one's children is also a great exercise in empathy for both parent and child.

Teaching Empathy

The above discussion may cause some parents to question: Is there any use to trying to teach children empathetic behavior, or is it all learned from experiencing empathy oneself? Indeed, there is some value to teaching empathy, in addition to providing empathetic experiences as the child is growing up and supporting good self-regulation (i.e., reducing the vulnerability to constant fight or flight reactions). Teaching is particularly helpful when it comes to the perspective-taking component of empathy.

As many teachers have observed, however, children are more likely to emulate what they see others do than what they are told to do. Thus, the first step in teaching empathy is to model empathetic behavior. In Canada, for example, there is a segment of the population known as "hockey parents". As ice hockey is a very popular sport, many parents invest large amounts of time, energy, and money in having their children participate in organized hockey so that they may aspire to, one day, playing in the National Hockey League. The possibility of this happening is rather remote, given the number of players, so the junior leagues are extremely competitive. Every year there are news stories of parents who sabotage players on other teams, encourage their children to use unscrupulous methods to win, and even attack coaches who are not effective in promoting their children's success. These parents role model a complete lack of empathy for one's fellow players, and an attitude of "win at all cost". By contrast, parents who emphasize team play, sportsmanship, and a love of the game are more likely to support the development of empathy in their children. In the long run, these children are also likely to continue to play the game for fun and good health, regardless of how far they advance in their competitive leagues.

Another aspect of modeling empathy is modeling respect for people of all backgrounds and abilities. If we don't want our children to be prejudiced, we need to avoid making stereotyped comments ourselves and nurture friendships across racial boundaries. If we don't want our children to consider those with different abilities "losers", we need to include these people in our communities and allow our children to interact with them. Honoring people for their unique contributions regardless of ability and integrating the disabled into mainstream activities are two ways of ensuring our children appreciate the courage it takes to overcome challenges, rather than marginalizing the challenged. Keeping an open mind about new people encountered and avoiding hostile biases concerning others can also model empathy. Giving others the "benefit of the doubt" unless they clearly show they do not deserve it is a nice, empathetic life lesson to impart.

In addition to modeling empathy and showing empathy to children, there are several ways of encouraging it. First, parents can help their children develop an interest in others' points of view. For example, when watching a movie or reading a book it is sometimes interesting to see if the child understands the motivation of the villain, as well as the hero, of the story. A good story shows how characters developed their attitudes and typical behaviors, and how they might yet change. Good stories are psychologically true to life in the sense that characters are complex, neither perfect nor completely evil. Understanding these characters can often support the development of understanding for other people. For example, one of my favorite recent films was *Maleficent*, the story of the motivations of the "bad fairy" in "Sleeping Beauty" (Stromberg, Woolverton, Roth, Jolie, Vieira, Hahn, et al., 2014). Crippled and rejected by her selfish lover, the fairy vows to take revenge by cursing his daughter. As she watches over the child's development though, her heart melts and she regrets her curse. Ultimately, she ensures the child's well-being at great cost to herself. She is an example of a flawed but not totally evil character, who both elicits and shows empathy.

Second, parents can help children understand what others might be thinking or feeling. For instance, when someone is excluded from a group, they might feel sad, angry, or lonely. They might wonder what they had done to deserve such exclusion. On the other hand, when someone is acknowledged for an achievement, they might feel proud, valued by their peers, or just relieved that the struggle to achieve a goal has concluded. When a child complains about a difficult peer relationship, see if he or she can understand the peer's point of view and emotions. When a child envies someone else getting an award, see if he or she can also relate to that person's struggle and feeling of validation.

Third, parents can encourage teamwork and solutions to conflict that benefit everyone. Given the need for coordination, projects involving teamwork sometimes take a long time to start, but they benefit from many different talents so are usually more productive in the long run. When there is conflict where a winner is declared, nobody really wins as the loser becomes determined to ensure a different outcome next time and the conflict continues. When there is a conflict where both sides achieve a result that they value, everyone wins and lasting peace is much more likely to occur. Most problems have "win-win" solutions if we are creative and persistent enough to find them.

Fourth, parents can alert their children to the common struggles all people share as they try to find their way in life. We all have our good days and bad days, successes and defeats, joys and sorrows. Dealing with life's ups and downs calmly and wisely is not easy for anyone, so it is usually unfair to denigrate or dismiss someone because of one negative interaction with that person. Moreover, even people who look very different from us or come from very different backgrounds usually share goals and aspirations similar to our own. Who wouldn't want to have enough money to pursue a favorite recreational activity? Who wouldn't want to see their children healthy and happy? Pointing out how others share the same joys, sorrows, and insecurities can be helpful not only in promoting empathy but also in alleviating self-consciousness. For example, the next time your child has to do an oral presentation, ask if there is anyone they know who is *not* nervous about such presentations. Recognizing the universality of certain emotions and trials helps all of us develop both empathy and a sense of connection with the rest of the human race.

Finally, although not always thought of as "teaching", parental guidance regarding various media exposures can have a significant effect on children's development of empathy. Knowing what is on children's "screens" and talking about it is essential. Avoiding all images of violence may be unrealistic, though parental controls allow for some limits, but placing those images in the context of human relationships can make a difference. For example, parents can help children distinguish between fantasy and reality, take the perspective of the victim as well as the perpetrator of the violence, and think about the impact of sharing violent or sexual images with others in order to avoid this practice.

In short, parents who talk to their children about others' points of view, others' emotions, "win-win" solutions, and the similarities (rather than differences) between people are laying the groundwork for their children's development of empathy. Limiting exposure to media that contradict these ideals is also important, especially in younger children.

The Child You Weren't Expecting

Children with special needs can pose challenges to our capacity for empathy: empathy toward the child, empathy toward our partners as we parent the child, and (for those outside affected families) empathy toward parents raising special needs children. Parental empathy toward the child is strained by grief about the loss of the "normal" child and the hopes and dreams attached to it, by anxious uncertainty about the child's future, and by guilt about the parent's possible contribution to the child's problems and ability (or inability) to treat them optimally. These emotions may repeat over the course of development. For instance, it is a cruel irony that even with optimal parental support, a child who develops at a slower rate falls further behind his or her peers each year. Moreover, "special needs" are not limited to developmental delay. In his award-winning book *Far from the Tree* (see Solomon, 2012), Evan Solomon describes a myriad of issues that can result in unexpected challenges with children: from physical challenges such as deafness to mental illness such as schizophrenia to other differences such as being transgender or having an unusual talent.

My Son

Even parents who are very emotionally attuned to their children can sometimes struggle to communicate empathy when the child has limited language skills. The child may be unable to communicate the source of his or her distress, or unable to understand the comforting words we try to offer. I discovered this a number of years ago soon after my husband passed away and my six-year-old autistic son was coming to terms with the loss. Every night, at 9.30 pm, he left his bed and went to the kitchen. He sat at the kitchen table with a spoon in his hand and said a single word: "Weetabix". He would not move and would not say anything else.

As he could not explain what was going on, I had to piece together the meaning of the ritual. Eventually, I realized that as my husband tended to work late, he came home around 9.30 pm. I was usually asleep by this time. My son, however, got up at that hour routinely and came to the kitchen to have milk and cereal with his father. Now that his father was gone, he got up as usual and waited for him and for his favorite cereal, Weetabix.

There was no point explaining the loss of his father to my son at that hour, as he hardly remembered what had happened by the next day. The most empathetic thing to do was to combine some milk and cereal in response to his request. I learned to use less milk, as that was the "right" way to do it according to my son. I also learned that once he finished his bowl he fell asleep at the table and needed to be carried to bed. I continued the ritual for a couple of months this way, until the day came when my son no longer woke up at 9.30 pm. Only then was he able to talk about losing his father. He asked a few questions every week or so, which I answered simply and honestly. Few emotions were expressed, but he seemed reassured. I learned that empathy can take many forms when children have special needs.

As mentioned earlier, raising a child with challenges can impact family relationships, and the relationship between the family and the larger community. It can be difficult, for example, for employers or colleagues to understand the number of medical appointments working parents must attend to care for children with multiple medical or developmental needs. It can be difficult for other parents to understand why the parent of a child with special needs may need more respite than they do from their children, or may be less able to participate in school meetings or other community activities. Thus, there is often an unintentional lack of empathy toward these parents. In my own experience as a single parent of a child with multiple medical and developmental needs, I recall sitting through meetings where people, without malice, made general announcements such as "Everyone should contribute to the bake sale", or "Quarterly conference travel should be expected to publicize our work", or "To be fair, night-time coverage should be compulsory and evenly divided among us". Creative solutions could sometimes be found (e.g., finding supermarket bake sale products or sending students to some conferences), but anything that was compulsory and rigid required a special discussion with the boss. In short, there seems to be an assumption in much of North American society that parents should be able to look after their children, their jobs, and their households with limited support from others. That assumption is clearly flawed when it comes to children with differences.

Within the family, parents who conscientiously attend to the special needs child risk neglecting spouses and siblings. When one child requires several times as much parental attention as the other, it is no longer possible to treat siblings fairly. In trying to show empathy toward the "normal" sibling, some parents overindulge that child (e.g., buying lots of toys in an attempt to compensate for the lack of time spent with the child), which is not helpful for his or her development. Other parents engage the child as a "helper" with the special needs child. The problem here is that children in this role sometimes consider themselves auxiliary parents, and so become defiant when parents try to set limits with them. Still other parents acknowledge the neglect, and attend to and empathize with the child whenever possible. In the long run, this is probably the least harmful approach.

When considering effects on the spousal relationship, recall the example of Dana and her husband, the high-achieving couple in Chapter 8. Their daughter's serious illness and subsequent disability challenged their philosophy of extreme individualism (as they had to accept help) and their biases against those less accomplished by conventional standards (as some of these people were very helpful to them). How else might their life have changed?

Dana (Continued)

It soon became obvious that the little girl would always be developmentally delayed. Despite the fact that she would never be self-sufficient like her mother, Dana saw something very special in her daughter. People invariably relaxed when they saw her winning smile. Dana began to appreciate how a vulnerable child can bring out the best in even the toughest adult. Her husband wasn't so sure. He was playful and kind to the little girl, but grumbled to his wife about how her illness had changed their long-term plans. Dana was incensed: "You and your plans! Think about people instead of plans for once!" The marital relationship became frosty.

A few weeks later, their daughter unexpectedly developed a seizure disorder, a late complication of her illness. A whirlwind of medical appointments and medication adjustments followed, and life became even more unpredictable. Dana's tolerance for unplanned events was higher than her husband's, but these events really challenged her ability to cope. She began to understand the anxiety he had experienced, as she now felt anxious herself. As the couple pulled together to get their daughter through this latest crisis, the relationship became mutually empathetic again.

As shown in this example, challenges posed by special needs children often accentuate attitudinal and personality differences between spouses. Very few parents are on exactly the same page when it comes to child-rearing, but when parenting challenges are minor they can readily accommodate their differences. When there are daily challenges in relation to the child, however, conflict can also become daily. In this case, such conflict threatened the relationship, until a further stress allowed Dana to understand her husband's perspective. In summary, raising special needs children poses different challenges to different parents, but empathy between parents is essential if the family is to continue to function.

And yet...as Dana found, children with challenges can contribute in unique ways to the lives of those around them. In a famous poem, Kingsley (1987) compares the experience of raising a special needs child to an unexpected detour on a trip: an air traveler has planned a trip to Italy, and is fully prepared for this destination, only to have the pilot announce that the plane is now landing in Holland. In describing the response to this change, the poet eloquently captures the idea that raising a child with differences is not necessarily a negative experience: it is simply an alternative experience from what was expected. Some might say this sentiment doesn't reflect the harsh realities of raising a special needs child, but I believe there is some truth to it. Such children can be a blessing. As empathetic parents, it may be helpful to remember that our children, regardless of their challenges, are not burdens. Rather, it is fitting each child's unique needs and abilities into the burdens of ordinary life that stretches our creativity and our resources.

Summary

- Benefits of developing empathy include lower vulnerability to depression, anxiety, and aggressive behavior, increased resilience, better school adjustment, and more cooperative behavior with peers.
- Children are most likely to develop empathy in the context of secure, empathetic relationships with parents.
- These relationships are characterized by caring, affection, and respect for psychological boundaries; parents often need support from other adults to maintain these relationships.
- Secure relationships may be challenged by child temperament and developmental change.
- A biopsychosocial approach to child development allows us to understand how different aspects of empathy can be supported in children.
- A stable, caring, supportive environment that promotes good health habits will facilitate the biology of empathy.
- Parental modeling of good self-care, healthy coping strategies, and attention to personal mental health supports the psychological development of empathy.
- Managing social influences on empathy requires parents to wisely manage family interactions, home and school interactions, and interactions between the child and the broader community; balancing empathy for the child with limits needed to optimize long-term development can be particularly challenging.

- Teaching empathy begins with modeling inclusive attitudes toward diverse people, and valuing cooperation rather than competition.
- To improve children's perspective-taking abilities, parents can talk about or read stories about others' points of view, encourage an appreciation of others' emotions, foster "win-win" solutions, emphasize the similarities between people, and limit violent or dehumanizing media exposures.
- Children with special needs can pose challenges to our capacity for empathy toward the child, toward our partners as we parent the child, and (for those outside affected families) toward parents raising special needs children.

Questions for Parents

Take a moment to think about how different influences on empathy might be affecting your child. Here are some questions to guide your thinking:

- Start with yourself: How might difficult past experiences be influencing your own capacity for empathy? How might current life stresses or problems be influencing it?
- How can you relate to your child with greater empathy? (e.g., Can you focus on strengths/likeable aspects of the child? Can you put yourself in the child's shoes? Can you relate with caring, affection, and respectful boundaries?) Do you need the support of other adults for this to work? Who might be able to help?
- If you have several children, think of the one who is most difficult to parent. How could you develop greater empathy for this child?
- What opportunities might there be to model empathetic, cooperative, and respectful behavior for your child, as well as good self-care and practices that promote a centered, empathetic approach to life?
- Does your child suffer from a physical or mental health condition that might interfere with the development of empathy? How could you address this issue?
- What family dynamics might be influencing your child's capacity for empathy? How could you address this issue?
- What life stresses outside the home might be influencing your child's capacity for empathy? Consider his or her relationships with teachers, peers, and other community members. How could you address this issue?
- How could you help develop your child's understanding of others' points of view and others' emotions?
- How could you encourage social problem-solving that results in "win-win" solutions?
- Could your child engage in activities outside of school that might foster empathy or a sense of community?

- Do you know what your child's "screen time" consists of, and are these media influences likely to increase or decrease his or her capacity for empathy?
- Do your spiritual/philosophical beliefs and practices foster an empathetic approach to life that your child can emulate?
- If you are raising a child with special challenges, do you need to show empathy toward this child in a different way than you show it toward others?
- If you are raising a child with special challenges, how is this affecting your relationship with your spouse, your other children, and your community?

References

Bakermans-Kranenburg, M., van IJzendoorn, M. and Juffer, F. (2003). Less is more: meta-analyses of sensitivity and attachment interventions in early childhood. *Psychological Bulletin*, 129, 195–215.

Bowlby, J. (1969). *Attachment. Attachment and Loss: Vol. 1. Loss*. New York: Basic Books.

Dickstein, S., Seifer, R. and Albus, K.E. (2009). Maternal adult attachment representations across relationship domains and infant outcomes: the importance of family and couple functioning. *Attachment and Human Development*, 11, 5–27.

Gordon, M. (2012). *Roots of Empathy: Changing the World, Child by Child*. Markham, ON: Thomas Allen Publishers.

Hastings, P.D., McShane, K.E., Parker, R. and Ladha, F. (2007). Ready to make nice: parental socialization of young sons' and daughters' prosocial behaviors with peers. *Journal of Genetic Psychology*, 168, 177–200.

Kingsley, E.P. (1987). *Welcome to Holland*. http://www.our-kids.org/archives/Holland.html Retrieved July 12, 2016.

Powell, B., Cooper, G., Hoffman, K., and Marvin, B. (2013). *The Circle of Security Intervention: Enhancing Attachment in Early Parent-Child Relationships*. New York: Guilford Press.

Raby, K.L., Steele, R.D., Carlson, E.A. and Sroufe, L.A. (2015). Continuities and changes in infant attachment patterns across two generations. *Attachment & Human Development*, 17, 414–428.

Schore, A.N. (2001). Effects of a secure attachment relationship on right brain development, affect regulation, and infant mental health. *Infant Mental Health Journal*, 22, 7–66.

Solomon, A. (2012). *Far From the Tree: Parents, Children, and the Search for Identity*. New York: Scribner.

Stromberg, R., Woolverton, L., Roth, J., Jolie, A., Vieira, M., Hahn, D., and Patel, P. (2014). *Maleficent* (film). Buena Vista Home Entertainment.

Zimmerman, P. (1999). Structure and functions of internal working models of attachment and their role for emotion regulation. *Attachment & Human Development*, 1, 291–306.

11 Implications for Leaders and Organizations

> Dream in a pragmatic way.
>
> Aldous Huxley

Much of this book has been focused on the personal development of empathy for others. It is important, however, to also be mindful of how our actions inspire or fail to inspire empathy in others. Therefore, I included this chapter on leadership, as leaders are often in a position to increase or decrease the capacity for empathy in their subordinates. We begin by examining a recent controversy concerning the value of empathy in political leaders, and its implications. Then, we revisit the example of an unhealthy organization described in Chapter 3 and contrast it with communities that inspire empathy. The differences are outlined in Table 11.1, and illustrated with a personal example of the "classroom community" created by an excellent teacher. A particular challenge to empathetic leadership and empathetic communities is posed by extremists and other individuals who consistently *lack* empathy for others. Finally, the broader implications of empathetic leadership for interconnected, global issues are explored.

Is Empathy Overrated in Political Leaders?

In a recent *New York Times* article (Tierney, March 21, 2016), the value of empathy in political leaders is debated. Psychologist Paul Bloom, on one side, argues that empathy results in favoritism rather than justice, and so should be avoided by fair-minded, principled leaders. The oxytocin-fueled tendency to show empathy toward one's own group and hostility toward those outside it (De Dreu, 2012) is highlighted, as are empathetic biases toward those perceived as victims (often resulting in undue aggression toward their adversaries), toward those who are attractive, and toward suffering individuals rather than suffering groups (sometimes undermining financial support for the latter).

On the other hand, as discussed in Chapter 2, in-group biases relate predominantly to oxytocin, the brain chemical linked to the emotional aspects of empathy (Usefovsky et al., 2015). Cognitive aspects of empathy relate to different brain chemicals, and are thus less vulnerable to this bias. Similarly, the inability to balance empathy for competing adversaries when one adversary is labeled a victim or to balance empathy for more attractive and less attractive people assumes that empathy is a purely emotional response. If this were true, a parent who sees two siblings fighting would always defend the child who is crying rather than seeing (based on cognitive as well as emotional aspects of empathy) how both children are vying for his or her attention. Thus, the argument that leaders should use reason rather than empathy to guide decisions may be based on a somewhat simplistic understanding of empathy as a purely emotional response. As reviewed in Chapter 1, empathy is not just an involuntary welling up of emotion in response to others' suffering. Rather, it is a complex and often deliberate attempt to understand others' experience, which includes several cognitive processes as well as an emotional response.

A further point made by psychologist Daryl Cameron and his colleagues is that the reduced empathy shown to groups versus individuals may reflect "compassion collapse". This is a phenomenon where people protect themselves from emotional or financial exhaustion by directing empathy preferentially toward situations where they feel they can help (in this case, those involving one person) rather than those they feel helpless to change (i.e., a large, overwhelming number of sufferers). When people are not expected to change the plight of the larger number, their empathy for this group increases. A leader who offers a hopeful approach to large-scale suffering that does not over-burden people may thus mitigate the "anti-group" bias. For example, some people are surprised to hear that extreme poverty could be eliminated globally if as little as 1.5 percent of the Gross Domestic Product of all nations were directed toward international development (Schmidt-Traub, 2015).

Finally, Bloom's emphasis on the negative effect of empathy-related biases on leaders ignores the many potential benefits that stem from empathetic leadership. These are described in the remainder of this chapter.

Leading Empathetic Communities and Organizations

Empathetic communities are characterized by many of the positive qualities of groups described by Yalom and Leszcz (2005), as discussed in Chapter 3 and outlined in Table 11.1. They are cooperative, mutually supportive and value the contributions of all members. They may be formal or informal. For example, students who socialize after a difficult examination, commuters who help each other when the train is stuck, or neighbors who rally around a family that has encountered sudden tragedy may constitute informal, small communities. Formal communities or organizations usually have longer term mandates, and often grow to include increasing numbers of people. Size and duration often pose challenges to continued empathetic behavior within the group and between the group and outsiders. Thus, sadly, organizations that lack empathy resembling the unhealthy clinic described in

Chapter 3 are common. Their members are competitive and focused on enhancing their own prestige; their leaders are removed from the concerns of their workers, prioritize bureaucratic procedures over doing work that is truly valuable to the mandate of the organization, and (not surprisingly) are competitive and focused on enhancing their own prestige.

Leaders who care about their subordinates as well as their organizations usually hope to avoid this fate. Such leaders can be found across demographic categories. Even though many of the examples below may imply business leadership, people in leadership positions can be found in educational, medical, religious, political, and other organizations. The same principles apply, regardless of the type of organization or community. In all cases, creating and maintaining empathetic communities and organizations is not easy. At minimum, leaders must consider the following issues: the value of the individual, the type of group interactions that are encouraged, the role of the leader, the types of solutions to problems that are promoted, and the philosophy of the group as a whole. Each will be discussed in turn.

Empathetic communities ensure that the basic needs of all their members are addressed. Food, shelter, clothing, essential health care…in short anything needed for one's basic human dignity is considered a right, not a privilege. Those who cannot afford these bare essentials may need help from other people, but these people recognize that those helped are still valuable human beings who can and will contribute to the community in various ways. The person who earns a modest wage supervising the school lunchroom may inspire the children she supervises in wonderful ways that are not reflected in her earnings. The person who lives at home because he can only manage a part-time job at a fast food restaurant may be a blessing to his frail, elderly parents. The refugee family may galvanize community efforts to integrate them into their new country. The young adult who is suddenly disabled may elicit admiration for his or her perseverance in the face of adversity, or challenge us to re-evaluate what "quality of life" really means for human beings. Empathetic communities do not define contributions solely based on dollars and cents. Some people achieve conventional success, others support those who have or will accomplish things, others bring the group together, and still others bring out empathetic or constructive responses in those around them. Empathetic communities benefit from the bounty of all of these talents.

Interactions within the empathetic community are characterized by mutual respect and mutual support. Not only is everyone's contribution valued, but the ability to achieve more collectively than individually is prized. One of the difficulties exemplified in the unhealthy clinic is the tendency for many organizations to pay lip service to cooperation while actually promoting competition. Many companies, for example, engage in team building exercises with their staff but only base promotions on individual achievement. In my own experience, medical services and even church committees are often organized in "teams", but awards are given only to individuals. If we truly value cooperation, then everyone in a cooperative group should be considered a "winner", regardless of whose name appears on the most publications, or who is most well-known and popular in the congregation. Otherwise, people start to circumvent the rules, undermine each other's efforts, use the ends to justify the means, and generally "look out for number one" rather than engaging in cooperative, empathetic behavior. In short, individual awards foster competition and resentment; celebrating collective achievements fosters empathy and true teamwork. If we know we will sink or swim together, we are more likely to make space for everyone in the lifeboat.

Another aspect of mutual respect often neglected in organizations is a tolerance for diversity of opinion. As organizations develop mission statements and other collective ideals, there is an unfortunate tendency for members to engage in "group think". In other words, members feel that in order to feel welcome in the organization, they cannot disagree with its leadership or with other members. Personal ethics may be set aside in favor of a sense of belonging to the group, and personal responsibility becomes diluted as people feel the group is responsible. The most egregious examples of this issue occur in cults, paramilitary groups, or other organizations that emphasize obedience to leaders and discourage dialogue, ultimately resulting in unethical behavior. Empathetic leaders, by contrast, are always open to questions and alternative points of view. The leader may need to choose the group's course of action at the end of the day, but drawing on the ideas and expertise of all group members usually results in the wisest choice. Furthermore, group members who feel they can disagree without being excluded are usually more truthful, happy, and loyal in the long run.

As parents must model empathy for their children, so leaders must do so for their subordinates. A leader who cares about the impact of the company's products and procedures on people, takes responsibility for his or her actions, and is willing to listen to concerns voiced by subordinates garners respect and ongoing dedication. Moreover, such leaders recognize that ethical behavior cannot be dictated from above through "sensitivity training" or other bureaucratic procedures. Rather, ethical behavior emerges naturally when leaders create environments where mutual respect and cooperation are valued. When people feel like they are making valued, meaningful contributions to an important collective goal, they work diligently together. When they feel like cogs in a large corporate machine, they do the bare minimum and ignore each other's needs. Because empathetic leaders value people more than procedures they bring out the best in human nature.

Providing empathetic leadership without becoming over-involved can be tricky though. Much like parents of adolescents, leaders must judge carefully how much responsibility to turn over to their subordinates. Competent workers often feel insulted by excessive supervision; novices often feel abandoned when little guidance is provided. Leaders who become involved in every internal dispute in the organization may be perceived as biased;

those who ignore workplace bullying as uncaring or cruel. Regular feedback from the "front lines" is needed in order to gauge the degree of supervision and involvement that is perceived as helpful. In addition, such feedback can often provide useful ideas on addressing the gap between lofty organizational ideals and the practical strategies needed to implement them. No wonder some bosses go "undercover", working side by side with their subordinates for a few days, in order to better understand their concerns!

Leaders who focus excessively on demands outside the organization (e.g., media presentations, lobbying for support for the organization or its mandate, meeting with various stakeholders, etc.) can be especially vulnerable to losing touch with their workforce. This alienation between managers and those they manage often results in decisions that are perceived as inappropriately controlling, non-consultative, or simply clueless and lacking in empathy. Therefore, if it is not possible for the same person to do both public relations and internal management well (e.g., due to the increasing size of the organization or the complexity of the issues), one or the other should probably be delegated for the sake of everyone in the organization.

Problem-solving in organizations that foster empathy tends to be a daily, humble, interpersonal exercise. Leaders recognize that their long-range plans offer a framework for future efforts, but may need to adapt to changing realities. Brainstorming where everyone's ideas are considered results in a myriad of creative solutions to problems that might not have occurred to the leader(s). Perhaps more importantly, people are invested in solutions when they have had a chance to participate in designing them. Motivation is enhanced, and everyone's strengths are applied to overcoming obstacles. The leaders may not be able to take personal credit for the results, but they have the satisfaction of knowing that their methods have fostered collective success and cooperation.

Finally, group philosophies that support empathy must include empathy for outsiders as well as those who are members of the group. As mentioned in Chapter 2, oxytocin and other brain chemicals support empathy for people we consider kin, but not for outsiders (De Dreu, 2012). Therefore, empathetic leaders must make a conscious effort to avoid favoring "insiders" over "outsiders" in disputes or competitions, to celebrate diversity of traditions and styles among group members and non-members, to emphasize similar human hopes and needs among all people rather than differences, and to include non-members in a positive way when envisioning future goals. For example, when deciding whose name goes first on a new patent or product, it is easy to minimize the contributions of someone who is peripheral to the organization and magnify those of a long-time, valued colleague unless there is an effort to resist this bias. On a more encouraging note, celebrating holidays from multiple faiths can acknowledge diversity, as well as resulting in sampling a delicious variety of foods. Common humanity is emphasized when friendships form across ethnic divisions. Seeing those outside one's group as potential consumers of one's products, potential participants in one's workforce, or potential leaders in new initiatives can all promote universality: the sense of being part of one human family. Moreover, supporting the development of empathy in groups may require reassuring fight or flight responses (see Chapter 6). Ideologies based on fearful visions of the future, for instance, easily lead to paranoia and a fear of outsiders. Such attitudes generally reduce empathy. Leaders that emphasize hopeful, unifying themes are much more likely to inspire empathy.

At first glance, it may seem that addressing all of these issues would complicate leadership to the point where it becomes unrealistic. However, this pessimistic view ignores the fact that many of these issues are related and are readily addressed when leaders simply make empathy a central theme in day to day interactions with those they lead. One leader who exemplified this approach was my third grade teacher, Mrs. Finney.

Mrs. Finney

When I was in elementary school, I was not a very popular child. I didn't wear popular clothes, I wore thick glasses, and I was uncoordinated so always got picked last for sports teams.

In third grade, however, I met Mrs. Finney. Mrs. Finney smiled warmly whenever I handed in my work. She always made bigger checkmarks than "Xs" when correcting it. She knew I was shy and awkward, but rather than telling me I needed professional help (as my second grade teacher did), she gave me a special, respectable job to do in class. I did it well, and was reassured that I belonged and could contribute to the group.

It wasn't that I was her favorite student: she seemed to like everybody. The boy with ADHD was "a real live wire" who made us laugh; the girl who was developmentally delayed was "a really good listener" who was always given extra time to explain her answers. Mrs. Finney saw the best in all of us.

The remarkable outcome was, our resentments faded as we saw the likeable qualities everyone brought to the class. I started to appreciate my classmates' quirks, even if they slowed down our lessons sometimes. I didn't feel the need to compete for Mrs. Finney's attention, because she already knew what I could do and I trusted that my report card would reflect this. Instead, I worked hard, helped others when I was done, and felt confident that we would all make it successfully to fourth grade. We did, and I never forgot Mrs. Finney.

I later learned that it was not just the personal attributes of Mrs. Finney that made third grade such a special year. Rather, Mrs. Finney was allowed to teach the way she did because of a supportive principal. He resisted pressure by the ministry of education to bring his school up to a rather arbitrary provincial standard on a test, and instead encouraged teachers to find creative ways of bringing out the best in their students. He also created an award system based on personal improvement, consistent attendance, and participating in the school community rather than rewarding only students with the best marks. Every student eventually won an award in at least one of these areas, and success became a shared experience for all. As this example shows, creating empathetic communities need not be complicated, but it usually requires wise, caring individuals at all levels of leadership.

What Should Leaders Do About Those Lacking Empathy Entirely?

Junior

Junior was considered "the runt of the litter" in his large, impoverished family. His father drank away his meager earnings and beat anyone who tried to stop him, including his wife. When his mother ran out of food, Junior had to forage for scraps in the local dump. In the winter, he cut down trees on a nearby hillside for firewood. He wasn't particularly close to his mother, as she behaved unpredictably with her children. Sometimes she hugged him affectionately, at other times she told him he was just as cruel as his father and pushed him away, and at other times still she was too disturbed by nightmares to interact with him much at all during the day. The atrocities she had witnessed when fleeing her homeland years before still haunted her. Junior felt he could not rely on her and had to fend for himself.

Junior hoped for a better life, but could see no way of achieving it. When he begged for money, the police shooed him away and beat him with clubs. When he foraged in the dump, he did not risk a beating but often got sick from spoiled food. He had no birth certificate, so was not allowed to enroll in school. Even if he could, his parents couldn't afford to buy him the uniform required. The wealthier people in town referred to children like Junior as "street urchins" and "vermin". A couple of Junior's friends had disappeared, and nobody bothered to investigate. Nobody seemed to care about children like Junior, and Junior cared little about anyone else.

Junior's life changed when a famous teacher came to town. He offered a free but secretly held lecture for all who would listen. Eager to learn, Junior attended. He heard that the wealthy were misguided non-believers who needed to be overthrown so that "the truth" could prevail. He heard that every person who joined the side of "the truth" would be rewarded handsomely, and would contribute in a meaningful way to a better society. Everybody, he was assured, had some useful talent to contribute. Junior joined the teacher's cause without hesitation. A few weeks later, he demonstrated his "talent" and his loyalty to the teacher by blowing himself up in a crowded market.

I named this character "Junior" deliberately, so as not to imply any particular nationality or religion. In doing so, I hoped to reflect the fact that extremists can emerge from any number of political or religious ideologies. If Junior was Muslim, he might have joined ISIS; if he was a member of my parents' generation in Germany, he might have joined the Hitler Youth. He could also be the follower of a powerful drug dealer. The particular ideology varies, but the central problem with people like Junior is the same: they value ideology more than human life, and certainly more than empathy.

Junior's life was marked by poverty, hopelessness, and alienation from mainstream society. His father modeled a violent approach to problems; his mother's traumatic history precluded a secure attachment relationship with him. Nobody seemed to care about Junior, and the attitudes of the wealthy and the local authorities reinforced this belief. In response, Junior didn't care much about others and felt rather worthless. He craved attention from someone who could make him feel worthy, regardless of the cost to himself or those around him. Junior's history created a "perfect storm" for extremism. The famous teacher's ideology, whatever it was, was merely a lightning rod.

You may wonder why Junior's story should matter to leaders. I believe it should matter because it provides clues to what fuels extremism and what actions will or will not reduce it. When we link extremist actions exclusively to a particular set of beliefs, we turn a blind eye to other elements that contribute to them. Elements such as poverty, alienation, and intergenerational trauma (which disrupts parent-child attachment) often contribute to the extreme lack of empathy we see in people like Junior. If these elements are present, Junior could be your child or mine. If these elements are ignored, extremism continues to flourish. Killing or jailing extremists without addressing these elements is unlikely to be effective. In fact, when wars are waged against extremists, the "collateral damage" to the local population may result in intergenerational trauma that fuels another generation of extremism.

Are there alternatives to this rather pessimistic view? History suggests there may be. After World War II, for example, the United States adopted The Marshall Plan (a.k.a. The Economic Recovery Plan of 1948; see Crafts and Toniolo, 1996), a substantial investment to rebuild infrastructure in Western Europe after Nazi Germany was defeated. It was expensive and took time to implement, but multiple stable democracies emerged in relation to this plan, and persist to the present day. Supporting non-extreme, empathetic societies is not easy, but if we want to prevent more cases like "Junior", it is a long-term leadership responsibility.

Even as we strive to improve social circumstances, people like Junior may not be a hopeless cause. The Aarhus Model, for example, is a mentorship program in Denmark that helps alienated youth develop empathetic relationships with people of similar background whom they respect, resulting in a feeling of inclusion in their communities (Powell, 2015). Since the program's inception, the number of youth that leave the country to become jihadist fighters has dramatically decreased.

Do We Need to Extend Empathy to All Life?

We usually think of empathy as the ability to take the perspective of another human being, yet empathetic relationships sometimes cross boundaries between species. We often form close bonds with the animals we keep as pets, and mourn them as we would close friends or family members when their lives end. Even if we cannot take their perspectives completely, we certainly care about their well-being, talk about their "personalities" as though they were human, and value the comfort and companionship they offer. Animals can also be considered our ancestors in evolutionary history, and it's surprising how much of our DNA we share with our closest primate kin (e.g., 96% for chimpanzees; Lovgren, 2005). In cultures that are highly connected to the natural world, animals are sometimes revered or considered "spirit guides" (Takatoka, 2016). In these societies, hunters often have ceremonies honoring the prey they take for food, and they never kill for sport.

Moreover, as we have learned more about ecology, our dependence on animals not only for food but also for their various roles in our ecosystems has become clearer. Even an insect we may consider annoying plays an important part in an interdependent system of life. The demise of the honeybee, for example, has seriously affected the growth of crops that rely on it for pollination (Nosowitz, 2016). The fossil fuels that provide much of our energy are derived from the decayed remains of ancient marine life. Plant life is equally if not more important. In addition to being a food source for animals and humans, plants often provide them with habitat, anchor the soil preventing erosion, and generate oxygen essential for us all. Therefore, some have argued that beyond empathy for individual creatures, we must regard the entire biome, and perhaps the planet itself, with empathy if we are to endure as a species (Chalquist, 2011).

Thus, the question "Do we need to extend empathy to all life?" is a rhetorical one. Clearly, it is essential that we do. If leaders are to encourage empathy for non-human life, however, a thoughtful approach is needed. Empathy for other creatures can be fraught with the same biases that sometimes affect human empathy, and environmentally friendly policies are unlikely to succeed if they are perceived as burdensome or unfair.

To review, potential biases include the kinship bias, the attractiveness bias, empathy that favors perceived victims, and empathy that favors individuals rather than groups. Kinship in this case, however, needs to be thought of in evolutionary terms. Thus, our closest kin in the natural world are other mammals. Not surprisingly, dogs and cats are among our favorite pets and the decision to euthanize one of these pets can be heart-wrenching. Disposing of a goldfish, on the other hand, is typically a less emotional experience. Similarly, many people (myself included) have few qualms about catching a fish or two for supper, but would feel awful about shooting a deer. The attractiveness bias is evident in our preference for "cute" animals. Most people acquire pets when they are young and have "cute" features, and donate money to animal-related causes more readily when shown pictures of creatures with an attractive appearance. The "victim bias" is evident in our difficulty empathizing with predators relative to prey, even though both are essential to balanced ecosystems. Ironically, humans themselves are now "top predators" in most ecosystems.

In summary, it would be easiest to experience empathy towards a cute, young, non-predatory mammal (e.g., young rodents, baby panda bears) and hardest towards fully grown non-mammalian predators (e.g., sharks, alligators, snakes). Zookeepers use these biases to their advantage when planning special exhibits, as do fundraisers for various wildlife-related causes. Environmentally responsible leaders, however, must remember that these biases are based entirely on emotional aspects of empathy. Once cognitive aspects come into play, these biases are reduced. Educating the public about interdependence within ecosystems and the crucial roles played by less emotionally appealing creatures is therefore essential.

The individual versus collective bias may be harder to address. Environmental issues often seem vast and overwhelmingly difficult to manage. What difference can one person make when the entire planet is at stake? Moreover, will empathy for other creatures or for the environment result in policies that threaten our jobs and our well-being? These are the questions leaders must answer if societies are to work towards harmonious integration with the natural environment rather than its ongoing destruction. Any initiatives that demonstrate how individual action can make a difference to other creatures or to the environment must be supported. For instance, choosing foods that are locally grown is a small change in lifestyle that can significantly reduce air pollution produced by the transportation of imported food. Similarly, we must support initiatives that allow stewardship for the environment to create jobs rather than destroy them. Designing such initiatives will challenge our intelligence and creativity for decades to come, but without them collective action that benefits the planet is unlikely.

The apparent cruelty of the natural world can pose a further obstacle to such action. Many people have beautiful, awe-inspiring experiences when they encounter nature walking in a forest, gazing from a mountain, or hearing the roar of the sea. Unfortunately, these may be offset by experiences of devastating illness or natural disaster that appear random and defy explanation. For example, I recall being incensed at the vines that were digging into the mortar on the walls of my house shortly after my husband died, and thinking (perhaps irrationally), "Nature's a bitch. I'll show her!" as I ripped them down. I associated the natural world with sudden disease and death, and with threats to my dwelling. Yet at the same time, petting my soft, purring cat was a great source of comfort and peace. This aspect of nature was obviously helpful but, overwhelmed with emotion, I couldn't see that. I imagine people who lose their homes in storms, floods, or wildfires might have this skewed view of nature as well.

Part of the problem, of course, is that nature is not really an entity that is for us or against us: nature simply is. It is the substrate of all life, including our own. Moreover, we are a part of nature, so natural events are never entirely random. For instance, pollutants we spew into the air contribute to global warming, which in turn contributes to more severe storms, wildfires, and other natural disasters than were present in the past. Diseases (at least those prevalent in North America) are partly linked to our genes, but also partly to unhealthy, sedentary lifestyles that remove us from the natural world for much of the day. Rather than blaming nature, we do better understanding how we have wounded nature, and wounded ourselves in the process. Then, we can return to regarding the natural world with the respect and curiosity needed to care for it effectively, and in so doing care for ourselves.

When leaders try to create programs and policies that honor the natural world, they must carefully consider how these programs and policies are likely to be perceived. If they are perceived as burdensome or unfair, they are likely to be resisted. For example, in some communities recycling programs are so complex that people spend hours every week cleaning and sorting various types of paper, food containers, and compostable products in order to avoid going over a maximum quota set for non-recyclable garbage. In busy, working families this time-consuming activity often becomes burdensome. As a result, the less fastidious recyclers may sneak around the neighborhood the night before trash day, distributing their excess garbage among the piles of their more fastidious neighbors. Clearly, this was not the outcome intended by authors of the recycling program. However, until the program is simplified (for example, by creating a better sorting process after the recycling is collected), people will likely continue to "bend the rules" this way.

Environmental policies are often perceived as unfair when they disproportionately affect a particular segment of the population. For example, some jurisdictions tax electrical power in order to support the development of renewable energy sources (so-called "carbon taxes"). This increase in the cost of electricity may have a modest impact on those who either use little power (e.g., private home owners) or for whom electrical costs represent a small fraction of the overall budget (e.g., large corporations). However, small businesses that are highly dependent on electricity (e.g., manufacturing plants, restaurants, or brightly lit recreation facilities) may struggle with the added cost, in some cases resulting in bankruptcy. It would seem important to find more equitable ways to generate revenue for clean energy initiatives.

In conclusion, extending empathy beyond humankind is possible, but requires leaders who can address the biases inherent in emotional aspects of empathy, inspire hope that small individual actions can make a difference globally, and find creative approaches to living in harmony with the natural world that are not experienced as burdensome.

The Interconnection of Global Problems and Empathetic Leadership

As discussed so far in this chapter, leadership that exemplifies and promotes empathy in organizations and communities can involve caring attention to the needs of group members, those outside the group, and even those outside our species. How would the world be different if all leaders behaved this way? Let's return to the example of Junior, and imagine the possible differences in his life story.

Junior (Alternate Version)

Junior was considered the "runt of the litter" in his large, impoverished family. Fortunately, his father was able to obtain a low-interest loan to start his own business selling work boots to local miners. Determined to make a profit and repay the loan, he worked hard to maintain sobriety. Some of the miners paid him in cash; others bartered for food which sustained the family. After a year there was enough money for a proper furnace, eliminating the need to raze the hillside for firewood.

As a number of local people had been traumatized by war, a mental health nurse was assigned to the district. She ran groups for survivors, including one for traumatized young women. Junior's mother participated, and was eventually able to see past her own distress to the needs of her children. When Junior had a tough day, she became a reliable source of support and encouragement. He trusted and cared about her, and started showing some trust and care towards others as well.

At first, Junior had to help his father in making boots, but as the business took off his father had the funds to pay for a school uniform, and an hour of a lawyer's time to get Junior's identification papers in order. Junior began his education. He walked by the homes of the wealthy with his head held high. He was certain he would make something of himself, and not be relegated to a life on the streets.

When a famous teacher came to town, Junior was curious and attended his lecture. The teacher's promises seemed too good to be true though, and his school mates warned him that some of the teacher's tactics were illegal. The local policeman, who had been trained in community relations, also advised Junior against joining the teacher's group and directed him instead towards a program where he could volunteer helping younger students. The youngsters looked up to Junior, and he enjoyed being able to make a positive difference.

Interestingly, the changes needed to turn Junior's life around were not complicated. The availability of a low-interest loan, a mental health nurse for the district, and a policeman educated in community relations were all that was required. As a result, Junior no longer posed a threat to his community (as he was not an extremist lacking empathy) or to the environment (as he no longer cut trees from the hillside causing erosion and possibly a landslide). The solutions were simple, but galvanizing the political will to implement them was not. It is much easier to blame and dehumanize the poor than to think of solutions that provide them with hope and self-respect. These solutions, however, may be the hallmark of empathetic political leadership.

Junior's example illustrates one further idea: the idea that global problems are inherently interconnected, so empathetic leadership in relation to one problem will often address others. As shown in Figure 11.1, peace, prosperity, and an environmentally sustainable world are mutually dependent goals. Poor people like Junior often degrade the environment in order to survive. Conversely, environmental degradation disproportionately affects the poor. For example, global warming has more devastating consequences for poorer countries than for wealthier ones, even though the latter create most of the pollution that fuels it (Mooney, 2016). Poverty also makes military solutions seem more appealing, as people may feel they have so little to lose that they might as well use violent means to fight for a better life. Armed conflict costs money, however, and that money cannot be used to fund solutions that might alleviate poverty. Armed conflict also leads to environmental degradation. The oil fires set in Kuwait during the first Gulf War are an obvious recent example (DeWeerdt, 2008), but all wars contribute to some extent to the destruction of the natural world. Conversely, environmental degradation often results in competition for scarce resources, fueling further conflict.

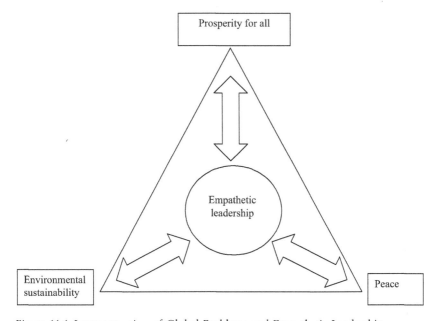

Figure 11.1 Interconnection of Global Problems and Empathetic Leadership

Empathetic leadership is central to reversing these negative cycles. When we prioritize empathy for others, we wage fewer wars as we cannot dehumanize our enemies. We think more carefully about how our actions affect the biosphere, our planetary community. We share our resources more equitably as we value all beings. As the disparity between rich and poor decreases, average health increases as well (Marmot, 2005). Given the interconnection of global problems, all of these changes are mutually reinforcing, ultimately contributing to peace, prosperity, and a sustainable environment for all. Some may think this picture is a bit overly optimistic, and perhaps it is. However, if every leader had this vision, perhaps it could become a reality.

Summary

- Some have argued that empathy may prompt leaders to make biased decisions, but cognitive aspects of empathy may mitigate the effects of empathy-related biases.
- The bias against empathy for large groups may be reduced when people are shown that group suffering can be alleviated without overburdening anyone.
- Review Table 11.1 to understand the characteristics of empathetic communities in order to foster their development.
- By undermining the development of empathy, poverty, alienation from mainstream society, and intergenerational trauma all provide fertile ground for extremist ideologies that can result in violent behavior; we must attend to these factors in order to combat extremism effectively.

Table 11.1 Empathetic Communities Versus Unhealthy Organizations

Empathetic Community	*Unhealthy Organization*
Leader inspires hope	Leader's ideology based on fear
Diversity is celebrated	Outsiders are perceived as threats
Everyone's contribution is valued	Winners and losers are clearly defined
Everyone's basic needs are addressed	"Losers" are neglected or fired
The success of the group is celebrated	Lip-service to teamwork; advancement based on individual achievement
Mutual respect	"Losers" are disparaged
Mutual support	Looking out for number one
Belonging and independent thought are balanced	Group think
Ethical behavior is a by-product of cooperative work and mutual respect	Ethics is dictated from the top
Humble, interpersonal solutions to problems	Grand plans for the organization; the ends justify the means
Universality	Insiders versus outsiders

- Extending empathy to non-human creatures and to the natural world more broadly is essential to our long-term survival as a species and, as in all forms of empathy, cognitive as well as emotional aspects are important to reduce various forms of bias.
- Demonstrating how small, individual actions can contribute to global sustainability is important if people are to remain hopeful.
- Personifying nature can sometimes undermine environmentalism, as people become preoccupied with the apparent cruelty of certain natural events.
- To succeed, programs and policies that honor the natural world must be carefully thought out to ensure that they do not place unfair burdens on some people.
- Because global problems such as poverty, war, and environmental degradation are interconnected, empathetic leadership aimed at addressing any one of them will contribute toward the solution of others.

Questions for Leaders

1. It is easier to develop empathy toward some people than others. Think of one or more person in your organization toward whom you have difficulty showing empathy. How can you ensure that your decisions are not biased against these people?
2. Using the ideas in Table 11.1 and the example of Mrs. Finney, what could you do to create a more empathetic environment in your organization?
3. What steps could you take to encourage people in your organization to show more empathy toward the natural world without feeling unfairly burdened by this task?
4. How do policies in your organization contribute to or detract from the ideal of peace, prosperity, and a sustainable environment for all? Are there small changes that would bring your organization closer to this ideal?

References

Chalquist, C. (2011). *Earth Empathy*. http://www.earthregenerative.org/earth-empathy/homepage.html Retrieved August 7, 2016.

Crafts, N., and Toniolo, G. (eds.)(1996). *Economic Growth in Europe since 1945*. Cambridge: Cambridge University Press.

De Dreu, C.K.W. (2012). Oxytocin modulates cooperation within and competition between groups: an integrative review and research agenda. *Hormones and Behavior*, 61, 419–428.

DeWeerdt, Sarah (2008). War and the environment. *World Watch*. 21(1), 14.

Aldous Huxley. (n.d.) BrainyQuote.com. https://www.brainyquote.com/quotes/quotes/a/aldoushuxl130029.html Retrieved October 4, 2016.

Lovgren, S. (2005). Chimps, humans 96 percent the same, gene study finds. *National Geographic News*, August 31 2005.

Marmot, M. (2005). Social determinants of health inequalities. *The Lancet*, 365, 1099–1104.

Mooney, C. (February 5, 2016). Why climate change is really, really unfair. *The Washington Post*, https://www.washingtonpost.com/news/energy-environment/wp/2016/02/05/why-climate-change-is-really-really-unfair/?utm_term=.8cddb6e2ee74 Retrieved August 8, 2016.

Nosowitz, D. (May 13, 2016). Honeybee deaths getting worse: we lost 44% of colonies last year. http://modernfarmer.com/2016/05/honeybee-colony-loss/ Retrieved August 7, 2016.

Powell, A. (July 2015). The Aarhus Model: how Denmark prevents jihad fighters. http://borgenproject.org/aarhus-model-denmark-prevents-jihad-fighters/ Retrieved August 21, 2016.

Schmidt-Traub, G. (2015). *Investment Needs to Achieve the Sustainable Development Goals*. Washington, DC: United Nations Sustainable Development Solutions Network Working Paper.

Takatoka (2016). *Spirit Guides and Totems*. Manataka American Indian Council, www.manataka.org/page291.html Retrieved August 7, 2016.

Tierney, J. (March 21, 2016). Empathy may be overrated in an election, and in a leader. *New York Times*.

Usefovsky, F., Shalev, I., Israel, S., Edelman, S., Raz, Y., Mankuta, D., et al. (2014). Oxytocin receptor and vasopressin receptor 1a genes are respectively associated with emotional and cognitive empathy. *Hormones and Behavior*, 67, 60–65.

Yalom, I. and Leszcz, M. (2005). *The Theory and Practice of Group Psychotherapy*, 5th Edition. New York: Basic Books.

12 Implications for Everyone

> You are a child of the universe. No less than the trees and the stars, you have a right to be here.
>
> Ehrman, 1927

In this chapter, we will discuss the implications of developing empathy that are relevant to people of all walks of life, review some key ideas to help in this endeavor, and provide some reasons for optimism about the human capacity for empathy. We conclude that, as the quote implies, we can all become children and caregivers of a more empathetic universe. To begin, let's review some important ideas in relation to the first case example in this book.

Revisiting the Coffee Server

The Coffee Server (Continued)

When the server in the preface overlooked my over-sized bill and paid for my coffee, she set a number of events in motion. First, I left the line-up feeling a bit foolish about my angry outburst, but also grateful that someone had, empathetically, gone out of her way to bend the rules on my behalf. I respected that behavior and resolved to treat others in a similar fashion. I listened more intently to my colleagues at the meeting I was rushing to attend, was more forgiving than usual with my patients who arrived late that day, and paid for another person's coffee the next day when she didn't have a small enough bill to do so. Furthermore, I felt good about doing all of these things, encouraging me to do more of them in future. In Haidt's words, the server prompted a "virtuous cycle" of empathy in me for quite a while after her initial helpful gesture (Haidt, 2003). In other words, altruism increases when we feel good, which makes us feel even better and more likely to continue behaving altruistically.

Beyond my own experience, however, others in the queue with me were affected as well. As a result of the server's actions, the line moved quickly and smoothly despite my payment problem. Therefore, everyone's day got off to a better start, and everyone was in a somewhat better mood heading into their usual duties. Positive mood is associated with a heightened capacity for empathy and with thinking styles that are broad and creative rather than narrowly focused on survival (Compton, 2005), which reduces fight or flight reactions, further increasing the chances of showing empathy. If even some of those people in the queue behaved more empathetically during the day, they could inspire others to feel understood, to work more cooperatively than otherwise, and to also respond to those around them empathetically. Thus, like ripples in a pond, the effects of a single empathetic act can spread to affect a host of people. When experiences of empathy are shared in books or through the media, the ripples spread even further. With the advent of the internet and particularly social media, the experiences are shared even more quickly and widely. Take another look at Figure 3.1: Social Influences on Empathy over Time. Just as the various circles of social influence can impact the development of empathy, the reverse is also possible: empathy can spread from one person to multiple spheres of influence.

Moreover, if some of the people in the coffee queue with me had children, they likely responded to them more patiently and affectionately that day than otherwise. As described in Chapter 2, experiencing an empathetic relationship with a parent in childhood sows the seeds for developing personal empathy in the long run. Feeling that we are cared for helps regulate unpleasant emotions physiologically, helps us develop psychological relationship models based on caring and mutual respect, and helps us feel we belong in our communities and in the world so we become more socially responsible citizens. Thus, the positive ramifications of an empathetic act can persist, even crossing generations.

Let's suppose for a moment that the coffee served at the establishment I frequent is produced by farmers who are paid a fair price for their crop (so-called "fair trade" coffee—Fair Trade USA, 2016). In this case, the server's ability to circumvent my outburst and ensure smooth procurement of beverages has even further reaching effects. The health, wealth, and well-being of the coffee growers increases each time a cup of coffee is sold. As their well-being increases, their capacity for empathy increases and affects those around them including their children, resulting in further "virtuous cycles" and further perpetuation of empathetic behavior across generations. Moreover, as discussed in Chapter 11, people who are hopeful of achieving success without resorting to violence typically avoid it, and people who are hopeful of meeting their needs without destroying the environment typically don't destroy it. Thus, directly or indirectly, our empathetic actions contribute to peace and to a sustainable environment.

There is one caveat to this good-news story: it doesn't work without faith. I'm not talking about religious faith, but rather faith that one's actions will make a difference even if the difference is not obvious at the time or even in one's lifetime. We may never know the positive outcomes associated with efforts to understand and help others, nor the negative outcomes associated with neglecting to do this. Occasionally, I have a patient write to me or call me expressing gratitude about how I changed his or her life with some brilliant statement I made years ago. Often, I have no memory of having made the statement. My intentions must have been good, but I had no idea at the time what impact my work would have. There are probably many more patients out there for whom I made a positive difference, but in most cases they don't call and so I never know about this. There are probably some for whom my work was not helpful, and in most cases I don't know about that either. Conversely, I'm sure there are people who have helped or inspired me along the way whom I forgot to thank. Thus, they might never know the impact of their actions. Much of the time, we must be content with knowing our intentions are good and empathetic, as the effects of what we say or do remain unknown. Carrying on despite that unknowing requires faith: faith that empathy has value, whether we ever see it or not.

An Attitude of Interdependence with Others and the World

Knowing the many positive effects of empathy, we are compelled to ask: "How do we develop it more consistently?" Much of this book has been dedicated to answering that question. Before summarizing some of the main points, however, it is important to highlight an assumption that underlies almost all empathetic behavior: the assumption of interdependence (previously described in Chapter 8).

Interdependence implies that we are distinct, unique individuals capable of contributing to each other's lives and to the world yet perpetually linked to one another and to other species in relationships that connect us and sustain us. Thus, we all have an impact and yet are all impacted by each other and by our environment.

Various metaphors have been used to describe this apparent paradox of existing as both autonomous and dependent beings. "The web of life" is a common phrase used in ecology, but perhaps it emphasizes the inter-connection more than the autonomy of its members. Others have described humans and other beings as unique pieces of a large puzzle or unique notes in a symphony. The value of these descriptions lies in their emphasis on the irreplaceability of each individual life. The puzzle is incomplete and the symphony discordant when even a single being is missing. These metaphors place less emphasis on connections and mutual dependence though. Perhaps "tapestry of life" resolves the paradox as well as can be. A tapestry only holds together as a result of the interweaving of its strands, yet each strand adds a unique hue to the final product. Moreover, the total picture created is dependent on both the color of the strands and the manner in which they are woven together.

How does this relate to empathy? Well, if we think of ourselves as unique and our relationships as interdependent or "interwoven", we cannot arrogantly claim to be totally independent, nor irresponsibly claim to be mere victims of circumstance. Rather, we see ourselves as both relying upon and influencing others who are different from ourselves and yet share many of our needs and hopes. Curiosity about differences coupled with respect and appreciation of what we share is fundamental to empathy. The assumption of shared characteristics allows us to trust others enough to not find them threatening, dampening fight or flight responses. Then, respectful curiosity about differences prompts us to ask questions, which lead to a better understanding of their points of view, and eventually allow us to step into their shoes, creating empathy.

Key Points for Developing Empathy

Beyond an attitude of interdependence, our journey through the biopsychosocial approach in this book has revealed a number of ways of developing empathy and overcoming obstacles to it. If we summarized some of the key points in a list of instructions, it might look something like this:

- Give people the benefit of the doubt: look for the best in each person.
- Remember your role models, mentors, and all people who made you feel valued more; remember your tormentors less.
- Be particularly careful when dealing with people who remind you of negative people/experiences in the past; take a few slow, deep, calming breaths before responding to them.
- If attitudes among your friends or within your family, place of work, community, or culture have a negative effect on your capacity for empathy, consider challenging them (at least in your own mind); conversely, see each of these settings as an arena of life where you can show greater empathy.
- Nurture self-compassion, especially when it comes to your physical health; find a daily time and a favorite method to calm your fight or flight response.
- Observe how those with disabilities contribute to your life and to the lives of others around them.
- Review the components of empathy shown in Figure 1.1; focus on developing the one that is most challenging for you.
- If needed, obtain help to better regulate angry, anxious, or depressive feelings; then model these coping strategies for your children.
- Cultivate an empathetic understanding of the other person in your closest relationships; emphasize what you share with them in the present; let go of past hurts if possible.
- See every encounter with a stranger as an opportunity for empathy; resist the temptation to use rude gestures in traffic.
- Treat your colleagues like the complex human beings they are, rather than a means of achieving your goals.
- Never be afraid to say you're sorry.

- Focus more on the aspects of your spiritual tradition or cultural ethos that enhance empathy and mutual respect than those that promote intolerance and competition.
- If you are a therapist, consider the ways you can both show empathy and foster it with your patients.
- If you are a parent, consider the ways you can both show empathy and foster it with your children.
- If you are a leader, consider the ways you can both show empathy and foster it with those you are leading.
- Expand your capacity for empathy to include non-human life and the planet.

For those who dislike dry lists, the following captures some of these ideas in a more poetic way:

> Cultivate a calm frame of mind, and pay attention to what happens on the sidelines of life. Most meaningful interactions happen while you're making other plans. Look for opportunities for random kindness. Allow for friendships outside your main social group. You may be surprised by the shared humanity you find, or the new insights. Model and show empathy to your children. The lives they live are our only guarantee of immortality, their discoveries allow us to relive our youth, and they are a delight to be cherished. See your adversaries as wounded children, for all have a kernel of goodness within, no matter how deeply buried. Emulate those who unify and heal. Whenever you can, replace fear with hope, take care of yourself compassionately, and seek ways to transcend the past. Remember that you are a "child of the universe", and so are all that you meet. Learn to accept help. Honor each person as a "thou".

That last bit about each person as a "thou" may be a bit unclear. Here are some examples:

- Regard every panhandler, disabled person, and person dependent on government assistance as a unique contributor to life's mosaic. Remember, you could be walking in their shoes but for the grace of God, fate, or whatever organizing principle you believe in. Appreciate their gifts, their courage, their ability to value life despite its limitations, and what they bring out in others.
- Regard every person who is different from you as a potential teacher. Human beings have complementary strengths and weaknesses; you may see in another qualities that you lack and could develop.
- Regard people who are similar to you as a reminder of the universal hopes and needs we all share. Listen to them, share their joy, and let them be a shoulder to cry on.

- Regard every grumpy, rude, insulting person as a beautiful, wide-eyed child whose spirit has been crushed by life events. This is hardest when facing those who abuse power. The person who issues an expensive traffic ticket when an impoverished mother explains that she has to get to the daycare by 6 pm as she can't afford the fine if she is late; the tax collector who insists on prosecuting bereaved families unless every last piece of paperwork connected to the estate return is correct; the boss who takes credit for others' work. Research the background of these people and you will find human beings who were disappointed or made to feel inadequate, and now have a compulsive need to wield power, even if they dehumanize, intimidate, or hurt people in the process. Try to remember that even these people are wounded children and need empathy, perhaps more than most.
- Regard with interest, humility, and deep respect all persons you encounter, whether daily or only once in a lifetime. Strive to understand them to whatever extent you are able.

These idealistic ideas may beg the question: How can we hope to change our negative attitudes and actions that interfere with empathy? In brief: Do whatever is necessary to make peace with the past. Do *not* do what comes naturally when stressed (i.e., the fight or flight reaction, with thinking narrowly focused on outcomes), but choose to honor relationships and global perspectives instead. Nurture health practices that can shift your focus away from self-interest, and towards a relational/global perspective. Focus on those values you cherish that promote empathy and inclusion of diverse individuals as "kin".

Another way of thinking about developing empathy is to consider two components. The first is nurturing one's personal capacity for empathy, and it has received the greatest attention in this book. As described in Part II, this involves attending to the biopsychosocial factors that can help or hinder empathetic behavior. As we regard other people with empathy more consistently, we can also hope for "ripple effects" described earlier in this chapter, as a result of those people behaving in a more kind and understanding manner with others. However, those effects are not guaranteed, so often we behave empathetically simply because it is the most helpful way to relate to other human beings moment by moment.

The second component of empathetic living is working towards policies that reflect empathy for all life. This means that rather than merely appreciating the beauty of nature, we must, as described in Chapter 11, address the interdependent problems of social inequality, violence, and environmental degradation. No one person can do all of these, but every person can make a small contribution toward addressing at least one of these issues. Some people would describe this second component as "compassion" rather than empathy, as the term empathy is used more when describing one to one relationships rather than broader social goals. Regardless of terminology, however, both components relate to an appreciation of the value of interdependence and of our individual efforts to contribute towards a kinder, gentler world.

Occasionally, these two components compete. For example, when writing this book with its goal of impacting a broad readership, I was acutely aware of the competing needs of my children, especially my son. Driving him back and forth through the snow to a cooking college in a neighboring town between patient appointments sometimes meant putting the book on the back burner for a while; later, helping him find a job had to proceed at a slower pace than ideal as I approached my deadline for the first draft. Usually, we are able to prioritize one or the other component at a given time, and address both eventually.

When in doubt though, pay attention to the person in front of you. The opportunity to support and encourage based on an empathetic understanding of that person may not come again, so seize it! Moreover, even the best efforts to improve the state of the world can become rigid, insensitive, and sometimes harmful ideologies if not tempered by empathy for the ordinary people affected by your plans. When it's unclear how to save the world, hold onto your ability to treat every person you meet with kindness, respect, and empathy.

Reasons for Optimism

I am optimistic that everything discussed so far in this chapter is possible. Some reasons for this optimism include knowing that: nature has designed us for empathy; empathy may be under-reported; we all have a great capacity for focusing on empathy despite difficult life experiences, and returning to empathy despite adversity; and finally, empathy sustains us, as empathetic responses are highly meaningful and man is a meaning-focused creature (see Frankl, 1984). Each of these reasons will now be described.

Designed for Empathy

For thousands of years, those who focused on the well-being of their group or tribe as well as their own survival were more likely to live to reproductive age (see Lewis, 1992). All it took was one harsh winter or one attack from a large predator for the friendless to succumb. Those who worked together tended to fare better, so their cooperative traits persisted in the gene pool. Thus, empathy for kin may be a legacy of our evolutionary past.

Wherever the substrates of empathy came from, however, they are abundantly evident in the brain. As described in Chapter 2, we have mirror neurons that support mimicry of others, different brain areas dedicated to perspective-taking, neurochemicals like oxytocin that support emotional aspects of empathy, other chemicals that relate to cognitive aspects (e.g., vasopressin, dopamine), and still others that improve our general ability to regulate strong emotions (e.g., serotonin), allowing for the emergence of empathy.

In primates, the biological priming for empathy is usually nurtured by a family environment that supports the physiology of emotion regulation and provides a model of empathy in relationships: secure attachment (Schore, 2001). Trusting that one is safe at home allows fight or flight reactions to subside, exploration to increase, and curiosity to emerge. When that curiosity is directed toward others, we begin to realize that those "others" may have perspectives that differ from our own. Striving to understand those perspectives, we begin to develop empathy. In addition to the immediate family, all those who support parents of young children, from caring friends or relatives to advocates for social policies regarding maternity/paternity leaves, contribute to secure attachment relationships and thus, indirectly, to the development of empathy in children.

Further empathetic experiences may occur outside the family. Teachers, coaches, close friends, and mentors can help nurture empathy, even in those situations where family circumstances are very difficult. A lucky few may also encounter programs specifically designed to nurture empathy (e.g., Roots of Empathy—see Gordon, 2012). As children mature, exposure to any philosophy that promotes mutual respect, appreciation of our shared humanity, and cooperative rather than competitive attitudes will further build upon past experience to highlight the value of empathy.

In summary, even though this book has talked about many factors that can interfere with developing empathy, there are also many opportunities in most lives to manifest this latent ability. With a little bit of nurturing, the seeds of empathy nature bestows can open and grow into blossoms.

The Under-Reporting of Empathy

There is a saying that only the bad news is reported, and there is some truth to this. When we turn on the television or surf the internet extraordinary events are more eye-catching than ordinary ones, and often events that involve violence or inhumanity are extraordinary and therefore highlighted. Everyday behavior involving empathy or altruism is neglected in this process, so we are often unaware of it. I've already alluded to acts of random kindness in the coffee server example, and these may be more common than one would think. The popularity of books of anecdotes about such acts (for example, the *Chicken Soup for the Soul* series—see Hansen and Canfield, 1993) speaks to our need to counter-balance the bias towards the negative typically found in news stories.

Perhaps even more prevalent than people who engage in random empathetic behavior, however, are people who choose to include empathy and altruism in their daily lives. My daughter, for example, dedicates one month a year to volunteer work at a wildlife sanctuary. I did not suggest or encourage this, as it is grueling and not without risk, but she finds it rewarding enough to put up with the long bus trip, rabies shots, lack of sleep, and many discomforts of the remote location. She returns covered in insect bites but beaming. She is one of many people who engage regularly in volunteer work or community service. In fact, rates of volunteerism are increasing in North America (Levy-Ajzenkopf, 2015), even though crime rates are reported more often.

A large number of professions or professional choices involve empathy or altruism as well. Empathy is central to psychotherapy, chaplaincy, social work, and many other professions. Altruistic behavior based on empathy is evident in many more. Firefighters risk their lives daily to rescue people from burning buildings; medical professionals work throughout the night to save the lives of strangers; legal aid lawyers work with little compensation to ensure that the poor are represented in court; and the list goes on. Furthermore, many professions allow people to mentor others, and mentorship relationships are often very empathetic, sometimes even repairing some of the emotional damage left by negative childhood experiences (see the examples of Ashley's choir teacher in Chapter 2 and Benny's coach in Chapter 10).

Sometimes one can also choose to pursue projects that benefit others in preference to those associated with more accolades. For instance, in my later years as a researcher I found myself pursuing more projects related to knowledge translation than basic science. As mentioned in Chapter 9, these projects involved training people in remote locations in evidence-based psychotherapy skills using telehealth technology. They were able to use these skills to treat children in their communities more effectively than before. I knew that the number of top-tier publications associated with this work would be small, so it would not enhance my professional status much, but felt compelled to do it anyways. Sometimes the satisfaction of knowing one is making a difference in the people's lives outweighs other considerations.

In summary, we might be surprised if we were aware of all the empathy and empathy-based behavior shown in random acts of kindness, volunteerism, helping professions, and professional choices. We often hear about community service in eulogies. Wouldn't it be nice to attend to it more while people are alive!

We Can Focus on Empathy When Life is Difficult

In Part II the biological, psychological, and social ways of nurturing and hindering empathy were reviewed. Most of us can improve in one or more of these areas. There are circumstances, however, where empathy must temporarily take a back seat to other, more urgent needs. Usually, this occurs when we face real danger to ourselves or our loved ones. Such dangers could include natural or man-made disasters, life-threatening illnesses or accidents, and any situation where we are deprived of food, shelter or another basic need. Most people quickly return to their former level of empathy though. In natural disasters, for example, people often help their neighbors even when their own homes are still threatened. When famine relief is provided, people often share the available food.

Empathy may be more consistently undermined by the cumulative effect of a large number of annoying, discouraging, and unnecessarily anxiety-provoking experiences. Being audited, accused of a petty crime, or "buried in red tape" to obtain access to necessary supports for a child are some examples that leap to mind. Each official involved in these experiences is not being deliberately cruel. In fact, in most cases he or she is simply following a set of procedures dictated by superiors. However, when people are forced to struggle through such experiences month after month and year after year, they become exhausted and rarely able to escape their own negativity and bitterness. Most cynical people were once empathetic and optimistic, but have been worn down by life's drudgery.

How then can we focus on empathy when life is difficult? There are many possible answers to this question. A few that come to mind include:

- By reminding ourselves that as long as we live better experiences are possible, and then doing what makes sense for everyone's well-being regardless of our own state of mind.
- By becoming willing to sacrifice the desire for personal satisfaction, vindication, or fairness in order to get past old resentments and contribute our unique abilities to our relationships and the world.
- By remembering that every positive interaction and every courageous response to our circumstances makes a difference, whether or not we can see that difference now, in the future, or even in our lifetime.
- By developing a perspective on life that goes beyond our own self-interest, and acknowledges our interdependence with each other and the larger biome.
- By modeling these ideas for our children.
- By recognizing that what makes life meaningful and bearable in the face of sorrow, injustice, and overwhelming fear is the knowledge that you can always get out of your head, respond empathetically to whoever stands before you, and try to make a positive difference. Perhaps that is an alternative definition of success.

Returning to Empathy

Many of us face times in life where, whether due to neglect or negative experiences, empathy seems a distant memory. We may feel we are too busy to indulge in daily practices that calm us and support an empathetic frame of mind. We may encounter people who claim to be proponents of empathy but treat their subordinates terribly. Sometimes seeing hypocrisy can do more to damage our capacity for empathy than witnessing overtly malicious acts. We may become preoccupied with getting the love we missed as children and treat our partners like surrogate parents, instead of the vulnerable, loveable human beings they are. We may feel compelled to disregard others' needs for fear of losing out on opportunities for personal advancement or success. We may be disoriented by traumatic events that are not only frightening but also lead us to question our own motives and character. As in the parable of the prodigal son who wasted his inheritance and ended up destitute (Luke 15:11–32 English Standard Version), we eventually long to return home to a kinder time and place, but are not sure if we have changed too much to belong there anymore.

Whether you have had one or all of these experiences though, the possibility of re-engaging with others empathetically is always there. Lifestyles that support an empathetic frame of mind can be nurtured. Hypocrites can be seen as wounded children, as can enemies. Negative assumptions from childhood that mar our current relationships can be challenged. Then, with effort and optimism new patterns of relating can be found. Knee-jerk competitive responses can be recognized as short-sighted, and replaced with attention to building trusting relationships which support long-term success.

If you are haunted by traumatic events, find someone who can help you process the complex emotions they elicit, and don't give up. Sometimes just as we've given up swimming and are about to drown, we find a current that pushes toward shore; sometimes when we are paralyzed by fear, we can bide our time until there is a chance to escape to safety; sometimes when the path seems to lead inexorably toward self-destruction, we can step off, sit on the grass, listen to the wind, and change course. That's not just poetic writing: I am alluding to some of my own most difficult experiences.

Forgiving ourselves may be the most challenging issue to address. It is often the issue that interferes the most with returning to a state where we feel we belong to the human race, and can once again be kind to ourselves and to others. And yet, it must be addressed if we are to overcome the self-preoccupation associated with guilt and *not* associated with empathy. Apologizing and making restitution for the harm done is a good place to start. It is sometimes surprising how accepting others become when we do this, but important regardless of their response. When restitution is no longer possible because the person has passed away or is unreachable, we are left with resolving to do things differently in future. Even the most horrible mistakes can be learned from, and sometimes learning is all we can do.

Lastly, nobody is too old or too set in their ways to change. If life experience has left you bitter and disenchanted with the human condition, pretend to have empathy. It's remarkable how differently people behave when they give themselves permission to play a new role. A colleague who seems like a stiff, formal old professor goes to a conference in Texas and takes up line-dancing; a shy person "comes out of her shell" when starting a new job where nobody expects her to be quiet; a teenager who spends his nights smoking marijuana instead of studying "steps up" and behaves responsibly when a parent dies and his siblings need him. Thus, if you don't feel empathy toward most other people, try to imagine what an empathetic person would say or do. Then, say it and do it. The responses you get may be surprising, and might even start a "virtuous cycle" that encourages your further development of empathy.

Walking the Path of Destiny

A few years ago, I was scheduled to speak at a conference in San Francisco and allowed myself an extra day to explore the sites. I had booked a tour of the city, and a tour of Alcatraz later in the day. During the city tour we stopped at Grace Cathedral. Like many old cathedrals, it inspired a sense of reverence and awe. I walked the labyrinth solemnly. No particular insights occurred during the walk though, probably because I knew I had a limited time to get back to the tour bus.

When it was time to take the boat to Alcatraz Island the heavens opened and it poured rain. This was an evening event, the waters in the bay were choppy, and there was initially some doubt about whether or not the tour would proceed. Eventually, the decision was made to proceed. The boat rocked and heaved on the waves. Many of us were nauseated by the time we arrived. Then we were marched up-hill to the prison in the dark downpour, much as new inmates would have been years ago. What followed was a self-guided walk with headphones that detailed a series of unsuccessful escape attempts from "The Rock". By the end, it was abundantly clear why most inmates were so resigned to their dismal fate.

Despite the miserable circumstances I found the trip enlightening. It reminded me of my labyrinth walk earlier in the day. Unlike a maze, a labyrinth has only one path. Thus, there is no choice but to walk that path. Much of life can be thought of as a prison or a labyrinth: the path is fixed, and the only choice one has is how to walk it. One can walk inconsiderately, ploughing through whoever gets in one's way, or one can walk kindly, passing fellow travelers on the path gently and with grace. One can walk deliberately, with dignity or shuffle along, discouraged by whatever unexpected turns occur.

Some people might protest that this is an overly fatalistic view of life, and perhaps it is, but I do not hold it without reason. My personal experience included spending years doing my utmost to succeed in my career and avoid close relationships so that I would not become "stuck" raising children with little support as I had seen my own mother do. When I finally succeeded professionally I felt secure enough to marry the man of my dreams. He died when the children were six and eight years of age. I became a single parent and, ironically, found myself raising children with little support.

Whether we are prisoners or judges, worshippers or builders of cathedrals, or ordinary folks just trying to make ends meet, there are limits to our control over our lives. We can modify life's path and meander here or there for a while, but ultimately the path is fixed. We can only choose how to walk it. Fortunately, walking it well by crafting the best response possible to each situation we encounter is something we can all do. Often that response is one that includes empathy for ourselves and others. This process, as Frankl (1984) described, provides a rich source of meaning in human life. There is an old saying that when life gives you lemons the best response is to make lemonade. A meaningful life is not just about making lemonade, but making a lemonade infused with your own unique recipe that makes it indescribably good.

Why not walk with dignity and respect for ourselves and others? Why not walk with child-like curiosity about ourselves, our path, and our companions on the journey? Why not encounter those companions with gentleness and grace? And, on occasion, why not put ourselves in our companions' footsteps and share in their journey?

Too often we think that in order to make a difference we need to accumulate accomplishments on some giant score-card of life. We fail to realize that lasting differences are not about high scores, or medals, or wealth, or 15 minutes of fame. Lasting differences are about the impressions left on others, uncaring or caring, hurtful or hopeful, which reverberate across space and time.

Reflective Questions

Review today's events this evening.

1 Which ones contributed to your capacity for empathy?
2 Which ones detracted from it?
3 How did you respond to these events?
4 Who was affected by your responses?
5 Based on your answers to 1–4, what do you hope to do differently tomorrow?

References

Compton, W.C. (2005). *An Introduction to Positive Psychology*. New York: Wadsworth Publishing, pp. 23–40.
Ehrman, M. (1927). *Desiderata*. Copyrighted by author.
Fair Trade USA. Products: coffee. www.fairtradeusa.org Retrieved August 16, 2016.
Frankl, V.E. (1984). *Man's Search for Meaning* (Revised and updated). New York: Washington Square Press.
Gordon, M. (2012). *Roots of Empathy: Changing the World, Child by Child*. Markham, ON: Thomas Allen Publishers.
Haidt, J. (2003). Elevation and the positive psychology of morality. In C.L.M. Keyes and J. Haidt (Eds.) *Flourishing: Positive Psychology and the Life Well-lived*. Washington, DC: American Psychological Association, pp. 275–289.
Hansen, M.V. and Canfield, J. (1993). *Chicken Soup for the Soul: 101 Stories to Open the Heart and Rekindle the Spirit*. Cos Cob, CT: Chicken Soup for the Soul Publishing, LLC.

Levy-Ajzenkopf, A. (2015). Giving, volunteering, and participating: latest survey results from Statistics Canada. https://charityvillage.com Retrieved August 19, 2016.

Lewis, D. (1992). *Millennium: Tribal Wisdom and the Modern World*. Toronto: Viking Canada.

Luke 15: 11–32. *The Bible. English Standard Version.*

Schore, A.N. (2001). Effects of a secure attachment relationship on right brain development, affect regulation, and infant mental health. *Infant Mental Health Journal*, 22, 7–66.

Index

Aarhus Model 184
abuses of power 198
acceptance commitment therapy 74
Adam 79–81
adaptive coping 98–100
addiction 76, 79–81
ADHD 163, 164
adrenaline 30, 91
advocacy 145, 146, 157–9
aerobic exercise 93
affective empathy *see* emotional empathy
age 49
Alcatraz 204
alcohol abuse 79–81
all life, empathy for 185–7, 198–9
Aloofa 28–9
altered stress responses 30
altruism 5, 8–9, 98, 193
ambition 134–5
ambivalent attachment 27
Aneesha 94–6
anger 90–2, 102; and empathy 94–6
animals 185–6
annoyance 17
anthropomorphic gods 127, 128–9
anti-bullying programs 162
anticipation 98–9
antisocial personality disorder 6, 76, 83–4
anxiety 76, 77, 101–2, 148–9; and empathy 92–4
appraisal-focused coping 99–100
Arjun 24–5, 114
Armstrong, K. 8, 52
Ashley 32–4
assertive responses 95–6
assessment 146–8

attachment 7, 22, 26–9, 32; insecure 27–9, 114–15; and reactions to illness 65–6; secure 26–7, 103, 115, 131, 165–6, 200
attending to others 11–12, 130, 132–3; mental health and 75, 76, 79–81
attentive listening 87
attitudes 61; social 133–40
attractiveness bias 185–6
attributional bias 87
authoritarian cultural norms 51
authoritative parenting 29–30, 42, 167
authority figures 140, 145; *see also* leadership; parents/parenting; therapists
autism 23, 67, 76, 81–3, 171–2; intensive therapy 159
avoidance of feared situations 93
avoidant attachment 27

"bad patients" 64–6
balance 109
basic needs 179
Batson, C.D. 9
Bauby, J.D. 68
behavior management 102
behavioral activation 77
beliefs *see* ideals and beliefs
benevolent reappraisal 131
Benny 163–4
biases 87, 95; empathy for other creatures 185–6; political leadership 177–8
biological substrates of empathy *see* developmental basis
biopsychosocial approach xiii; developing empathy with children 162–7
biopsychosocial assessment 147
blame 138

Bloom, P. 177, 178
Bob 117–18
body *see* physical aspects
Bombeck, E. 99
Bonhoeffer, D. 73
Bonita 117–18
boundaries 165–6; psychological 10–12, 75, 76, 84–6
Bowlby, J. 7, 26
brain 21–2, 57–8, 199–200
brainstorming 181
breathing from the diaphragm 63
"broaden and build" theory 7
broader autism phenotype 82
broken dreams 135–6
Buber, M. 6, 108, 132
bullying 92, 168
burnout 96–8
Byrne, R. 154

callous and unemotional people 83–4
Cameron, D. 178
Can I Catch It Like a Cold? 79
Canada 51, 169
capacity for empathy 110
carbon taxes 187
caring 165–6
catastrophic events 154–7
cell metaphor 47–8
centering on the moment 61
Charter for Compassion 52
Cherokee folk wisdom 63
children: developing empathy with 162–7; helping them manage strong emotions 101–4; importance of empathy in 161–2
Circle of Security intervention 166
clinical psychology 6–7
codes of conduct 15
coffee server xii, 113, 193–5
cognitive behavioral therapy training 158
cognitive biases *see* biases
cognitive empathy (perspective-taking) 9–10, 11–12, 22–3, 177–8; mental health and 75, 76, 81–3; teaching empathy 169–70
cognitive strategies for anxiety 93
collaborative religious coping 131
collective well-being 4–5
common struggles 170–1
communication: difficulties 68, 171–2; of empathy 11–12, 75, 76, 86–7; in families 41

communities: influences on empathy 38, 39, 45–8; leadership 178–83; voluntary activities 168–9; well-functioning 47–8, 190
community involvement 51–2
compassion 8, 52, 198; self-compassion 57–62
compassion collapse 178
competing loyalties 149
complementarity 109–10
component processes of empathy 9–12, 153; and mental health 75–87
confidentiality 146
conflict 170; between siblings 39–42, 104, 167
connecting with patients 151–2
connections/freedom balance 109
constitutional factors (nature) 21, 22, 23–6, 62–3, 199–200
content of therapy 153–7
contrarian view 12–15
cooperation 179–80
coping strategies 98–104, 131, 165; for children 101–4
coping styles 64–6
Coplan, A. 10
counter-transference 114
Courtney 118–20, 121
cults 45
culture 38, 39, 48–52; cultural characteristics and norms 50–2; cultural differences 48–50; reactions to illness 64
curiosity, empathetic 139

daily hassles 96–8
Dana 135–6, 173–4
Danny 24–5
Darren 137–40
dating 48–9
Davis, P. 121
defense mechanisms 98–100
degrees of empathy 25–6
dehumanization of others 96
Denmark 184
depression 76, 77–8; in a parent 78–9
de-reflection 74–5
desensitization 93
designed for empathy 199–200
detachment 151
developing countries 134
developmental basis 21–37, 62–3, 199–200; constitutional factors 21, 22,

23–6, 62–3, 199–200; environmental factors 21, 22, 26–30, 32–4, 62–3, 200
diagnosis of mental illness 146
Diamond, J. 134
different abilities, people with 169, 171–4
difficult life experiences 201–2
diffusion of responsibility 44
disability 50; witnessing 67–8
disfigurement 50, 68
disorganized attachment 27
diversity of opinion 180
divisive ideals 127–30
Dorothy 43–4

early environment 22, 26–9
eating disorders 57–8
education 4; level of 50
Ehrman, M. 193
Einfühlung 6, 68
electricity 187
elevation 7, 132–3
embodied cognition theory 22–3
emotion-focused coping 99
emotional empathy 9–10, 11–12, 22–3, 177–8; and mental health 75, 76, 83–4; teaching empathy 170
emotional states that suppress empathy 30–1
emotional valence 110; negative 111, 112, 118–22; positive 111–12, 113, 115–18
endorphins 23, 60, 63
enjoyable activities 63
environmental factors (nurture) 21, 22, 26–30, 32–4, 62–3, 200; early environment 22, 26–9; later environment 22, 29–30
environmental degradation 189–90, 198
environmental movement 5
environmental policies 187
envy 96
ethnicity 48–9
ethnocultural empathy 48–9
evolution 199
exercise 60
expectations: of ourselves 61; of relationships 113–14
exposure 13, 93
external locus of control 87
extremism 45, 183–4
extrinsic spiritual orientation 128, 129

fair trade 194
faith 194–5

"faked" physical symptoms 66–7
family 15, 38, 39–44, 52; *see also* parents/parenting
fatalism 87
favoritism 177
fear 90–2; anxiety and empathy 92–4
fight or flight reactions 5, 27, 30–1, 90–107; anger and empathy 94–6; anxiety and empathy 92–4; coping strategies 98–104; fear and anger 90–2; perceived scarcity, daily hassles and burnout 96–8
Finney, Mrs 182–3
Fleming, B.D. 49
flexibility 87
flooding 93
food bank 130
food deserts 69
forgiveness 51, 120–1, 132; self-forgiveness 78, 203
formal communities/organizations 178
Francis of Assisi, St xii, xiv
Frankl, V. 154–5, 205
freedom/connections balance 109
Freud, S. 5, 74
"frozen in time" relationships 115–18
future-focused ideals 127–30
future goal-defined relationships 115, 117–18

gangs 45
gender 49
generalized anxiety disorder 148
genetics 23–4, 32–4, 62–3, 199–200
global problems 5; interconnection of 188–90, 198–9
goals: future goal-defined relationships 115, 117–18; self-serving 14; of therapy 148–50
Golden Rule xiv, 5, 57, 127
government policy, protesting 159
gratitude 68, 132
Gray, J. 49
grief 121, 122, 172
group think 180
groups 177–8; small 38, 39, 40–1, 44–5, 52
guilt 59, 78; survivor guilt 157

habits 61, 98
Haidt, J. 7, 132–3, 193
Hank 64–5
hard truths 13
hateful ideologies 96, 138

Helen 127–9
high-influence relationships 110, 111, 113–22; hurtful 111, 118–22
hockey parents 169
Hoffman, M.L. 25–6
hope 132
humanity 7
humility 130–3
humor 99
hurtful people 111, 118–22
Huxley, A. 177
hyperventilation 93
hypo/hyper-arousal paradox 21, 31–4

I-Thou relationships 6, 108, 132, 197–8
ice hockey 169
ideals and beliefs 126–42, 154; extremism 45, 183–4; future-focused, divisive or self-serving 127–30; ideologies, psychological needs and empathy 126–7; patient's world view not shared by the therapist 137–40; present-focused, inclusive or humble 130–3; social attitudes and empathy 133–7
illness 31; mental health professional's perspective 66–7; reactions to 63–6; witnessing 67–8
imminent danger 146
inclusive ideals 130–3
inconsiderate patients 150–1
individual bias 185–6
individual well-being 5–6
individualism 4, 5, 133, 134–6
influence in relationships: high 110, 111, 113–22; low 110, 111–13
influences away from empathy 15–18
informal communities/organizations 178
insecure attachment 27–9, 114–15
intellectual empathy *see* cognitive empathy (perspective-taking)
intentions, therapist's 152–3
interactions within communities/organizations 179–80
interconnection of global problems 188–90, 198–9
interdependence 51–2, 64, 65, 133, 136–7, 150, 195–6
internal locus of control 87
inter-subjectivity 6, 22, 108–9

Jack 60–2
James, W. 128
Jason 148–50

Jennifer and her sons 39–42
Joel 83–4
John 129–30
Juanita 76–9
Junior 183–4, 188–9

Kabat-Zinn, J. 59
Keisha 84–6
Ken 101–2, 102–4
key points for developing empathy 196–9
kind strangers xii, 111–12, 113, 193–5, 200
Kingsley, E.P. 174
kinship bias 15, 185
Klein, N. 52
Kohut, H. 6–7
Kornfield, J. 57
Kyle 102–4

labyrinth walking 101, 204
later environment 22, 29–30
leadership 47, 48, 96, 145, 177–92; empathetic communities and organizations 178–83; interconnection of global problems 188–90; and the natural environment 185–7; and people entirely lacking in empathy 183–4; political 177–8
Leszcz, M. 44
Levenson, R.W. 48
life, empathetic approach to 204–5
life experiences, difficult 201–2
limits of power and knowledge 131–2
"locked in" state 156–7
logotherapy 154–5
Lois 65
low-influence relationships 110, 111–13

Maleficent 170
malnourishment 68–9
Mandy 115–17
MAO-A gene 23–4, 32
Marco 86–7
Marshall Plan 184
Marvin 16–18
Mary 163–4
mass communication 4–5
materialism 51
Matheson, R. 126
mature defense mechanisms 98–100
meaning 205
meaning-focused therapy 154–5
media 171

medical principle 5–6, 74
meditation, mindfulness 59–62, 74–5, 100–1
mental health 73–89; assessment 146–8; attending to another person 75, 76, 79–81; cognitive perspective-taking 75, 76, 81–3; communicating empathy 75, 76, 86–7; components of empathy and 75–87; diagnosis of mental illness 146; historical perspective 73–5; impact of mental illness on other people 146–7; parents' 165; preoccupation with oneself 75, 76–9; psychological boundaries 75, 76, 84–6; relating to another person emotionally 75, 76, 83–4
mental health care systems 145, 146, 157–9
mentalization 74–5
mentorship 34, 163, 184, 201
Merton, T. 108
meta-cognition 74–5
Micah 132
Michael 115–17
Milgram, S. 51, 122
mindfulness 59–62, 74–5, 100–1
mirror neurons 6, 21–3
mirroring body language 87
missed appointments 150–1
modeling: empathy 165, 169, 180; healthy coping 103–4
modification of the treatment approach 152
moral conduct 12–13, 15
motivations, understanding 170
mutual respect 179–80

national influences 38, 39, 48–52
natural disasters 201–2
natural world 5, 131, 168–9; empathy for all life 185–7, 198–9; environmental degradation 189–90, 198; environmental movement 5; environmental policies 187
needs: basic 179; psychological 126–7, 129
negative emotional valence 111, 112, 118–22
Nelson, J.M. 7
Nolton 81–3
norms: cultural 50–2; family 42

obedience 51
obsessive compulsive disorder 139–40

official procedures 202
openness to external influences 42
organizations: influences on empathy 38, 39, 45–7, 52; leadership 178–83; unhealthy 45–7, 178–9, 190
outsiders 44–5, 52, 133–4, 177–8, 181–2
oxytocin 23, 44–5, 52, 63, 133, 177

panic 92; attacks 93
parasympathetic nervous system 63
parent-child dyad 38, 39
parents/parenting 145, 161–76; attachment *see* attachment; authoritative parenting 29–30, 42, 167; children with special needs 171–4; child's resemblance to parent, or to someone in the parent's past 24–5; depression in parents 78–9; developing empathy with children 162–7; helping children manage strong emotions 101–4; hurtful parents 120–1; lacking in boundaries 84–6; parenting within a system 167–9; stable emotional environment 103, 139, 165; teaching empathy 169–71
Pargament, K.I. 131
passive-aggressive behavior 95
past pattern-defined relationships 115–17
patient's world view not shared by therapist 137–40
peace 189–90, 198
perceived scarcity 31, 96–8
PERMA 7, 149
personal issues, therapist's 152
personality disorders 74
perspective-taking *see* cognitive empathy (perspective-taking)
perspectives on empathy 3–20
philosophy of a community/organization 181–2
physical aspects 57–72; mental health professional's perspective 66–7; reactions to illness 63–6; self-compassion and the body 57–62; social determinants of health and of empathy 68–9; strengthening biological substrates of empathy 62–3; witnessing illness and disability 67–8
physical comfort 62–3
plants 185
political leaders 177–8

Index

positive emotional valence 111–12, 113, 115–18
positive psychology 7, 75, 149
potential danger to others 146–7, 149
poverty 68–9; global 178, 189–90
prayer 61
pregnancy 66
preoccupation with oneself *see* self-transcendence
present-focused ideals 130–3
printing press 4
Prinz, J.J. 12–13, 15
privately funded care 158
problem-focused coping 99, 100
problem-solving 42, 181
process of therapy 150–3
prodigal son parable 131, 203
professional choices 201
professions 201
prosperity for all 189–90, 198
protest against government policies 159
psychiatry 5–6, 6–7
psychological boundaries 10–12; mental health and 75, 76, 84–6
psychological needs 126–7, 129
psychopathy 6, 32
public relations 181

quick-temperedness 95

rage 92
random acts of kindness xii, 111–12, 113, 193–5, 200
reassurance of safety 130–1
reconciliation 51
recycling programs 187
regret 78
relating to another person emotionally *see* emotional empathy
relationships 7, 108–25, 127; defined by past patterns or future goals 115–18; high-influence 110, 111, 113–22; hurtful 111, 118–22; low-influence 110, 111–13
relaxation techniques 63, 93
remorse 78
resemblance to a parent (or someone in the parent's past) 24–5
resource scarcity, perceived 31, 96–8
respect 169; mutual 179–80
responsibilities: family 41; leadership 180–1
restitution 203
retaliation 122

returning to empathy 202–4
Richard 92–4
ripple effects xiii, 7, 193–5
Rogers, C.R. 6, 145
roles: family 41; leadership 180–1
Roots of Empathy program 30, 162, 168
rules: families 42; organizations 45–7

safety, reassurance of 130–1
Scale of Ethnocultural Empathy 49
scarcity, perceived 31, 96–8
scrupulosity 139–40
secure attachment 26–7, 103, 115, 131, 165–6, 200
Selena 118–21, 122
self-compassion 57–62; encouraging 59–62
self-esteem 3
self-forgiveness 78, 203
self-observation 149
self-psychology 6–7
self-reflection 74–5
self-respect 61
self-serving goals 14
self-serving ideals 127–30
self-transcendence 8, 11–12, 130–2; mental health and 75, 76–9
Seligman, M.E.P. 7
sensory experience, heightened 68
serotonin 23
sexual activity 63
sexual orientation 50
siblings: of children with special needs 173; conflict between 39–42, 104, 167
Sienna 10–11
similarities between people 170–1
slow/imperceptible change 153
small groups 38, 39, 40–1, 44–5, 52
social attitudes 133–7, 150; not shared by patient and therapist 137–40
social determinants of health and of empathy 68–9
social inequality 189–90, 198
social influences 38–54, 194: communities and organizations 38, 39, 45–8; national and cultural 38, 39, 48–52; small groups 38, 39, 40–1, 44–5, 52; triads and families 38, 39–44
Social Stories 82
socioeconomic level 50
sociopaths 120
Solomon, A. 47, 67, 171
somatic symptoms 66–7

Soto, J.A. 48
South Africa 51
special needs, children with 171–4
spirituality xiv, 7, 126–7, 127–33, 154; differences between patient and therapist 137–40
spousal relationship 167–8, 173–4
stable home environment 103, 139, 165
stages of empathy development 25–6
Stern, D. 21
stories 170
strangers, kind xii, 111–12, 113, 193–5, 200
strengths 6, 7, 44, 74–5
stress 62–3, 79–80; altered stress responses 30; daily hassles and burnout 96–8; religious coping strategies 131; in therapists 150
stress hormones 95
strong emotions, coping with 98–104
sub-groups 45, 47
sublimation 98
substance abuse 76, 79–81
success 81
suffering 154–7
supervision 180–1
suppression 98–9
surrogate families/partners 162
survivor guilt 157
sympathy 8
symptom eradication 5–6, 74
systems 41–2; parenting within a system 167–9

Tammy 58–9
tapestry of life 195
teachers: empathetic leadership 182–3; perspectives 168
teaching empathy 169–71
teamwork 170, 179–80
teens 167
telehealth technology-based training 158, 201
temperament 166–7
ten commandments 15
test anxiety 93–4
theory of mind 67, 82
therapeutic relationship 150–3
therapists 145–60: advocacy 145, 146, 157–9; assessment 146–8; content of therapy 153–7; goals of therapy 148–50; process of therapy 150–3; who don't share the patient's world view 137–40
Theresa of Avila, St 90
"thou": regarding each person as a "thou" 108, 197–8; *see also* I-Thou relationships
thrill-seeking 163, 164
time-out behavior management 102
totalitarian regimes 45
transference 113–15
trauma 115; due to war 121, 122; and and insecure attachment 28–9; logotherapy 154–5; protection from 104
treachery 119–20
triads 38, 39–44
tribalism 4, 133–4
trust 85
truth and reconciliation commissions 51
"tunnel vision" 31
tyrants 96

under-reporting of empathy 200–1
unexpected death 155–7, 172
unhealthy organizations 45–7, 178–9, 190
universality 182; of emotions and trials 170–1
unkind strangers 112
useless gestures 13, 15

Vaillant, G. 7, 98
value of individuals 179
Vanier, J. 47, 67
victim bias 177–8, 185–6
violent games/media 96, 163, 164, 171
virtues 7, 132–3
virtuous cycles xiii, 7, 193–5
Vischer, R. 6, 68
volunteering 51, 130, 168–9, 200–1

Walking Buffalo, Chief xii
Wang, Y.W. 49
war 122, 184, 189–90
wealth inequality 50–1
web of life 195
Weetabix ritual 172
Welcome to Holland (Kingsley) 174
well-functioning communities 47–8, 190
What Dreams May Come (Matheson) 126
whiners 152
win-win solutions 170

Yalom, I. 44

Taylor & Francis eBooks

Helping you to choose the right eBooks for your Library

Add Routledge titles to your library's digital collection today. Taylor and Francis ebooks contains over 50,000 titles in the Humanities, Social Sciences, Behavioural Sciences, Built Environment and Law.

Choose from a range of subject packages or create your own!

Benefits for you
- » Free MARC records
- » COUNTER-compliant usage statistics
- » Flexible purchase and pricing options
- » All titles DRM-free.

Benefits for your user
- » Off-site, anytime access via Athens or referring URL
- » Print or copy pages or chapters
- » Full content search
- » Bookmark, highlight and annotate text
- » Access to thousands of pages of quality research at the click of a button.

REQUEST YOUR **FREE** INSTITUTIONAL TRIAL TODAY
Free Trials Available
We offer free trials to qualifying academic, corporate and government customers.

eCollections – Choose from over 30 subject eCollections, including:

Archaeology	Language Learning
Architecture	Law
Asian Studies	Literature
Business & Management	Media & Communication
Classical Studies	Middle East Studies
Construction	Music
Creative & Media Arts	Philosophy
Criminology & Criminal Justice	Planning
Economics	Politics
Education	Psychology & Mental Health
Energy	Religion
Engineering	Security
English Language & Linguistics	Social Work
Environment & Sustainability	Sociology
Geography	Sport
Health Studies	Theatre & Performance
History	Tourism, Hospitality & Events

For more information, pricing enquiries or to order a free trial, please contact your local sales team:
www.tandfebooks.com/page/sales

Routledge
Taylor & Francis Group
The home of Routledge books

www.tandfebooks.com